Approaches to Teaching H.D.'s Poetry and Prose

Approaches to Teaching H.D.'s Poetry and Prose

Edited by

Annette Debo

and

Lara Vetter

The Modern Language Association of America
New York 2011

85 Broad Street, New York, New York 10004
www.mla.org

To order MLA publications, visit www.mla.org/books. For wholesale and international orders, see www.mla.org/bookstore-orders. The EU-based Responsible Person for MLA products is the Mare Nostrum Group, which can be reached at gpsr@mare-nostrum.co.uk or the Mare Nostrum Group BV, Doelen 72, 4831 GR Breda, Netherlands. For a copy of the MLA's risk assessment document, write to scholcomm@mla.org.

Approaches to Teaching World Literature 118
ISSN 1059-1133

POD 2026 (first printing)

Library of Congress Cataloging-in-Publication Data

Approaches to teaching H.D.'s poetry and prose / edited by Annette Debo and Lara Vetter.
p. cm.—(Approaches to teaching world literature, ISSN 1059–1133 ; 118)
Includes bibliographical references and index.
ISBN 978-1-60329-102-6 (hardcover : alk. paper)—
ISBN 978-1-60329-103-3 (pbk. : alk. paper)
1. H. D. (Hilda Doolittle), 1886–1961—Study and teaching.
I. Debo, Annette, 1964– II. Vetter, Lara Elizabeth, 1968–
PS3507.O726Z5 2011
818'.52—dc22 2011018576

CONTENTS

Acknowledgments ix

Preface 1

PART ONE: MATERIALS

Courses and Contexts 5

Editions 8

Modern Reception History 12

Other Primary Texts by and about H.D. 14

Critical and Reference Materials 15

Multimedia and Internet Resources 16

Teaching H.D. with Texts by Others 18

Classroom Assignments 20

PART TWO: APPROACHES

Introduction: Biographical Contexts 25
Annette Debo and Lara Vetter

H.D. and Modernism

Companions of the Flame: Teaching H.D. with Other Modern Poets 32
Mara Scanlon

Mapping *Sea Garden* 40
Lesley Wheeler

Portraits of an Artist: Introducing Students to H.D.'s Poetry 49
Lisa Rado

Ticking Differently: H.D.'s Time in Philadelphia 56
Adalaide Morris

Myth, Religion, Psychoanalysis

Teaching H.D. and Spirituality 63
Jane Augustine

God or Goods? Teaching *Tribute to Freud* in an Undergraduate Course on Critical Theory 70
Elizabeth Hirsh

Excavating H.D.'s Egypt 77
Marsha Bryant and Mary Ann Eaverly

Approaches to Teaching *Helen in Egypt* 84
Cyrena N. Pondrom

Sexuality, Feminism, Race

Teaching Sex and Sexuality in H.D.: "I Had Two Loves Separate" 92
Susan McCabe

Teaching H.D.'s *Trilogy* from Transnational Perspectives 100
Mary K. DeShazer

Teaching Race in H.D.'s Work 107
Rebecca Walsh

War and Trauma

H.D. and the British Modernist Tradition: *Kora and Ka*, Mythopoesis, and England's Great War 114
Bret L. Keeling

Teaching H.D.'s Work in a War Literature Course 120
Raffaella Baccolini

Burnt Offerings or Incendiary Devices? Ambivalence, Trauma, and Cultural Work in *The Gift* and *Trilogy* 127
Madelyn Detloff

Teaching *Trilogy*: H.D.'s War and Peace 135
Susan Stanford Friedman

Intertextual and Interdisciplinary Approaches

"She Showed a Way to Penetrate Mystery": Teaching H.D. and Denise Levertov 142
Donna Krolik Hollenberg

Robert Duncan's *The H.D. Book* 148
James Maynard

Teaching H.D. in the Creative Writing Classroom 153
Heather H. Thomas

Projecting H.D.: Film, Criticism, and Visual Culture 160
Rachel Connor

The Cinematics of H.D.'s Poetry 166
Charlotte Mandel

Hilda Digital: Teaching H.D. in Cyberspace 172
Helen Sword

Notes on Contributors 179

Survey Respondents 183

Works Cited 185

Index 203

ACKNOWLEDGMENTS

We would first like to offer our immeasurable gratitude not only to our brilliant contributors but also to the H.D. community at large for their generous response to this volume. So many teachers and scholars carefully completed lengthy questionnaires, offered their syllabi and assignments, shared their insights, and documented their teaching triumphs. Their overwhelming response has filled this book with detailed teaching techniques, necessary cultural information, and innovative pedagogical approaches, creating a volume that will inspire instructors new to H.D.'s work and enhance the teaching of even the veterans among us. It has been a truly collaborative endeavor, reaching across the country and across the oceans to instructors from all over the world.

We would also like to thank our colleagues at Western Carolina University and the University of North Carolina at Charlotte for their support through our extensive writing and editing process. We owe Jennifer Veilleux special thanks for her indispensable research assistance and exquisite attention to detail.

This book would not exist without our consistently supportive and patient editor, Sonia Kane, who has fielded our numerous questions with timeliness and good humor. She and the rest of the MLA staff, including our expert associate editor Sara Pastel, have navigated us through a smooth publication process. Anonymous readers of the manuscript offered invaluable suggestions that greatly improved the volume, and we thank them for their time and effort.

Above all, we would like to thank our families, who endured our absorption in this volume, our near-obsessive focus on H.D., and our many deadlines. Annette's gratitude goes out to Steve, Zac, and Ben, and Lara's to Kirk and Finley, for their unwavering encouragement and seemingly endless patience.

PREFACE

One of the first poets to write free verse in English, the poet Hilda Doolittle (known by her initials, H.D.) had a career that spanned over five decades. Her early imagist lyrics, her experiments in prose, her late modernist epic poems, and her Greek translations position her as a key figure in literary history. She enjoyed fame as an *imagiste* in the early 1910s—she, Richard Aldington, and Ezra Pound collaborated on the tenets of that important movement—and in the latter half of the twentieth century, after her death in 1961, H.D. rose to the forefront of modernist women writers recovered into the canon.

Shortly after H.D.'s death, serious scholarly attention to her poetry was initiated by Vincent Quinn's 1967 Twayne book on H.D. and *Contemporary Literature*'s 1969 special issue on H.D. Soon after these publications, in 1975, Susan Stanford Friedman's article "Who Buried H.D.? A Poet, Her Critics, and Her Place in 'the Literary Tradition'" began the fruitful application of feminist theory to her work. Since then, studies on H.D. have flourished, as she has received increasing attention from scholars, and her work is included in all the major anthologies. Her previously unpublished poetry and prose continue to be published by New Directions, Duke University Press, New York University Press, and the University of Florida Press, and several new editions of her letters to such figures as Sigmund Freud, Robert Duncan, Norman Holmes Pearson, and Richard Aldington have recently appeared. In addition, the growing number of reference books devoted to her work—including Harold Bloom's volume in the Bloom's Modern Critical Views series, Michael Boughn's *H.D.: A Bibliography, 1905–1990*, and volumes of collected critical essays—is a testament to her significance to literary study.

Since the 1970s, H.D.'s poetry and prose have begun to appear on syllabi, for high school students, undergraduates, and graduate students. As an integral part of creating this volume, we sent surveys to teachers at all levels. In the many responses we received, we found H.D.'s work in an impressive range of courses across the country and overseas. Classes in American modernism, British modernism, modern poetry, gender and sexuality studies, major authors, women's writing, literature of war, comparative literature, the classics, and mythology are among the many courses respondents described to us. H.D.'s writing is also taught in lower-level surveys of both American and British literature, in creative writing workshops, in critical theory courses, and in advanced composition courses. In some courses, H.D. is read for a week or two; in others, instructors focus entirely on her work, including graduate and undergraduate honors seminars on H.D.'s engagement with modernist writing and culture; and undergraduate and graduate students have written theses devoted to her. One high school teacher describes a course in which she spends twelve class periods on H.D.'s nonfiction prose and poetry.

This volume is divided into two parts. The first part, "Materials," presents resources useful to instructors of H.D.'s work. The section "Courses and Contexts" draws on the results of the survey sent to instructors of H.D. and on our experiences in the classroom, and it describes some challenges and rewards of teaching her work. "Editions" discusses the various editions of H.D.'s poetry and prose that are available; "Modern Reception History" offers a sense of H.D.'s "rediscovery" in the 1980s and situates her within the modernist canon. Several sections are devoted to primary and secondary resources that assist teachers preparing to teach H.D.'s work, and "Teaching H.D. with Texts by Others" offers suggestions for works that are fruitfully taught alongside H.D.'s. "Classroom Assignments" supplements the essays in part 2, "Approaches," by relating some of the exercises and assignments contributed by the many respondents to our survey.

AD and LV

Part One

MATERIALS

Courses and Contexts

In preparing this volume, we sent questionnaires to teachers at the graduate, undergraduate, and high school levels; their responses offered a wealth of information. Many instructors teach H.D. from the perspective of gender and sexuality studies; however, H.D.'s oeuvre accommodates a wide range of other critical approaches. Teachers use theories of performance, trauma, psychoanalysis, sexuality, cultural studies, and textual studies to illuminate for students the intricacies and nuances of her writing. Many take advantage of H.D.'s analysis with Sigmund Freud and her engagement with psychoanalysis in her poetry and prose to introduce students to one of the twentieth century's most important cultural and intellectual figures through a writer who both lauds and questions his thinking. Most frequently, instructors report that they employ a combination of approaches. "I emphasize possibility, play, fun—the detective work of 'getting' the intertextuality and the rewards of such a pursuit," one teacher writes to us. "To demonstrate to the students the variety of approaches and ways 'in' to a poem suggests that all readings are necessarily partial." Many stress that H.D.'s writing encourages an organic approach to critical theory, in which various theoretical frameworks arise naturally from the reading: "While our readings will thus almost inevitably cross the distinctive terrains of gender and psychoanalysis, or rely on some version of a dialectical reading practice, that movement tends to be generated inductively, ideally within H.D.'s own terms."

Teachers of her work explore an array of themes. H.D.'s pervasive focus on issues of gender and sexuality is cited most often by those responding to our questionnaire, with her poetic responses to war and violence running a close second. Intertwined themes of history, memory, and modernist mythology recur throughout the surveys; the function of art and aesthetics is another refrain. So often in H.D.'s writing, these various thematic threads are interwoven. As one instructor remarks, the speakers of H.D.'s poetry rewrite Western narratives from the perspective of the woman artist: "I trace that theme through many of the familiar narratives from cultural narratives of 'the feminine' to the Judeo-Christian narratives of male prophets and a female-subordinate creation, to the parallel and sometimes antithetical mythic structures [H.D.] identifies from Babylonian, Egyptian, Gnostic, Greek, Roman sources." Other instructors prefer to focus on poetic form rather than a specific topic or theme. As one writes, "We tend to focus on the historical and formal presuppositions and effects of the poetics, explicitly framing the question of *how* to read it before presuming that we can." Another teacher comments that "the images in [H.D.'s] work suggest the difficulty of capturing beauty in words and expressing ideas that are often elusive."

One reason we proposed compiling this volume is that at first H.D.'s work can seem quite difficult for students to comprehend and for instructors to teach. Instructors express frustration, for instance, with how overwhelming and impenetrable the long epic poems *Trilogy* and *Helen in Egypt* can seem to students initially, but they are delighted that students eventually respond well upon delving into the richness of the poems. It is imperative that instructors emphasize H.D.'s work's complexities within the context of the modernist movement more generally; without this contextualization, students can find her writing opaque and resist its allusiveness. They may react vehemently against what they perceive as elitism inherent in this kind of writing, though such a response can generate productive conversations about the avant-garde and its reception. It is helpful to talk with students about why modernist poetry and prose refuse a simple interpretation or an easy answer. A brief historical overview of the period—with a focus on rapid urbanization and industrialization, unprecedented immigration, radical social reform movements, policies of eugenics and rising racial tensions, technological warfare on a scale never seen, scientific discoveries and theorizing that disrupted traditional conceptions of time and subjectivity—can illuminate the rationale for a fragmented, disorienting, and indeterminate form in a time of anxiety and chaos. Like Gertrude Stein's, H.D.'s reiterative style—her tendency to revisit issues and scenes from multiple perspectives—can be off-putting for some students, so some discussion of the role of repetition in modernism can be useful. For students who feel overwhelmed at the indeterminacy of many modernist works, instructors advise an approach more focused on exploring the literature than on explaining it.

Most teachers report that, in general, teaching poetry is far more challenging than teaching fiction. Teachers almost universally acknowledge that students express anxiety about deciphering modern poetry—with its compression, its ambiguities, and its elusiveness—a form of expression alien to their everyday reading experiences. Many students come into our classes, even at the upper division or graduate level, with little training in reading and interpreting poetry, so instructors should be prepared to offer them a brief and focused tutorial and to model close readings of a few poems. An explanation of H.D.'s palimpsestic method is key to helping students figure out the myriad layers of meaning embedded in her poetry and the multiple strategies of interpretation required to disentangle these layers. A discussion of imagism and the beginnings of modern poetry is also crucial to teaching her early lyrics. Pairing a few imagist poems with some examples of more conventional nineteenth-century Romantic or sentimental poems can highlight for students the ways in which modernists saw themselves as creating a revolutionary kind of poetry.

From her earliest imagist poetry to her autobiographical novels to her late epic poems, H.D.'s prose and poetry are rich in allusions to Greek, Roman, Egyptian, and pre-Semitic mythologies. Her texts rely not only on the well-known Judeo-Christian tradition but also on the language of the occult, spiritualism, and a host of obscure or esoteric religious traditions. Her palimpsestic poems rapidly traverse distant historical eras, at times in the space of a mere line or stanza, and collapse ancient and modern time. Most respondents to our survey stressed that students should be reassured that allusions are not something to be feared and that tracking them down can be fun. In fact, in H.D.'s writing, in the words of one respondent, "the context so often clarifies the allusion." Instructors encourage students to read through a poem once without regard to the allusions—"without worry about detail, just experiencing the music of the poetry and the beauty of the images"—and to let a second reading guide them to reference books if needed. Close reading of the text will reveal a great deal of meaning even without notes on the allusions.

In subsequent readings, though, knowledge of H.D.'s allusions greatly enriches the texts, and students relish unpacking their meanings. They soon realize that H.D. employs allusions with purpose, that her style reflects her thematics. "With H.D.," another teacher writes, "I try to use the impossibility of tracing down and understanding every reference and resonance as a way to discuss her syncretist and palimpsestic methods." As some point out, allusiveness may well be less of a problem in today's information age, since most students have ready access to the Internet. Teachers can lecture or distribute handouts to the class on important allusions, but many assign various allusions to students who then conduct a kind of scavenger hunt, so that ultimately the whole class constructs collaboratively an annotated text, either by posting online or by sharing in class the fruits of their research. This strategy empowers students and introduces them to the joys and rewards of research.

H.D.'s approach to gender and sexuality can sometimes pose problems for undergraduate and graduate students alike. While male students may respond to H.D.'s critique of war, they may feel uncomfortable with her reimagining of Western patriarchal narratives and assertion of a female poetic voice. Conversely, female students may resent passages that portray female characters who are passive or self-destructive, for H.D.'s prose in particular can be brutally realistic in its depiction of the power dynamics of gender relations. These reactions can produce fruitful class discussions about gender, and illuminating the complexities of H.D.'s attitudes about gender can alleviate some of the anxiety. Calling attention, for instance, to the deities in the first poem of *Trilogy*, who combine the attributes of male and female, can problematize what seems to be an unwavering focus on female divinity in the second two poems, interrupted in the third poem, *The Flowering of the Rod*, by Kaspar, who is granted the power of vision. Similarly, addressing H.D.'s complicated relationship to Freud and other male figures in her life can underscore for students that feminism is a concept that needs historicizing. Some dialogue with students about the issues of canonization and the position of the woman writer in the early twentieth century may be necessary as well to combat patronizing biographical sources students may encounter in print or online.

Despite the difficulties, though, teaching H.D.'s work affords great rewards for both instructors and students. Our respondents wrote in glowing terms about those aspects of H.D.'s poetry and prose that students found most engaging. Students react positively to the early lyrics of *Sea Garden*, which critique conventional constructions of beauty and femininity. Undergraduates, one teacher reports, "almost uniformly are awed by how much emotion and commentary on deep human issues H.D. can pack into what looks on the surface like a simple nature poem." Another instructor observes that the early imagist poems—sparse and singularly focused—are especially effective in teaching today's generation, "who are used to processing image bits, one after another, in computer games, graphic novels, and so on." Perhaps the most frequently taught of H.D.'s texts, *Trilogy* resonates with male and female students immediately, since they find it "a moving and profound response to war and violence in an age, when, unfortunately, both loom ominously in their own lives." In this epic poem of war and peace, written from a woman's perspective, students find intriguing the rewriting of Western religious narratives rendered in language that is both evocative and eloquent. The tendency among many modernists to conceptualize art as a vehicle of healing and reconciliation in a fragmented, chaotic universe finds particular expression in *Trilogy*. Likewise, the poignant poems of the 1920s that assume the voices of forgotten female mythological figures, recasting their stories from alternative perspectives, spark students' interests. Moreover, H.D. was a fascinating figure, and the story of her life draws many students into an appreciation of her work. Some respondents write encouragingly that their students enjoy H.D.'s autobiographical prose—*The Gift*, *Paint It Today*, *HERmione*, and *Asphodel* in particular—though many find the memoirs, written in vignettes, more appealing to less advanced students. Students find compelling these late memoirs of Freud (*Tribute to Freud*) and Pound (*End to Torment*) in their depiction of the ways in which H.D. engages and argues with these powerful figures.

Editions

H.D.'s lyrical poetry is frequently taught, and many teachers use the definitive *Collected Poems, 1912–1944*, edited by Louis L. Martz, which arranges H.D.'s poetry chronologically by volume. It begins with the five volumes that H.D. published as *Collected Poems* in 1925: *Sea Garden* (1916), *The God* (1913–17), *Translations* (1915–20), *Hymen* (1921), and *Heliodora* (1924). *Red Roses for Bronze* (1931) is next, followed by H.D.'s uncollected and unpublished poetry. The volume concludes with *Trilogy* (1944, 1945, 1946). Available here in the context of much of her career are her best known and most often taught poems: "At Baia," "The Dancer," "Demeter," "Eurydice," "Fragment 113," "Garden," "Heat," "Helen," "Heliodora," "Leda," "The Master," "Mid-Day," "Orchard," "Oread," "Pear Tree," "The Pool," "Sea Rose," and "Sheltered Garden." Teachers characterize this edition as widely available, comprehensive, and affordable, and they point out that it offers a wide range of poetic genres, including imagist lyrics, mythic revisions, a long poem, and even translations. Martz also edited H.D.'s *Selected Poems*, which includes many of her popular lyrics, as well as selections from her translation *Euripides: Ion* and her later volumes *Trilogy*, *Helen in Egypt*, and *Hermetic Definition*. Some instructors prefer this smaller and less expensive edition, especially for undergraduate classes.

H.D.'s two epic works, *Trilogy* and *Helen in Egypt*, are also frequently taught, *Trilogy* more so than *Helen in Egypt*. New Directions released a 1998 edition of *Trilogy* that includes an introduction and readers' notes by Aliki Barnstone. The notes are intended for readers rather than scholars, in keeping with the publisher's goals. Many teachers find these notes especially useful for their students; others invite students to extend Barnstone's notes with their own research into H.D.'s wide-ranging allusions. New Directions's 1973 edition of *Trilogy* is no longer in print, though many teachers still offer their students its foreword, written by Norman Holmes Pearson—H.D.'s literary executor, Yale ally, and close friend. This foreword introduces *Trilogy* with a discussion of the biography of H.D., her correspondence, and notes she specifically wrote for Pearson about poetic sources and inspiration. *Helen in Egypt* is also available in a New Directions edition, first published in 1961 and still in print. Its introduction, by the poet Horace Gregory, is useful if dated in the light of recent scholarship. Some teachers mention teaching *Hermetic Definition*, H.D.'s final book of poetry, first published in 1972 and still in print.

Many instructors reported that it was useful to supplement the teaching of H.D.'s poetry with her *Notes on Thought and Vision*, written in 1919 and published in 1982 by City Lights in an edition still available. An aesthetic manifesto penned as a series of vignettes, the book describes the relationships between artistic creation, spirituality, and sexuality. This short text is introduced by Albert Gelpi, who discusses the book in terms of H.D.'s biography as well as theories of psychoanalytic thought and the occult.

Most of H.D.'s fiction and prose is now in print, some recently published for the first time. H.D. wrote several autobiographical novels set in the 1910s, a tumultuous period in which she had an affair with Frances Gregg, became engaged to Pound, moved from Pennsylvania to London, married Richard Aldington and lived with him in an apartment neighboring that of D. H. Lawrence, saw her husband go off to war, had a child with Cecil Gray, and met Bryher, her lifelong companion. *HERmione* (or, as H.D. titled it, *HER*) was first published by New Directions in 1981. Written during the late 1920s and completed in 1930, *HERmione* takes place entirely in Pennsylvania, addressing Hermione's coming of age through her relationships with her family, George Lowndes (based on Pound), and Fayne Rabb (based on Gregg). The short opening essay, "Pandora's Box," is written by H.D.'s daughter, Perdita Schaffner, and offers reflections on the figures fictionalized in the novel who peopled her childhood.

Paint It Today (*Paint It To-day*) is a fragmentary novel, composed in 1921 and published by New York University Press in 1992 as part of its series The Cutting Edge: Lesbian Life and Literature. Another rendering of H.D.'s life, *Paint It Today* follows Midget (based on H.D.) as she leaves the United States for Europe with Josepha (based on Gregg) and then meets Althea (based on Bryher). Cassandra Laity, the editor, offers notes and a critical introduction, which explores H.D.'s lesbian relationships depicted in this text. First published by Duke University Press in 1992, *Asphodel* covers much of the same autobiographical ground. In it Hermione leaves the United States for an expatriate existence in Europe, and the novel ends after Hermione's marriage to Jerrold dissolves and she finds salvation in a relationship with Beryl, who promises to care for her and her young daughter. The editor, Robert Spoo, includes a brief but useful introduction, an explanation of his editing guidelines, and an appendix identifying the biographical references in this roman à clef and offering a background sketch for each.

Bid Me to Live, often taught even though it is out of print, was first published in 1960 and most recently reissued in 1983 by Black Swan Books. Completed much later than *HERmione*, *Paint It Today*, or *Asphodel*, this novel is set in 1918 and chronicles the World War I interactions of a Bloomsbury group of writers, based on H.D., Aldington, D. H. and Frieda Lawrence, Dorothy "Arabella" Yorke, Gray, and Pound. The 1983 edition features Schaffner's "A Profound Animal," one of her prose pieces reflecting on her life as H.D.'s daughter. Schaffner offers insights into the novel, reading it explicitly as autobiography and tying it to her mother's later life as well as to her single encounter with her biological father, Gray. Also included in this edition are an afterword by John Walsh, publisher of Black Swan, and excerpts from H.D.'s "Notes on Recent Writings," reflections H.D. had written at Pearson's request.

Two other novels written in the 1920s, a prolific period of fiction writing for H.D., are noted frequently by our respondents. *Pilate's Wife*, revised in 1934 and the late 1950s, was published in 2000 by New Directions. This historical novel is a revision of the murky biblical story of Pilate's wife, whom H.D. names Veronica. Joan A. Burke edited the text, which includes a critical introduction. *Palimpsest*, although not in print, is nonetheless taught by a surprising number of instructors. This text was initially published in 1926 by Contact Press and then reissued in 1968. Perhaps a novel, perhaps a trilogy of stories, *Palimpsest* compiles three narratives with intertwining themes: one set in ancient Rome after its conquest of Greece features a thinly disguised H.D. and Aldington; another set in present-day London focuses on a woman poet in a time of war; and a third follows the travels of Helen Fairwood as she tours Egypt. Of particular interest to our respondents is Fairwood's story, "Secret Name: Excavator's Egypt," because of its use of Egyptian references.

H.D. wrote a series of short stories and novels about the late 1920s and early 1930s, a period in which she, Bryher, and Kenneth Macpherson lived together and collaborated on film. In *Kora and Ka* and *Nights*, short novellas that are beginning to appear on syllabi, the ties to H.D.'s life are much less fixed than they are in the earlier fiction. Privately published in 1934 in a run of one hundred copies, *Kora and Ka* was reissued in 1996 by New Directions. Spoo's edition includes a critical introduction. A study of the impact of war on civilians, *Kora and Ka* follows John Helforth, who suffers from a breakdown and severe writer's block, and depicts characters loosely based on Macpherson and Bryher (both, at times, H.D.'s lovers). *Nights* was privately published by the Dijon printer Maurice Darantière (as was *The Usual Star*, which has not been republished in its entirety), initially in 1935 and reissued in 1986 by New Directions. Divided into halves—a fictional preface by its publisher and "author," John Helforth, and the manuscript of the novel written by the protagonist, Natalia—*Nights* traces a series of sexual encounters between Natalia and her new lover, David, in the wake of a betrayal of a character based on Macpherson. Schaffner's introduction for this volume not only situates it in the context of her life with H.D., Bryher, and Macpherson in the late 1920s but also acknowledges that this volume moves further beyond autobiography than some of H.D.'s other fictional texts.

The Gift, composed during World War II and completed in 1944, is a fictionalized account of H.D.'s childhood in Bethlehem, Pennsylvania, and her Moravian heritage. This frequently taught text is available in two editions, the 1982 reader's edition from New Directions and the 1998 critical edition from the University Press of Florida. The novel in the reader's edition, as Charlotte Mandel has observed in a review of the novel, was "severely—and silently—truncated," about one-third of the manuscript being excised (344). This early edition does include a useful introduction by Schaffner, titled "Unless a Bomb Falls . . . ," which contextualizes the novel in terms of her mother's life during the London Blitz as well as her familial heritage. The 1998 edition, edited by Jane Augustine, restores the entire text of *The Gift* and includes notes by H.D. It also includes an explanation of its editing criteria, a critical introduction, and extensive editorial notes.

Two memoirs are popular choices for instructors. *Tribute to Freud*, perhaps H.D.'s most frequently taught prose text, consists of two parts, "Writing on the Wall" and "Advent." "Writing on the Wall," written in London in 1944, was published in *Life and Letters Today* from 1945 to 1946 and as a single volume in 1956. In 1974 and 1984 printings, "Advent" (constructed in 1948) was added to make the New Directions edition that is available today. Although sometimes still straightforwardly read as a portrait of psychoanalysis with Freud, *Tribute to Freud* is another of H.D.'s fictionalized memoirs—a laudatory account of Freud as well as an acknowledgment that Freud's theories exact a price sometimes too high to pay. The foreword, written by Pearson, relates the text to H.D.'s life and body of work. Also included are a few letters from Freud to H.D. A more expanded source for this correspondence is Susan Stanford Friedman's *Analyzing Freud: Letters of H.D., Bryher, and Their Circle*.

End to Torment, written in 1958, is ostensibly a memoir about Pound, but its primary focus is H.D., her early years in the United States, and her memories of the young Pound, before he became the fascist who deeply troubled her. Published in 1979 by New Directions, the edition, still in print, offers a foreword by Michael King and closes with a printing of "Hilda's Book," poems written by Pound for H.D. from 1905 to 1907, at the beginning of their long friendship.

Many teachers also use H.D.'s work in film in their classes. The only extant feature film is *Borderline*, which stars H.D., Paul Robeson, Eslanda Robeson, and Bryher, but the short film *Monkeys' Moon* was rediscovered in 2008. (The availability of both films and stills are described below in "Multimedia and Internet Resources.") H.D. contributed to the early and influential film journal *Close Up*, which was published from 1927 to 1933 and edited by Macpherson, Bryher, and H.D. Some research libraries hold the journal's entire run, which was republished in ten volumes by Arno Press in 1971, along with a foreword by Herman G. Weinberg and a cumulative index. This edition is no longer in print. But currently available is the anthology Close Up, *1927–1933: Cinema and Modernism*, edited by James Donald, Anne Friedberg, and Laura Marcus, which offers selections from *Close Up*, including eight of H.D.'s eleven contributions and an introduction to her film work by Marcus. The anthology also contains H.D.'s "The *Borderline* Pamphlet" (under its more accurate title, "*Borderline*: A POOL Film with Paul Robeson"), which offers a plot summary, commentary on the film's production, and a thematic analysis, all written to market the film. Within this essential book on modernism and film, Donald, Friedberg, and Marcus have compiled particularly helpful appendixes, which list the contents of *Close Up* by issue, offer notes on *Close Up*'s contributors and correspondents, present a publishing history of the journal, list the books POOL published, and put *Close Up* in its historical context in a substantial chronology of modernism.

There are British editions also available for many of these texts.

Modern Reception History

After H.D.'s death in 1961, the first special journal issue dedicated to her was published by *Contemporary Literature* in 1969. Edited by L. S. Dembo, this issue offered scholars a new look at H.D.'s extensive body of work. In the 1960s, critical attention to H.D. had declined in some respects—*Helen in Egypt* received only five reviews—while in others H.D. was well appreciated. She was awarded the Award of Merit Medal for Poetry by the American Academy of Arts and Letters in 1960, demonstrating that her fellow poets held her in high esteem, and her work was lauded in an October 1961 panegyric published by Horace Gregory in the *New York Times Book Review* following her death. Two critical books had been published on H.D. in the 1960s, Thomas Burnett Swann's *The Classical World of H.D.* in 1962 and Vincent Quinn's Twayne book *Hilda Doolittle (H.D.)* in 1967. But the *Contemporary Literature* special issue called for more intensive critical attention and did so by offering essays by established and up-and-coming scholars like Dembo, Norman Holmes Pearson, Joseph N. Riddel, Norman N. Holland, Bernard F. Engel, Linda W. Wagner, and A. Kingsley Weatherhead; by sampling H.D.'s poetry, fiction, and correspondence; and by providing scholars with commentary on H.D.'s position in the canon and a substantial bibliography of primary and secondary sources. The journal issue did indeed spark new scholarship, and, when combined with the emergence of feminist literary theory, it provided impetus toward reasserting H.D.'s place in the literary landscape.

In 1975, Susan Stanford Friedman's essay "Who Buried H.D.? A Poet, Her Critics, and Her Place in 'the Literary Tradition'" brought H.D. to the attention of feminist critics involved in the pivotal recovery movement of neglected women writers and of those interested in feminist theory, which so fruitfully illuminates H.D.'s themes and texts. The convergence of the recovery movement—which helped propel H.D.'s many unpublished or out-of-print texts to publication—the creation of women's literature classes, the diversification of theoretical approaches to include feminism, and the evolution of feminism itself formed a rich setting for H.D. studies to develop. Scholarship on H.D. poured forth in the 1980s: Jean Gould's *American Women Poets*; Friedman's *Psyche Reborn* and *Penelope's Web*; Alicia Suskin Ostriker's *Writing Like a Woman* and *Stealing the Language*; Rachel Blau DuPlessis's *Writing Beyond the Ending* and *H.D.: The Career of That Struggle*; Shari Benstock's *Women of the Left Bank*; Mary K. DeShazer's *Inspiring Women*; Albert Gelpi's *A Coherent Splendor*; Angela DiPlace Fritz's *Thought and Vision*; two volumes of Sandra M. Gilbert and Susan Gubar's *No Man's Land*; Gary Burnett's *H.D. between Image and Epic*; Deborah Kelly Kloepfer's *The Unspeakable Mother*; and Bonnie Kime Scott's *The Gender of Modernism*; plus book chapters, critical articles, reference articles, and reviews. The latter half of the 1980s was particularly energized by the many celebrations of the centennial of H.D.'s birth in 1986 through conferences; special journal issues; Friedman and DuPlessis's collection of essays *Signets*; Harold Bloom's *H.D.* volume in the Modern Critical Views series; and Michael King's *H.D.: Woman and Poet*, a second collection of significant essays that also includes a selected annotated bibliography. The 1980s also produced two full-length biographies (Guest; Robinson), *Collected Poems* and *Selected Poems*, and new editions of H.D.'s fiction, thereby providing scholars with a wealth of new primary and secondary texts.

Since then, the critical attention paid to H.D. has only increased. In the 1970s, the *MLA International Bibliography* records just 45 entries, including 6 dissertations. By 2010, however, the MLA lists 680 publications, 121 of which are dissertations. In many respects, these studies have followed the trajectory of feminist theory: recovery and validation, representation of women's voices and concerns, a consideration of racial and ethnic identity, a focus on sexuality, and a reflection on the role of colonialism. Additional current concerns in H.D. studies include women's or civilian representation of war and trauma; the impact of Egypt, both material and mythologized; spirituality in all its representations; nation and colonial identity; film studies; lesbian and queer sexuality; poetics and aesthetics; and comparative work, especially with poets influenced by H.D. The output of scholars keeps growing with the publication of more special journal issues, newly edited primary texts, editions of letters, Michael Boughn's *H.D.: A Bibliography, 1905–1990*, and additional reference books—all a testament to H.D.'s significance to literary study.

For an account of H.D.'s critical reception before 1969, see Jackson Bryer; Friedman also comments on H.D.'s reception in her 1986 *Dictionary of Literary Biography* entry (144–46).

Other Primary Texts by and about H.D.

H.D. wrote about her life in many of her fictional texts, and she occasionally wrote commentary on her writing, generally for Norman Holmes Pearson, who asked her to provide contexts for her texts—influences, timing, connections, inspirations. Much of this writing is only available in the H.D. Papers at Yale University's Beinecke Rare Book and Manuscript Library, but "H.D. by Delia Alton," a reflection by H.D., was published in the *Iowa Review*.

H.D.'s daughter and friends also wrote about her. Perdita Schaffner wrote a number of short memoirs about H.D., herself, and their family. Many are included in editions of H.D.'s texts and are described above in the "Editions" section. In addition to those, Schaffner wrote "Merano, 1962," which describes her one brief meeting with Ezra Pound in Brunnenburg after his release from St. Elizabeths Hospital and her friendship with his daughter, Mary de Rachewiltz. "Running" was published in the *Iowa Review*'s 1986 special issue, and it reminisces primarily about the later years of H.D.'s life, Pearson's influence, and the explosion of H.D. scholarship. Michael King's collection *H.D.: Woman and Poet* includes "Keeper of the Flame," in which Schaffner muses on her role as the daughter of a woman artist being rediscovered by literary scholars. "A Sketch of H.D.: The Egyptian Cat" was published in Susan Stanford Friedman and Rachel Blau DuPlessis's collection *Signets*. This short essay, which previously appeared in H.D.'s *Hedylus*, offers insights into H.D.'s identity as a writer, a mother, and a person. Schaffner also wrote the introduction for H.D.'s children's book, *The Hedgehog*, in which she clarifies the genesis of the book; she also wrote a brief sketch for *New Directions for Women* ("They").

Bryher wrote two memoirs that include reminisences of H.D. *The Heart to Artemis* begins in 1894, the year of Bryher's birth, and traces Bryher's life through 1940, her daring escape from Switzerland, and her subsequent arrival on the doorstep of the Lowndes Square flat she shared with H.D. during World War II. *The Days of Mars* picks up at the moment of that arrival in 1940 and covers the war years, coming to a close in 1946 with Bryher's return to Switzerland. Silvia Dobson also wrote about H.D. and included selections from their correspondence in her articles "Cloud of Memories: Books H.D. Shared with Me, 1934–1960"; "Remembering H.D."; "'Shock Knit within Terror': Living through World War II"; and "Woof and Heave and Surge and Wave and Flow." In addition, Pearson gave a significant interview to L. S. Dembo, "Norman Holmes Pearson on H.D.: An Interview," which was included in *Con-*

temporary Literature's 1969 special issue on H.D. (See Friedman and DuPlessis's *Signets* for a more substantial listing of texts concerning H.D. [459–61].)

H.D. wrote volumes of correspondence, writing to some people, like Bryher, several times in one day. Her letters are beginning to appear in print. Book-length editions exist of selected correspondence between H.D., Sigmund Freud, and Bryher during the years that H.D. was in analysis with Freud (Friedman, *Analyzing*); between H.D. and Pearson from World War II, when they solidified their friendship, through the end of her life (Hollenberg, *Between History*); and between H.D. and Robert Duncan, whose poetry she greatly influenced (Bertholf). Caroline Zilboorg has edited three volumes of the correspondence between H.D. and Richard Aldington: *The Early Years in Letters*, *The Later Years in Letters*, and *Their Lives in Letters*. Several articles also offer selected letters and commentary on H.D.'s relationships with Denise Levertov (Hollenberg, "'Within the World'"), Adrienne Monnier (Zilboorg, "Letters"), John Cournos (Hollenberg, "Art"), Dobson (Tinker), F. S. Flint (Pondrom, "Selected Letters"), and May Sarton (Mandel, "Letters").

Another source for a variety of texts is the *H.D. Newsletter*, edited by Eileen Gregory, which published eight issues between 1987 and 1991. Memoirs, notes, and full-length critical articles are available there. A full table of contents is available at www.imagists.org/hd/hdnlet.html.

Critical and Reference Materials

The most inclusive bibliography of H.D.'s primary works is Michael Boughn's *H.D.: A Bibliography, 1905–1990*, which can be especially useful for teachers wishing to present H.D.'s poems in their original contexts, the little magazines and modernist journals that published them. Teachers might also find helpful Virginia Smyers's catalog of H.D.'s library preserved at the Beinecke Library. The most frequently cited sources for teachers are the major monographs on H.D. written from the 1980s to the present, including those by Claire Buck, Diana Collecott, Rachel Blau DuPlessis, Susan Edmunds, Susan Stanford Friedman, Eileen Gregory, Cassandra Laity, and Adalaide Morris. Two collections of essays on H.D., Friedman and DuPlessis's *Signets* and Michael King's *H.D.: Woman and Poet*, are also recommended highly by our survey respondents, several of whom mention two essays from *Signets*: Friedman and DuPlessis's "'I Had Two Loves Separate': The Sexualities of H.D.'s *HER*" and Susan Gubar's "The Echoing Spell of H.D.'s *Trilogy*." In addition to biographical and critical scholarship written by prominent H.D. scholars, *Signets* includes photographs of H.D. as well as Friedman's timeline that ascribes dates to the composition and publication of all of H.D.'s work. More photographs are reproduced in the two book-length biographies (Guest; Robinson) and in Friedman's *Penelope's Web*.

Readers should also be aware of special issues of scholarly journals devoted to H.D., beginning in 1969 with *Contemporary Literature*, edited by L. S. Dembo. The years near H.D.'s centennial saw many special issues, including the following: Friedman and DuPlessis edited a second special issue in *Contemporary Literature* (1986); Thomas H. Jackson edited an issue celebrating H.D. and Marianne Moore for *Poesis* (1985); the *Iowa Review* offered a lengthy issue edited by Morris (1986); Collecott edited an issue for *Agenda* (1987–88); and DuPlessis edited yet another special issue, this time for *Sagetrieb* (1987). Almost a decade later, *Sagetrieb* offered a flurry of H.D. scholarship in special issues edited by Donna Krolik Hollenberg and Gregory (1995) and Burton Hatlen (1996). In 1987, *San Jose Studies* ran a special issue devoted to Emily Dickinson and H.D., edited by Fauneil J. Rinn, and in 2004 *Paideuma* devoted a special issue to Marianne Moore and H.D., which Hatlen edited.

While most respondents shied away from assigning secondary texts to undergraduates beyond basic biographical material, the list of texts recommended for graduate students mirrors that for teachers given above. Appearing most prominently are books and articles by Friedman and DuPlessis, as well as Alicia Suskin Ostriker's essay "No Rule of Procedure" in *Signets*. For undergraduate and graduate students puzzling through H.D.'s allusions, several sources on mythology were recommended, most notably Thomas Bulfinch's *Bulfinch's Mythology*, Edith Hamilton's *Mythology*, William Smith's *Smaller Classical Dictionary*, E. A. Wallis Budge's *The Egyptian Book of the Dead*, and Barry B. Powell's *Classical Myth*. Other respondents, however, related that they gave students handouts with basic information on Greek mythology or encouraged them to purchase a mythological dictionary.

Trilogy is perhaps the most frequently taught text of H.D.'s oeuvre, and its dependence on allusions can be initially daunting. Many instructors recommend Aliki Barnstone's introduction and notes to her edition of *Trilogy*, though students should be encouraged to build on Barnstone's work by creating their own annotations. Also helpful in preparing to teach this epic poem are essays by Albert Gelpi, Gubar, and Ostriker in *Signets*, as well as Morris's treatment of sound in the poem in *How to Live / What to Do*. Many also suggest recent work on *Trilogy*'s geopolitical critique, inaugurated by Susan Edmunds's *Out of Line*.

Multimedia and Internet Resources

There are numerous multimedia and Internet resources available for the study and teaching of H.D.'s work. First and foremost, the official *H.D. (Hilda Doolittle) Home Page* (www.imagists.org/hd/) features a range of information, including biographical and bibliographical essays and links; electronic texts of some of H.D.'s works not available elsewhere, as well as new and reprinted scholarship on her work; information about the H.D. International Society and how to join its Listserv; and a calendar of events related to the study of H.D. Selected articles from the *H.D. Newsletter* (1987–91) can be found on this site, as well as Louis Silverstein's invaluable chronology of H.D.'s life. Also particularly useful for teachers and students of H.D. have been the recent efforts by the Beinecke Rare Book and Manuscript Library, at Yale University, to digitize materials from their collection of H.D. Papers. These high-resolution images are available for downloading. Included here are photographs of H.D., her family, and her friends; images of manuscript pages from several of her works; stills from the movie *Borderline*; and reproductions of pages from the "H.D. Scrapbook," which contains collages of photographs and cutouts as well as the nudes taken of H.D. and Bryher in California in the 1920s. The site also includes *Monkeys' Moon* (1929) ("Digital Images").

Several respondents to the survey named two other useful sites. Cary Nelson's *Modern American Poetry* (www.english.uiuc.edu/maps/), designed as a multimedia companion to his *Anthology of Modern American Poetry* and maintained at the University of Illinois at Urbana-Champaign, contains an entry on H.D. compiled by Marsha Bryant. The entry reprints excerpts from scholarship on particular poems by H.D., biographical and bibliographical information, and electronic texts of poems ranging from the mid-1910s to the mid-1920s. Similar entries on a vast array of twentieth-century poets at this site can fruitfully supplement a unit on H.D. The Academy of American Poets's *Poets.org* (www.poets.org) offers a biographical entry on H.D. that includes links to electronic texts of her poetry; to an audio recording of a reading from *Helen in Egypt*; and to essays on related topics such as imagism, modernism, and other poets (e.g., Amy Lowell, D. H. Lawrence, and William Carlos Williams). A longer recording of *Helen in Egypt* is available at *PennSound* (Bernstein). The recording, made in Switzerland in 1955, is abridged and differs at times from the published poem. H.D. made the recording at the behest of Norman Holmes Pearson and, after making it, continued to revise *Helen in Egypt*, which was published in 1961.

Many survey respondents also recommended that students use the Internet to research allusions from and contexts for H.D.'s poems and prose, as well as to locate images of Greek, Roman, and Egyptian art and architecture. Several instructors reported directing students to online sources for historical information on World War I and World War II. Students can easily access a variety of resources on mythology and religion, including the University of Virginia Electronic Text Center's text of the King James Bible. The Perseus Digital Library at Tufts University offers electronic versions of classic Greek and Roman texts translated into English. For information on Helen of Troy, one instructor recommended the site *Greek Mythology Link*, by Carlos Parada, author of the *Genealogical Guide to Greek Mythology*. The Moravian Church's Web site makes available historical information that students and teachers alike might find useful.

There are also multimedia resources available for teaching H.D. that are not online. An audio recording of H.D. reading parts of *Helen in Egypt* is available on cassette tape for purchase from *The Writer's Center*. *Borderline* became available in 2007 for purchase, as part of the Criterion Studio DVD collection *Paul Robeson: Portraits of the Artist*. Other movies H.D. reviewed in *Close Up*, such as Carl Dreyer's *Passion of Joan of Arc* and G. W. Pabst's *Joyless Street*, can supplement classroom units on H.D.'s notions of visuality and film. Finally, one respondent wrote that she had taught H.D.'s *Trilogy* with Richard Danielpour's *An American Requiem*, which features tenor and mezzo-soprano renditions of parts of the poem.

Teaching H.D. with Texts by Others

According to our respondents, H.D. is taught primarily in one of two contexts: as modernist (British and American) and as woman writer. A useful way to introduce students to modernist poetry is to teach H.D.'s early lyrics with those of Richard Aldington, Amy Lowell, Mina Loy, Marianne Moore, Ezra Pound, and William Carlos Williams. Pound's "In a Station at the Metro" and "L'art, 1910" can be paired with H.D.'s "Oread," which Pound claimed to be both the ideal imagist and perfect vorticist poem; one instructor adds that H.D.'s poems from *Sea Garden* work well with Lowell's poem about gardens, "Patterns." Pound's essay on imagism (in *Literary Essays*), his essay on vorticism that appeared in the *Fortnightly Review*, and his edition of Ernest Fenollosa's essay on the Chinese ideogram can serve as useful background for teachers and could be assigned to upper-division or graduate students. Perhaps the most frequently cited poet taught with H.D., though, is T. S. Eliot. In fact, several instructors teach entire courses devoted to the two. *The Waste Land* and *Trilogy* create nice bookends to a course on modernism, as students progress from World War I to World War II. The two modernist long poems engage with ancient mythological traditions to "shor[e] against [the] ruins" the "fragments" of Western civilization in a time of global warfare (Eliot, *Collected Poems* 69). Eliot's "Tradition and the Individual Talent" is also helpful in distinguishing his vision of modernism from that of Pound, H.D., and others (*Sacred Woods*).

H.D. frequently appears on syllabi devoted to the American expatriates, including Eliot, F. Scott Fitzgerald, Ernest Hemingway, Pound, and Gertrude Stein. In a course on the modernist long poem, H.D.'s *Trilogy* and *Helen in Egypt* might be taught with Eliot's *The Waste Land* and *Four Quartets*, Pound's *The Cantos*, Williams's *Paterson*, and Robert Duncan's *The H.D. Book*. Another course on the American long poem combines these texts by H.D. and Eliot with Walt Whitman's "Song of Myself" (*Leaves*) and the work of more contemporary poets such as Claudia Emerson, Ntozake Shange, and Derek Walcott. One instructor pairs *Trilogy* with Langston Hughes's *Montage of a Dream Deferred* to provoke discussion about montage as poetic method, while another class features

H.D.'s epic with Cynthia Hogue's *The Incognito Body*. On H.D. and notions of the visionary, teachers recommend teaching *Trilogy* with her artistic manifesto *Notes on Thought and Vision* and writings by W. H. Auden, Lawrence, and William Butler Yeats.

H.D.'s fiction also appears on syllabi for modernist classes with the works of Djuna Barnes, Jane Bowles, Emily Holmes Coleman, Ford Madox Ford, Charlotte Perkins Gilman, Hemingway, James Joyce, Lawrence, Dorothy Richardson, Stein, Oscar Wilde, and Virginia Woolf. One course on queer modernisms reads H.D.'s *Paint It Today* with Barnes's *Nightwood*, Radclyffe Hall's *The Unlit Lamp*, E. M. Forster's *Maurice*, Stein's *The Autobiography of Alice B. Toklas*, and Sylvia Townsend Warner's *Mr. Fortune's Maggot*. Another teacher pairs H.D.'s *HERmione* with Joyce's *Portrait of the Artist as a Young Man* in a course on the modernist *Bildungsroman* and *Künstlerroman*. H.D. wrote in her later years that she had composed *Pilate's Wife* in part as a response to Lawrence's *The Man Who Died*, and teaching these short novels together provokes stimulating conversations about these two biographically linked writers.

Many sent us syllabi for courses on women's literature that feature H.D.'s writing. H.D. is taught with Barnes, Coleman, Loy, Moore, Richardson, Edith Sitwell, and Stein in courses on women modernists. One class on modernism and psychoanalysis spends a unit on H.D.'s *Tribute to Freud*, Stein's *The Making of Americans*, and Moore's "The Mind Is an Enchanting Thing"; a similarly themed course pairs H.D.'s writing with that of Lawrence. Emily Dickinson and H.D. are often taught together, and one instructor teaches a course on Dickinson, H.D., Sylvia Plath, and Adrienne Rich. Other courses that feature modernists with later poets teach H.D. and other early-twentieth-century writers—including Lowell, Edna St. Vincent Millay, and Moore—with later poets such as Muriel Rukeyser and Denise Levertov. Texts by other late-twentieth-century women writers read with H.D. in gender studies courses include Angela Carter's *The Bloody Chamber*, Audre Lorde's *Black Unicorn*, Anne Sexton's *Transformations*, Leslie Marmon Silko's *Storyteller*, and any number of Jeannette Winterson's novels.

Feminist revisionist mythmaking is a popular topic for a course or a unit within a course. Instructors teach H.D.'s poetry with works by Margaret Atwood ("Circe / Mud Poems" in *You Are Happy*, "Bluebeard's Egg"), Octavia Butler ("Bloodchild"), Elizabeth Cook (*Achilles: A Novel*), Rita Dove (*Mother Love*), Carol Ann Duffy (*The World's Wife*), Debora Greger (*God* and *Desert Fathers, Uranium Daughters*), Maxine Hong Kingston ("White Tigers" in *The Woman Warrior*), Levertov's many volumes, Lorde (*Black Unicorn*), and Rich ("Diving into the Wreck"). Creative nonfiction books such as Rachel Blau DuPlessis's *The Pink Guitar* and Alicia Suskin Ostriker's *Feminist Revision and the Bible* offer useful theoretical frameworks. H.D.'s poems that take on female personae from mythology lend themselves to wonderful comparisons with both ancient sources, such as Ovid, and contemporaneous and modern-day poems about the same myth. One course asks students to read book 10 of the *Odyssey* with

H.D.'s "Circe" and Atwood's "Circe / Mud Poems" and then to look at Ovid's story of Orpheus alongside H.D.'s "Eurydice," Rainer Maria Rilke's *Sonnets to Orpheus*, and Jorie Graham's "Orpheus and Eurydice." An extremely productive classroom exercise is to have students compare (in writing or in discussion) various poems about Leda: these might include poems by H.D., Barbara Bentley, Lucille Clifton, Nina Kossman, Robert Graves, Lawrence, Rilke, Helen Van Duyn, and Yeats. Yet another is reading together Edgar Allan Poe's "To Helen," Yeats's "No Second Troy," and H.D.'s "Helen." In this vein, Kossman's *Gods and Mortals: Modern Poems on Classical Myths* is an excellent source.

Instructors report a number of other contexts for H.D.'s work. A course on modernism, war, and insanity brings together H.D.'s writing with works by Barnes (*Nightwood*), Eliot (*The Waste Land*), Fitzgerald (*Tender Is the Night*), Hemingway (*The Sun Also Rises, A Farewell to Arms,* and *The Garden of Eden*), Lawrence (*Sons and Lovers* and *The Rainbow*), Pound (*Cantos*), and Stein (*Everybody's Autobiography* and *The Autobiography of Alice B. Toklas*). One teacher uses Victorian poetry by women to set the stage for H.D.'s early lyrics and *Trilogy*, including Elizabeth Barrett Browning's "The Virgin Mary to the Child Jesus," Charlotte Brontë's "Pilate's Wife's Dream," and Christina Rossetti's Sappho poems. Another instructor teaches a unit on the persona poem that features H.D.'s poetry with dramatic monologues by Robert Browning, Eliot's "Journey of the Magi," Williams's "The Widow's Lament in Springtime," and Pound's "The River Merchant's Wife: A Letter." We read about yet another course that looks at H.D., Lawrence, and Flannery O'Connor in terms of their treatment of Christianity.

Classroom Assignments

To supplement assignments and exercises described in part 2, "Approaches," here we draw from our own experience and cull from all the teaching materials we received from our correspondents to highlight some of the more innovative ideas. Though we learned from all the materials sent to us, we wish to extend special thanks to these teachers for contributing the discussion questions and assignments that appear in this section: Marsha Bryant, Kimberly Engdahl Coates, Christine E. Coffman, Miranda B. Hickman, and Bret L. Keeling. It became clear in this process that H.D.'s writing inspires a wide array of approaches and assignments: explications, position papers, seminar papers, creative parodies, multimedia presentations, and more.

Assignments requiring students to compare H.D. with other writers or to analyze her use of mythological figures are common and extremely fruitful (see "Teaching H.D. with Texts by Others," above, for possible pairings). Instructors shared with us a variety of directive questions as well, which can be used in classroom discussion or as paper topics. Some of these questions apply to many of H.D.'s texts, such as asking students to explore her revisionary mythmaking through Helen; to characterize H.D.'s response to war (Is her poetry redemptive? How do the world wars both devastate and inspire H.D.?); to consider whether "feminine language" is a term that can be applied to H.D.'s writing; or to clarify the role of imperialism in her texts. Coffman asks students to consider how the urban experience is linked to the modes of perception exploited in a given text through its relation to temporality, modernity, imperialism, gender, or sexuality. Coates encourages her students to think about how H.D.'s work illustrates modernism's role in unsettling the assumptions of literary practice, assumptions about the linearity of narrative, the sanctity of authorial control over the text, generic definitions and limits, the security of textual boundaries, and the relation of theme to narrative form. She also encourages students to take into account how H.D.'s novels discover that the self is largely a social construction. Coates asks if the expatriate experience clarifies the construction of the self and how the expatriate experience is imagined as a way to rewrite or to disavow old cultural scripts. Hickman offers similarly challenging questions, asking students to explore how H.D.'s early poems treat the idea of a "new beauty," a line from "Sheltered Garden" in *Sea Garden*. She also suggests that students look at the attitudes toward math and science implied in *Tribute to Freud* and *HERmione*; read H.D.'s representation of the body in *Notes on Thought and Vision*; scrutinize the portrayal of Miss Ames in *Bid Me to Live*, a militant suffragette from the prewar period, reflecting on how she is viewed by the bohemian circles in which Julia Ashton moves; and construct an argument about what H.D.'s *Nights* suggests about the discipline of psychoanalysis in comparison with its prologue or with *Tribute to Freud*.

Several instructors mention forming panels in class around controversial topics. Bryant uses *Trilogy* to launch a debate among her students. Three to four students respond to a discussion topic, based on one of H.D.'s shorter poems or "the Lady" sequence in *Trilogy*. She might ask students to debate how H.D.'s Lady of *Tribute to the Angels* intersects with the Christian figure of Mary, mother of Jesus. Ultimately, she wants to know if H.D.'s extended use of the Mary figure in *The Flowering of the Rod* works toward or against her revision of religion in *Trilogy*.

Teachers also described creative projects that have worked well in their classes. Several teachers ask their students to define the conventions of modernist poetry, specifically imagism, and then write a poem that fits those conventions. Alternatively, some instructors ask students to parody one of H.D.'s poems, as another way to understand form. Inspired by Allen Ginsberg's "Sunflower Sutra," one of Bryant's students wrote an especially fine parody of H.D.'s "Sea Rose." Students might be asked to engage *Helen in Egypt* or *Trilogy* in a creative project that takes shape in a medium other than the written word—a song, a painting, a sculpture, or a short film—as Keeling does. Another larger, visual project Bryant shared with us asks students to be creative, to become practicing modern artists following H.D.'s example of triangulating self, myth, and history in her work, applying an approach recommended by Helen Sword in "Teaching in Color." For their projects, students take this list of ingredients and mix it in some visual medium: three visual images (drawing, painting, photographs, hieroglyphs, ideograms); five to eight literary quotations, two of them from H.D.'s work; at least two mythic references (traditional, popular, or legendary figures); at least one event of historical significance; at least one autobiographical event narrated in the first person, authentic or invented; at least one psychological or psychoanalytical allusion; and additional elements of their choice. Bryant reports that this project yields a text that is meaningful on multiple levels.

Part Two

APPROACHES

Introduction: Biographical Contexts

Annette Debo and Lara Vetter

H.D. had personal connections to many of the major poets and artists of her time, and much of her work resonates biographically. But, more important, she was an integral part of the international movement known as modernism; helped found imagism, the early avant-garde free verse movement; and was witness to, and recorder of, many of the pivotal historical moments of the first six decades of the twentieth century. An early innovator of experimental form in poetry and prose, H.D. also traverses an extraordinary terrain of modernist thematic concerns in her writing. With T. S. Eliot and Ezra Pound, she shared a keen interest in comparative mythology and ancient models of civilization, but her writing diverges from theirs in her focus on female deities suppressed in the modern era. Dubbed the "perfect bi[sexual]" by her analyst, Sigmund Freud (Friedman, *Analyzing* 497), H.D. depicted heterodox sexualities that break definitively the strictures and silences of the Victorian era, offering, as did Gertrude Stein and Radclyffe Hall, alternative models of love and family. An avid student of the new field of psychoanalysis, H.D. followed her modernist peers in transmuting psychoanalytic principles into artistic ones. If, as Leon Surette has argued, "[e]veryone 'dabbled' in the occult" in this period (36), H.D. is no different; her life's work continually returns to the role of the mystical in a modern industrial society seemingly and increasingly devoid of faith. The two world wars are typically seen as constituting the temporal boundaries of the modernist era, and H.D.'s lifelong examination of the power and destructiveness of war includes epic poetry on the origins of war as well as prose ruminations on the politics of the personal—the impact of war on the home front. Her poetry was central to the beginnings of modernism, and she continued to write for nearly five decades after her lyrics launched imagism.

Hilda Doolittle (1886–1961)

On 10 September 1886, Hilda Doolittle was born to Charles Doolittle, professor of astronomy and mathematics at Lehigh University, and Helen Wolle Doolittle in Bethlehem, Pennsylvania, a town founded by Moravians, a mystical Protestant sect to which her mother's family belonged. Her Moravian childhood is fictionalized in her 1940s novel *The Gift*. The only girl of six children, H.D. had three brothers and two half brothers by her father's first marriage. When her father became professor of astronomy at the University of Pennsylvania, H.D. and her family moved to Upper Darby, a suburb of Philadelphia, where she attended a Quaker school considered a top preparatory school. In 1905, H.D. matriculated at Bryn Mawr College, one of the Seven Sisters known for its academic rigor, where she first met a woman who would prove to be another central modernist figure, Marianne Moore, initiating one of H.D.'s most important literary relationships. At Bryn Mawr, H.D. pursued science and mathematics, following in the footsteps of her father and brothers, but at the end of her third semester, she withdrew after performing poorly in several classes. During the 1908–09 academic year, she took courses at the University of Pennsylvania, where she again found the academic success she had achieved in secondary school.

It is in Philadelphia that H.D. first met Pound at a Halloween ball in 1901, as well as William Carlos Williams in 1905 and Frances Josepha Gregg around 1910. H.D. and Pound became engaged around 1905, an intermittent tie that never resulted in marriage, and the bisexual love triangle of H.D., Pound, and Gregg is touched on in H.D.'s autobiographical novels *HERmione*, *Paint It Today*, and *Asphodel*. It was also in Philadelphia that H.D. began to write poetry, as she and Pound studied together the pre-Raphaelites, the decadents, and Balzac. Pound dedicated his earliest poems to her in a handmade volume entitled *Hilda's Book* (H.D., *End to Torment* 67–84). H.D. and Gregg, a student at the Pennsylvania Academy of Fine Arts, wrote poetry to each other and read A. C. Swinburne's verse together, especially entranced by his poetry with references to lesbianism. Pound and Gregg remained important influences on H.D.; Gregg, who died in a bombing in World War II, figured significantly in H.D.'s erotic imagination, and Pound haunts H.D. late in life, witnessed by her memoir *End to Torment* and her poem "Winter Love" (in *Hermetic Definition*), works that chronicle their early relationship.

In 1911, H.D. began her expatriate life when she sailed to Europe on the *Floride* with Gregg and Gregg's mother and decided, like many other American writers and artists of the period, to remain. In London, through Pound, she was introduced to many early modernist luminaries, including Eliot; the British poets Richard Aldington and William Butler Yeats; the English novelists May Sinclair, Violet Hunt, Wyndham Lewis, and Ford Madox Ford; and the future fellow imagists F. S. Flint, John Gould Fletcher, and John Cournos. In 1912, H.D., Pound, and Aldington decided on the principles of imagism, a short-lived but highly influential vanguard movement that produced some of the first vers libre in English. Eschewing the emotional excess of much nineteenth-century verse as well as the rigid forms of traditional poetry, imagist poetry was dedicated to direct treatment of objects, sparse language, and rhythm based in music rather than prescribed conventional meters. H.D.'s verse served as principal exemplar of the movement; published in Harriet Monroe's *Poetry* in 1913, H.D.'s poems "Epigram," "Hermes of the Ways," and "Priapus" formally launched imagism. Another journal, the *Egoist* (known as the *New Freewoman* until 1914), became a voice for the movement, and H.D. was assistant editor for one year, a position turned over to Eliot in 1917. Pound oversaw the 1914 imagist anthology *Des Imagistes*, but he eventually ceded the movement to the American poet Amy Lowell, and three additional anthologies of imagist poetry were produced during the years of World War I. Through Lowell H.D. met the British novelist D. H. Lawrence in 1914, who for a time shared her residence in Bloomsbury. Her autobiographical novel *Bid Me to Live* chronicles her relationship with Lawrence, whose views of spirituality and gender both inspired and infuriated her. H.D. was published widely in many prominent little magazines and journals on both sides of the Atlantic, and her first poetry volume, *Sea Garden*, appeared in 1916. She also worked extensively in the 1910s on translations of Euripides, Sappho, and other ancient Greek dramatists and poets, fascinated, as so many modernists were, with ancient Greece and comparative mythology.

In 1913 H.D. traveled to Italy with her parents and Aldington, whom she married in London in October of that year in a brief civil ceremony witnessed by her parents and Pound. Aldington fought at the front during World War I, and the couple separated by the end of the war; they divorced formally in 1938 but remained frequent correspondents for the rest of their lives. The war years were traumatic: H.D. suffered the stillbirth of her and Aldington's daughter in 1915 and the deaths of her brother Gilbert, a soldier, in 1918 and her father in 1919. While Aldington carried out an intense affair with Dorothy (Arabella) Yorke, H.D. conceived a child with the musician Cecil Gray. Frances Perdita was born on 31 March 1919 and named for both Gregg and the heroine of William Shakespeare's *A Winter's Tale*. H.D.'s life during World War I is fictionalized in several novels, including *Paint It To-day*, *Asphodel*, and *Bid Me to Live*, and her experience of that war continued to resound in her writings of World War II and the Cold War.

In 1918, H.D. had tea with an avid fan of her poetry, the English writer and wealthy heiress Annie Winifred Ellerman (known as Bryher), the daughter of the shipping magnate Sir John Ellerman. This meeting resulted in the most significant romantic relationship of H.D.'s life and a lifelong companionship. Having nursed H.D. through the influenza outbreak of 1919, Bryher journeyed with her to the Isles of Scilly, to Greece (with the sexologist Havelock Ellis in tow), to New York (to reunite with Moore), and to the California coast, where they took nude photographs of each other, the basis of several collages in the "H.D. Scrapbook" produced in the late 1920s and early 1930s. H.D.'s mystical experience in the Isles of Scilly led to the composition of her aesthetic manifesto *Notes on Thought and Vision*, which explores her theories of the spiritual, intellectual, and somatic development of artistic consciousness. This mystical experience and three others are detailed and analyzed in her 1940s prose texts *Majic Ring* and *Tribute to Freud*.

The early 1920s saw the publication of new volumes of poetry that delve into Greek mythology from a woman's perspective—H.D.'s famed "revisionist mythmaking" (Ostriker, *Stealing* 222–28)—*Hymen* and *Heliodora*; the verse drama *Hippolytus Temporizes*; and the formal beginning of H.D.'s prolific fiction writing (under a variety of noms de plume) that ranged from a retelling of the days of Christ (*Pilate's Wife*) to a mythic narrative of ancient Greece (*Hedylus*). This decade also brought more international travel, as H.D., Bryher, and H.D.'s mother visited Italy, Greece, Constantinople, and Egypt. These trips fueled H.D.'s keen interest in several ancient cultures at a time when most modernists remained focused on Greece. H.D. knew the British Museum's famed Egyptology collection well, and her 1923 visit to the then recently excavated sites of Karnak and Luxor in Egypt provided further inspiration for her use of Egyptian mythology, architecture, and sacred spaces in her prose work *Palimpsest* and her epic poems *Trilogy* and *Helen in Egypt*. Also during this time, H.D. met Mary Butts, the scandalous British novelist she much admired, and was photographed by the surrealist artist Man Ray (Silverstein). Likewise, H.D. circulated among many young artists who became foundational modernist figures, such as Ernest Hemingway, James Joyce, Nancy Cunard, and Dorothy Richardson. H.D. and Bryher were also part of the legendary lesbian literary circles of the time and enjoyed friendships with Alice B. Toklas, Stein, Sylvia Beach, and Adrienne Monnier.

Bryher was rapidly becoming a major patron of modernist art and literature. Under pressure to appear more conventional to her family and to shield her relationship with H.D., she married twice in the 1920s. Her first marriage was to the writer Robert McAlmon, with whom she established a key modernist imprint, Contact Press, and her second was to one of H.D.'s significant lovers, the bisexual filmmaker and writer Kenneth Macpherson. With Macpherson, H.D. and Bryher became interested in cinema, and the three began to spend time in Berlin with German filmmakers such as Georg Pabst. The threesome formed the POOL group, which produced several silent films, including *Borderline* (1930), starring H.D. and the internationally renowned African American star Paul Robeson. Barred entry into the United States because of its portrayal of an interracial sexual relationship, the film explores racism, violence, and racial identity, themes H.D. also addressed in a marketing piece for the film (now known as "The *Borderline* Pamphlet") and in her short story "Two Americans" (published in 1938 in *The Usual Star* and reprinted in 1987). Funded by Bryher and edited by Bryher and Macpherson, *Close Up* was born, the first journal to treat film as a serious art form. *Close Up* was published from 1927 to 1933 and distributed throughout Europe and the United States, featuring articles by its editors, H.D., and a number of modernist writers and filmmakers such as Sergei Eisenstein, Hanns Sachs, Richardson, Stein, and Moore.

The 1930s also marked H.D.'s increasing interest in psychoanalysis. She underwent analysis first with Mary Chadwick and Sachs and later with Erich Heydt in the 1950s, but H.D.'s sessions with Freud in 1933 and 1934 have received the most attention. Freud's theories of the history of civilization, of gender and sexuality, and of family and trauma proved tremendously illuminating in a time when H.D. felt stifled creatively and anxious about the darkening world stage, although, as she wrote famously in her memoir of the experience, *Tribute to Freud*, "the Professor was not always right" (98). In Vienna, H.D. was faced with the growing Nazi presence in 1933, the year Hitler became chancellor and the Gestapo was founded, and she documented the ominous presence of armed Nazi guards and the showers of paper swastikas on the streets where she walked. Despite the gravity of the historical moment, H.D. found help in her sessions with Freud, who is considered a model for Theseus (the older, wise guide) in *Helen in Egypt* and who is figured in the poem "The Master." During this decade H.D.'s mother passed away, as did Bryher's parents. H.D. and Aldington's divorce became final in 1938, and in 1939 H.D. drafted sections of *Bid Me to Live*, the last of her novels to recall the World War I period. The commonplace that H.D. went through a dry spell in the 1930s is untrue; she published the poetry volume *Red Roses for Bronze* (now available in Martz's edition of *Collected Poems*); several novellas; her one book for children, *The Hedgehog*; and more than twenty short pieces, including a serialization in *Life and Letters To-day* of part of her memoir of Freud, *Writing on the Wall* (in *Tribute to Freud*).

Though she received many offers of refuge from Americans, H.D. chose to remain in London when England entered World War II, withstanding the Battle of Britain, the Blitz, the later doodlebugs and V2 flying bombs, sleepless nights, bombed buildings, injured friends, and severe food and fuel shortages. Despite her embarrassment that the United States had not entered the war earlier—H.D. even uncharacteristically published "A Letter from England" in the *Bryn Mawr Alumnae Bulletin* encouraging Americans to act—at the war's conclusion, she hoisted an oversized American flag into her window. The daily terrors and deprivations of the war years were incredibly generative for H.D. Her famed war epic, *Trilogy*, was published in three parts: *The Walls Do Not Fall* in 1944, *Tribute to the Angels* in 1945, and *The Flowering of the Rod* in 1946. In the midst of the chaos, she also produced a chronicle of the war, *Within the Walls*; an autobiographical novel of her childhood, *The Gift*; a thin volume of poems, *What Do I Love?*; a study of English Renaissance writers, *By Avon River*, that merged poetry and prose; and a novelization of her experiments with séances, *Majic Ring*. Immediately following the war, she completed three additional novels that plumb heterodox spiritualities but also stress more politicized themes found in the texts of other late modernists, such as the origins of war, the palimpsestic nature of history, and the politics of gender. *The Sword Went Out to Sea (Synthesis of a Dream)* at once fictionalizes her experience of the war and delves into the violent history of British nationalism; *White Rose and the Red*, like *By Avon River*, contemplates literary history, this time in a fictionalized story of Dante Gabriel Rossetti's wife, Elizabeth Siddall; and *The Mystery* delves into the history of the Moravian church.

During the war, H.D. developed a close friendship with Norman Holmes Pearson, who was serving in the Office for Strategic Services (OSS), which would become the CIA after the war's conclusion. On his return to Yale University after the war, as Yale built its impressive modernist holdings, Pearson offered H.D. a "shelf" at the Beinecke Rare Book and Manuscript Library, where she deposited her first editions, published but uncirculated material, manuscripts, letters, diaries, photographs, legal documents, films, and more—enough to fill not just a shelf but boxes upon boxes. Providing encouragement and an enthusiastic audience tightly connected to the literary academy, Pearson convinced H.D. to revise old manuscripts, to reveal her sources and inspirations, to pen reminiscences, and even to produce an audio recording of *Helen in Egypt*. Pearson oversaw the publication of *Selected Poems* in 1957, which showcased some of her best early work as well as her mature, more complex poetry. In the last five years of her life, she composed still more poetry, including *Vale Ave* and the poems that would make up *Hermetic Definition*: "Sagesse," "Winter Love," and "Hermetic Definition." Her second epic, *Helen in Egypt*, was also composed in the mid-1950s and published in 1961; reputedly a copy of it was placed in her hands days before her death. The reminiscences requested by Pearson of the aging H.D. included not only several autobiographical texts but also an essay commenting on her life's postimagist work, "H.D. by Delia Alton," and a memoir about Ezra Pound, *End to Torment*.

As the modernist canon was constructed during the Cold War, H.D. repatriated in 1958, recovering her American citizenship, which had been stripped from her by American law when she married the British Aldington. This choice cemented her place in the American literary canon and made her eligible for American literary awards, a flurry of which followed in the few remaining years of her life. In 1958 H.D. was awarded the Harriet Monroe Memorial Prize from *Poetry*; she was a finalist for the National Book Award in both 1958 and 1962; she received the Brandeis University Creative Arts Award for Poetry in 1959; in 1960 Bryn Mawr awarded her the Citation for Distinguished Service, akin to an honorary doctorate; and she became an honorary member of the Poetry Society of America. Her crowning moment of critical acclaim was in 1960, when the American Academy of Arts and Letters awarded her the Award of Merit for outstanding achievement in poetry, the first time it was ever awarded to a woman.

H.D. spent the last decade and a half of her life living independently in Swiss clinics and residential hotels in Küsnacht, Lausanne, and Lugano, even though she continued to travel, largely with Bryher, to the United States, Paris, Rome, Venice, and elsewhere in Europe. Abdominal surgery in 1953 and a broken hip in 1956 curtailed her mobility, and from 1955 to 1961 she largely resided in the Klinik Brunner. In June 1961, she suffered a stroke, closely followed by a heart attack. Weakened by a virus that fall, H.D. died on 27 September 1961. Bryher chose to bury H.D.'s ashes in Bethlehem in Nisky Hill Cemetery, up the street from her childhood home. Her simple gravestone, often adorned with seashells left by visitors, is engraved with lines from her poem "Epitaph," which Pearson read at a memorial service in the Moravian church she attended as a child:

> so you may say,
> "Greek flower; Greek ecstasy
> reclaims for ever
>
> one who died
> following
> intricate songs' lost measure."
> (*Collected Poems* 299–300)

Other Biographical Sources

This brief sketch is largely drawn from and usefully supplemented by several good biographical sources for H.D. The most accessible and accurate source is Susan Stanford Friedman's 1986 entry in the *Dictionary of Literary Biography*. With the help of fourteen carefully reproduced illustrations, this thirty-five-page article summarizes H.D.'s life and body of work. Friedman situates H.D. not only biographically but also within wider historical and literary contexts, carefully delineating H.D.'s constant movement throughout Europe, her complex erotic attachments, and her persistent literary production. Another invaluable biographical resource is the late Louis Silverstein's six-part "H.D. Chronology." Silverstein methodically cataloged H.D.'s voluminous papers at the Beinecke Rare Book and Manuscript Library at Yale University, an undertaking that gave him an expansive understanding of her life. He compiled the chronology over many years and with the combined contributions of many H.D. scholars.

Herself Defined: The Poet H.D. and Her World, by the poet Barbara Guest, offers a largely accurate account of H.D.'s life in a reader's edition—that is, the volume contains a selected bibliography but no scholarly documentation. Published in 1984, this biography sensitively grapples with the immense amount of material, published and unpublished, about H.D. and offers readers a cogent account of H.D.'s life. Janice S. Robinson's *H.D.: The Life and Work of an American Poet* is not recommended. Gillian Hanscombe and Virginia L. Smyers offer biographical information about H.D. in *Writing for Their Lives*, which focuses on the networks of modernist women writers. The authors trace two themes—women's financial and literary patronage and the connection between being a writer and adopting a fluid sexual identity—through several women writers' lives. One chapter is dedicated to H.D., another to Bryher, and both women are mentioned throughout. Because a Wikipedia entry is never finalized and may be edited by anyone, the one on H.D. can at times contain inaccuracies that can be difficult for students to identify.

Other critical works add some occasional details to these biographical accounts, but most rely on the existing research, such as Shari Benstock's *Women of the Left Bank*, which offers a useful contextualization of H.D. and Bryher in the lesbian circles of Paris. Friedman and Rachel Blau DuPlessis's *Signets* offers some significant quasi-biographical material: "A Photobiography of H.D." (well-reproduced and carefully captioned photographs of H.D. and significant people in her life), "Herself Delineated: Chronological Highlights of H.D." (a condensed version of Silverstein's timeline of H.D.'s life), and "Dating H.D.'s Writing" (a chart offering composition and publication dates for H.D.'s texts; an updated version appears in Friedman's *Penelope's Web*).

Companions of the Flame: Teaching H.D. with Other Modern Poets

Mara Scanlon

Narratives about modern poetry have been dominated by masculine lineages and alliances: Walt Whitman to William Carlos Williams, Carl Sandburg, and Louis Zukofsky; Williams versus T. S. Eliot; and Ezra Pound as the consummate insider-outlaw, a poetic player with his hand in every mix. In such narratives, those who do not easily fit this main plotline can be seen as important but marginal, interesting but not essential. Here I posit that H.D., now recognized as a significant and innovative poet, might be placed right in the conceptual center of a course on modern poetry; the graphic on the next page suggests only some of the promising connections that emerge if we think about H.D. in the company of her fellow modern poets (see fig. 1). Suddenly, new alliances appear: H.D. prophesizes like Pound, emphasizes the concrete like Williams, practices linguistic innovation like Marianne Moore, excoriates war like Wilfred Owen, rejects the hegemonic like Gertrude Stein, and shifts from the lyric to the epic like Langston Hughes.

When I teach such a class, I work from collections of individual poets rather than from a general modern poetry anthology, illustrating what I see as some of the most important concepts, movements, strategies, or styles of the period but also tracing a poet's variety or growth over time. Thanks to the critical work of the last twenty years, all the poets I include might now be widely considered major, to use a vexed term, but I do approach the class with a framework drawn from "the new modernisms," which complicates traditional canonical assumptions about what modernism looked like aesthetically and ideologically. The most common pool I use in designing my undergraduate modern poetry class consists of H.D., T. S. Eliot, Robert Frost, Langston Hughes, Marianne Moore, Wilfred

Fig. 1. Locating H.D. in a web of modernists

Owen, Ezra Pound, Gertrude Stein, Wallace Stevens, William Carlos Williams, and William Butler Yeats, from which I strategically choose about seven or eight at a time.

From the group of poets we study, the class is able to take up topics including but not limited to the following: imagism and its related manifestos and movements; the shift from spare lyric to long poem or epic; gender; revisions or rejections of formalist compositions and meters and the turn to alternatives such as the musical or the rhythms of spoken languages; revisionary mythology; the role of little magazines; sexuality; the effect of World War I and sometimes World War II; expatriatism or nationalism; vision, prophecy, and the occult; race; the rejection of or nostalgia for old ideologies, structures, and codes and the concomitant search for new gods or goddesses; (in)equalities, forms; (in)stability, identities, or linguistic practices; access to publication; the subjective mind; and stylistic markers such as fragmentation, the metapoetic, multivocality, discontinuity, allusion, and wordplay. In addition to class discussion, I assign frequent, short writings (five hundred words) that can prompt focused analysis of one poet or poem or can take up a honed comparison (e.g., compare one significant aspect of the Lady in Eliot's "Ash-Wednesday" with the Lady in H.D.'s *Tribute to the Angels* [*Trilogy*]). The topics generally emerge through more than one writer, creating a semester in which we delve deeply into individual poets but also begin to track patterns of connection and disjunction among them. Certainly across the body of her work in poetry, fiction, creative nonfiction, and film, H.D. engages every topic in the list above, but even in a limited text like *Collected Poems, 1912–1944* we can find a surprisingly large number of them.

The three modernists with whom H.D. has been most consistently discussed and for whom, consequently, there exist good critical resources are Ezra Pound, William Carlos Williams, and Marianne Moore (see, e.g., Ostriker, "What"; Pondrom, "H.D." and "Marianne Moore"; Baccolini; Twitchell-Waas; Korg; Phelan; Orange), and it is fair to speculate that the reasons may be as much biographical as textual. Pound and H.D. for much of their adult lives had a relationship that waxed and waned but was never psychologically or professionally distant. Their collaboration (with Richard Aldington and F. S. Flint as well) in theorizing imagism is well examined, as is their intimate and fraught relationship with Williams, whom they both met in young adulthood. H.D. and Moore met at Bryn Mawr, and H.D.'s instrumentality in publishing Moore's work, as well as the availability of some of their letters in *The Selected Letters of Marianne Moore*, makes a study of the two women rich, especially for studying communities of artistic women in that time period. My intention here is to focus on some of the pedagogical methods and benefits of studying H.D. with these poets.

As noted, it can be hard to move beyond the biographical in pairing H.D. with Pound and Williams, since the story of Pound's so–called discovery of the poet he would mock to Williams in a 1920 letter as "the refined, charming, and utterly narrow minded she-bard 'H.D.'" (*Letters* 157) is nearly iconic in the history of imagism, a movement that Eliot said was "usually and conveniently taken as the starting-point of modern poetry" (qtd. in Bornstein 28). Critics are not yet done arguing which of the three poets most typifies imagism, whether Williams is appropriately included, and whether those early lyrics mark H.D.'s poetic high point. But in the classroom it may be effective to identify more straightforwardly the clear modernist turn toward image-object-objective correlative from poetic narrative or subjective expression ("No ideas / but in things," writes Williams [*Selected Poems* 145]) and to have the students explore the theories of imagism in action across early lyrics (1912–23) from Pound, Williams, and H.D., not testing viability or perfection but rather seeking a working sense of what this poetic turn actually looked like. Students can see how the poem can, in Pound's words, include "the moving image" and not become static (*ABC* 36); how Williams's interest in the imagination's encounter with the objects of the natural world (paired easily with Stevens and Moore) compares with Pound's or H.D.'s use of a natural image to carry emotion; what a "superfluous word" seems to be and how H.D.'s use of repetition or Williams's colloquial voice may be understood within, or as resistant to, the imagist directive to avoid such superfluity (Pound, "A Few Don'ts" 201). The drive in imagism is toward linguistic precision, and reading H.D., Pound, and Williams together can also establish an interesting tension with H.D.'s refusal of such precision in her long poems.

Rhythm, what Eliot called "the real pattern in the carpet" (qtd. in Vendler 79), deserves special attention when reading Pound, Williams, and H.D. together. Pound insisted that "rhythm MUST have meaning" (*Letters* 49), and Williams's experiments with the variable foot and with rhythm using natural pause were highly influential on later groups like the Black Mountain poets. While in Pound's "The Return," his use of line and rhythm is so close to H.D.'s that the poem might be mistaken as hers ("See, they return; ah, see the tentative / Movements, and the slow feet" [*Selected Poems* 24]), by the time Pound writes "The River-Merchant's Wife: A Letter" and certainly "Hugh Selwyn Mauberley," he moves to a line and rhythm more sentence based ("He strove to resuscitate the dead art" [61]) than H.D.'s typically compressed and incantatory forms ("we met / but one god, / one tall god with a spear-shaft" [*Collected Poems* 61]). Even in the early lyrics Williams provides an interesting middle ground, using very tight, short lines but modeling his larger syntaxes on spoken sentences ("Among the rain / and lights / I saw the figure 5" [*Selected Poems* 36]), a form that both loosens and fractures significantly by *Paterson*. Comparing the rhythm created by syntax and line can add nuance to our understanding of voice, emotional representation, and form. The strictures of imagism and the working maxim that modern poets reject formal poetry ("To break the pentameter," says Pound famously, "that was the first heave" [*Cantos* 532]) may mute discussion of H.D.'s formal poetic strategies, a discussion that reading with these poets (and others like Owen) could reactivate. In addition, Moore can be easily linked to the discussion, though her poetics are generally seen as dissimilar and she felt marginalized "to not be able to be called an 'imagist'" (qtd. in Vendler 78). Her so-called syllabic meter (determining lines by syllables rather than poetic feet—a term she disclaimed and a technique she said was secondary to her conception of the stanza) is a striking modernist variation and, in retaining the syntax of the spoken sentence simultaneously with the disrupted line, provides an excellent comparison with the metric techniques of the other three poets.

Teaching H.D. with Pound, Williams, and Moore can also provoke a discussion about the subject matter of modern poetry and its relation to the mythic past and to the present portrayed in canonical modernism as deficient and bankrupt. In H.D. and Pound we can see an affinity for classical and mythic figures, stories, and images, even if they are significantly revised. In Williams and Moore, conversely, we see an interest in the everyday—the news, the American city, the animals in the zoo, the patient or shopkeeper. Students might also be asked to decide whether there are significant patterns that distinguish or unite the American modernists who did not expatriate from those who did.

Building more explicitly on a consideration of Moore and H.D. as modernist companions, I ask students to compare what the (traditionally male-dominated) discourses, methods, assumptions, or figures of science and of myth hold for the two poets and in what contexts and manners they are mobilized. In each, the object or image or persona can be a safe vehicle for presenting the self, a risky venture for women modernists, whether they adopted genderless initials or were indefatigably identified by the honorific "Miss." Students, like critics, may find useful a comparison of the armored and protected in H.D. and Moore. Moore's "Paper Nautilus," who "constructs her thin glass shell" in defiance of "[w]riters entrapped by / teatime fame" (*Complete Poems* 121), or "The Snail" is constructively examined with the "shell-fish" and shrouded worm lyrics of H.D.'s *The Walls Do Not Fall* ("I sense my own limit, / my shell-jaws snap shut" [*Trilogy* 9]), or with the imagery of rocks, shrines, gardens, and body armor that emerges, and frequently confines, in *Sea Garden*. In both Moore and H.D., students can be asked to trace a (submerged to explicit) critique of masculine power—martial, poetic, political, sexual, or cultural—that is essential to enrich traditional narratives of modernism.

Thinking about H.D. in conjunction with less obvious poet-partners is equally valuable. For instance, the World War I poet Wilfred Owen, who died tragically just days before the war's end and whose work was almost entirely unpublished in his lifetime, is often read in courses on war literature but rarely discussed with H.D., though her traumatic experience of war is well documented. Led by his loyalty to the soldiers in the trenches, Owen bitterly denounced, including in gendered ways, the inexperience of those who did not fight, such as in the poem "The Send-Off," where men board a train for duty:

> So secretly, like wrongs hushed-up, they went.
> They were not ours:
> We never heard to which front these were sent.
>
> Nor there if they yet mock what women meant
> Who gave them flowers. (46)

Owen's poetry read in company with *The Walls Do Not Fall* opens a rich discussion of various issues, such as authority (Who can write about war or claim first-hand experience of it?); gender; a band of "initiates," to use H.D.'s word (*Trilogy* 21), or of brothers, to use the term commonly invoked for soldiers; trauma and violence; and the rejection of old truisms about war's glory, denounced by Owen as "[t]he old Lie" in his famous poem "*Dulce et Decorum Est*" (55).

Thematically, the two poets complement, intensify, and sometimes contradict each other. Owen's quiet despair over war offers a productive contrast to the somewhat frenzied incantations of H.D.'s *Walls* and the sense of possibility that accompanies fear and destruction there. His consideration of the traps of masculinity in poems like "Disabled" can be discussed in relation to H.D.'s negotiation of the feminine in "Sheltered Garden" or "Orchard," among many other poems, in showing the interrogations of gender and sexuality in the period. Furthermore, a poem like "Loss," from H.D.'s *Sea Garden*, in which the homoeroticism between male soldiers emerges in an apostrophe from one man to his beautiful dead companion, can illuminate the similar complexes of eroticism, grief, and violence in poems like Owen's tender, brutal lyric "Arms and the Boy" or the pastoral revision "Futility."

In addition to providing thematic comparisons, Owen's poetry resonates with H.D.'s in his intense use of sound and half rhyme. More formal than many other modernists, Owen still revises expectations of rhyme patterns. Some characteristic pieces are written in couplets that end with dense, reverberating sound created by multiple consonances, as in "Strange Meeting": escaped/scooped, eyes/bless, moan/mourn, grained/ground, laughed/left, spoiled/spilled, killed/cold (35–36). In a piece like this, the closure of the couplet form and the repetitive sounds of the half-rhymed line endings create a claustrophobic or claustrophonic, occasionally choking lyric appropriate to the poem's setting, an underground trench or tunnel, an underworld in which the speaker meets face-to-face the enemy he killed in the prior battle.

H.D.'s use of repetition and half rhyme can signal entrapment but may also sound like incantation. Consider a poem like "Helen," in which the three short irregular stanzas (five, six, and seven lines) bear a great deal of repetition (e.g., "white" four times, "Greece" three times) and numerous internal couplets and other lines that are rhymed and half-rhymed: hates/face, reviles/smiles, still/ills, unmoved/love, feet/knees/cypresses, maid/laid (*Collected Poems* 154–55). Similar strategies can be read in "Sheltered Garden," where, again, half rhymes and assonance or consonance—like enough/breath, last/hill-crest, resin/astringent/pinks, or cloth/frost/straw—illustrate easily aural experimentation in free verse (*Complete Poems* 19–20). Eliot's poetry, at times equally incantatory, can be effortlessly included in such study as well. I have frequently found it useful to have students write close imitations of poets like H.D. and Owen, asking them to show some mastery over the sounds, stanzaic patterns, or rhythms adeptly manipulated by these modernists.

Before turning from form and related issues, I would note that H.D.'s close attention to language's sound can also fortify a study with Gertrude Stein. H.D.'s fiction more explicitly takes up female sexuality and lesbian desire, important issues for Stein, than does her poetry. But both women's poetry encodes such desire, and both poets also disrupt traditional usage and continuities of language, frequently through sound manipulation, in exposing language's inadequacy for what must be said or conceived. For instance, H.D's well-studied alchemy in *Tribute to the Angels*, in which she "distill[s]" the "word most bitter, *marah*" through subtle shifts of sound and meaning ("mer, mere, mère, mater, Maia, Mary") into "Mother" (*Trilogy* 71), is a manipulation of sound and language resonant with Stein's punning, even in a more accessible poem like "Susie Asado" ("Sweet sweet sweet sweet sweet tea. / Susie Asado. / Susie Asado is a told tray sure" [*Selected Writings* 549]). The extent to which Stein pushes the limits of available syntax and vocabulary also might remind us of the moment in H.D.'s *Tribute to the Angels*, cantos 13–14, when the poet's "patron" tells her to "invent" a name for an essence she tries to describe, an order that she resists by talking about it in terms of color, fragrance, and pulse (*Trilogy* 76–77). Many modernist writers struggle with a sense that language's structures and vocabularies will no longer suffice, leading to intense fragmentations of form and syntax in poems such as Eliot's *The Waste Land*, and the sound play of Stein and H.D. can be considered on this spectrum of linguistic revision.

Revisionary poesis is a primary connection between H.D. and another modernist with whom she may be infrequently considered, Langston Hughes. Consider a poem like "Aunt Sue's Stories" from Hughes's early volume *Afro-American Fragments* (in *Selected Poems*). On the porch at night, he tells us, "Aunt Sue cuddles a brown-faced child to her bosom / And tells him stories" (6), stories about "black slaves" working, walking, singing, stories that the

> . . . dark-faced child, listening,
> Knows . . . are real stories.
> He knows that Aunt Sue never got her stories
> Out of any book at all. (6)

A poem like this, in which the power of what is in books is usurped by the nurturing, female, African American storyteller, resonates with a poem like H.D.'s *Tribute to the Angels* in its claim to new narrative authority:

> she carries a book but it is not
> the tome of the ancient wisdom,
> the pages, I imagine, are the blank pages
> of the unwritten volume of the new.
> (*Trilogy* 103)

In both cases, the collapse of prior hierarchies long associated with modernist nostalgia instead nudges open a sense of possibility (even if sometimes knotty) in writers like H.D. and Hughes, and the comparison builds a reason for the class to deeply interrogate assumptions about what modernism really looks like if we engage it complexly.

For both H.D. and Hughes, the enabled voice of a previously silenced speaker is one place that such possibility is powerfully registered. In H.D.'s "Eurydice," the title speaker expresses nearly unbearable grief and anger at being swept back to the underworld for the "arrogance" and "ruthlessness" of her husband, Orpheus (*Collected Poems* 51), insistently questioning why he looked back as she charges him with narcissism: "what was it you saw in my face? / the light of your own face, / the fire of your own presence?" (52). But rather than remain merely reflective, Eurydice emerges as a compelling, self-sufficient speaker: "At least I have the flowers of myself, / and my thoughts, no god / can take that" (55). Figuring herself sexually and intellectually, Eurydice speaks from a myth in which she has been routinely rendered collateral damage in the story of Orpheus's artistic power and own grief.

While gender often prompts H.D.'s revision, race more frequently motivates that of Hughes. One can barely identify a poem of Hughes in which the syntax, rhythm, and content do not signal the voice of a fresh lyric speaker whose words revise prior complacencies, prejudices, and narratives. Engaging the potent traditions of pastoral and nostalgia for the antebellum South, for instance, the singer in "Song for a Dark Girl" says of her lynched lover:

> Way Down South in Dixie
>   (Break the heart of me)
> Love is a naked shadow
>   On a gnarled and naked tree.
>   (*Selected Poems* 172)

In the multiple speakers of *Montage of a Dream Deferred,* Hughes sounds the voices of the poor, the hopeful, the unnoticed and displaced, the joyful, the beaten down. Some claim control of their narratives like the speaker of H.D.'s "Eurydice," and some do not, a point that is worth analysis. In either case, reading the poets together enables a rich discussion of revision, possibility and deferral, and shifting social identities.

Positing just these few readings of H.D. in the company of other modernist poets is a difficult exercise, since the web of possible readings becomes more rather than less dense as one teases out a small number of threads. Much to the benefit of students of modernism, however, H.D. may be appropriately read centrally enmeshed in the forms, themes, and strategies of modernism as it responds to its time.

Mapping *Sea Garden*

Lesley Wheeler

Anthologies have their uses, but as Neil Fraistat has argued, poems also deserve to be encountered in one of their native habitats, the original single-author collection (3–11). Poets and editors shape these collections purposefully, creating juxtapositions and narrative passages that can open even elliptical poems to the light. *Sea Garden*, H.D.'s first book, makes a wonderful case study for this kind of "contextural" reading (Fraistat 3); it not only contains many powerful early lyrics but also provides a compelling example of the poetry volume as an ecosystem, in which the poem-organisms coexist in delicate interdependence. A sustained examination of *Sea Garden* illuminates important patterns of sound and image, a motif of spiritual searching characterized rhetorically by apostrophe, and complex pronomial strategies. The volume's title foregrounds a liminal landscape by way of paradox, but the book is an environment, resonant with echoes, that demands exploration. *Sea Garden* is a text best approached not in shards but as a whole work.

Since the best pedagogies for *Sea Garden* highlight this wholeness, this essay offers an assignment I have used successfully on single volumes by a variety of authors: I require my undergraduate students to create a one-page visual representation analyzing recurring elements of the collection. Through this process they not only learn how a poetry collection might be organized but also develop fresh and useful insights about H.D.'s preoccupations and tactics. In cultivating a narrow area of mastery, they also become more comfortable with the challenges of modernism and poetry generally.

Backgrounds

Sea Garden was first published in London in 1916 by Constable and Company; Houghton Mifflin brought out the American version a year later. Constable also published anthologies of imagist poetry and was Amy Lowell's London publisher. The first edition of *Sea Garden* is only held by a few research libraries, but the New Directions *Collected Poems* reprints the volume's poems in their original order, so the text is readily available.

Imagism originated with a group of writers in London—T. E. Hulme, F. S. Flint, and several others—who, in resistance to the tastes of their day, championed free verse, Chinese and Japanese poetry, and French symbolist verse. They met Ezra Pound, who sympathized with their aims, in 1909. Hilda Doolittle and Richard Aldington became part of this network early in 1912 (H.D. had arrived in England during the previous year), although H.D.'s work came to define the movement and gives the original group its retrospective importance. H.D. and

Aldington shaped imagist aesthetics through their passionate interest in Greek poetry, especially the evocative fragments of Sappho's surviving work. Pound, who served as foreign correspondent to the new magazine *Poetry*, sent work by H.D. and Aldington to its editor, Harriet Monroe, in fall 1912 under the label "Imagiste," and the movement was thereby officially launched. The anthology *Des Imagistes* was published by the Poetry Bookshop in 1914 and edited by Pound, whose interests then shifted to vorticism, and the American poet Amy Lowell became imagism's champion. Three more anthologies were published in 1915, 1916, and 1917 under the title *Some Imagist Poets*; Aldington was largely responsible for their arrangement (Zilboorg, *Early Years* 17).

In "A Retrospect," Pound defined an image as "that which presents an intellectual and emotional complex in an instant of time" (*Literary Essays* 4); this emphasis on instantaneous transmission pervades imagist poetry, which relies heavily on visual imagery. His other precepts, which he credits to discussion with H.D. and Aldington, stress the importance of concreteness, economy, and musical rather than strictly metrical rhythms (3). The poems of *Sea Garden* are, in fact, full of concrete details, usually captured in one- or two-syllable words that resonate with multiple meanings. As Burton Hatlen puts it, H.D.'s poems respect

> the integrity and otherness of the object, *refusing* to reduce the object to a function of the perceiving consciousness, even as they also recognize the object as a point of concentration, a node of energy.
> ("Imagist Poetics" 112)

H.D.'s "free verse," however, often seems haunted by ancient Greek meters, especially the choriamb (/◡◡/)and the minor ionic (//◡◡) (see Nims on these "maverick" feet). Further, although many of these pieces are brief and their diction is tightly controlled, H.D.'s style is not precisely economical, especially across an entire volume. Periodic repetition of sounds, words, and images within and across poems creates an incantatory effect and stresses the cycles of this landscape—the pulse of the waves, the turn of the days and seasons.

H.D.'s involvement with imagism coincided with her early development as a poet and her marriage to Aldington. Most of the poems in this collection were, however, written in a more troubled time, after the opening of World War I in August 1914 (Friedman, *Penelope's Web* 60). By the time Constable accepted *Sea Garden* for publication in February 1916, H.D.'s marriage was also strained. In May 1915 H.D. gave birth to their daughter, who was stillborn. As H.D. prepared her first book for printing in spring 1916, Aldington, facing military conscription, tested their professed ideal of free love and open marriage by conducting an affair (Zilboorg, *Early Years* 18–23). Although *Sea Garden* is not explicitly autobiographical, these difficult circumstances pervade the work.

H.D.'s publications in *Poetry* and *Des Imagistes* brought her to the attention of poets and critics; her first book expanded her audience and increased her reputation. *Sea Garden* received reviews in influential venues, including the *Times Literary Supplement*, the *Egoist*, *Poetry*, and the *New York Times Book Review*. These notices emphasize the exquisiteness but also the escapism of her early lyrics (Friedman, *Penelope's Web* 58–60). Further, Michael Boughn's bibliography documents the increasing number of reviews that her later poetry collections garnered, as if this first round of attention secured her a permanent place on the literary map.

H.D.'s books never reached the large popular readership earned by Edna St. Vincent Millay's succession of slim volumes. In fact, in part because of her reliance on fine presses with small print runs, H.D.'s prominence ebbed after the modernist period until feminists recovered her work during the last decades of the twentieth century. Yet she remained a poet's poet with significant influence on her contemporaries and on later writers (Hollenberg, Introduction xi). Friedman persuasively suggests that T. S. Eliot's poetics of impersonality was rooted in the effacement of autobiography in H.D.'s early work (*Penelope's Web* 46), and H.D.'s investments in Hellenism, vers libre, and harsh beauty helped establish the hallmarks of poetic modernity for writers on both sides of the Atlantic.

The very arrangement of *Sea Garden* may have influenced other poets. Most original single-author collections of the period resemble *Sea Garden* in grouping similar poems together. Poetry volumes tend to be largely unified in their thematic preoccupations, vocabulary of image, and formal and rhetorical strategies—sometimes by deliberate design, but sometimes because the poems are typically composed within a limited period. One common arrangement in the 1910s was to begin with a longish poem, usually a particularly ambitious and famous one, and to bunch thematically similar poems after it: two first books from 1917, Eliot's *Prufrock and Other Observations* and Millay's *"Renascence" and Other Poems*, follow this model. Robert Frost, because he had a large backlog of poems before he achieved book publication, ordered his poems by genre: lyrics appeared in *A Boy's Will* (1913), narrative pieces in *North of Boston* (1914). Occasionally volumes from this period exhibit a strong conceptual structure, such as Lowell's *Sword Blades and Poppy Seed* (1914), divided into poems that cut and poems that dream, or Williams Butler Yeats's *Responsibilities* (1914), framed around a narrative progression from mythic Ireland to a defiled modernity.

Sea Garden's periodic structure, involving intermittent flower poems and references to natural cycles, is quite unusual in the period. Shortly after it was printed, however, at least two careful readers of H.D.'s work produced volumes that follow a similar blueprint. While William Carlos Williams's 1913 book, *The Tempers*, jumbles different styles and topics together, his far superior 1917 collection, *Al Que Quiere!*, uses recurrence much as *Sea Garden* does: three poems called "Pastoral" are spaced throughout the book, as well as multiple portraits of patients and apostrophes to "my townspeople." Marianne Moore creates a comparable rhythm in her 1924 *Observations* by dispersing the dedicatory poems ("To a Chameleon," "To a Steam Roller," etc.) rather than grouping them together. While modernists and their reviewers rarely discuss the shapeliness, or lack of it, in volumes of verse, poets were intermittently obliged to consider it as they arranged their books. *Sea Garden* may have provided a fresh model for poets and editors engaged in this work.

Creating Maps

In winter 2007, I asked twenty-five English majors to "map" *Sea Garden*.[1] This seminar-style class treated nineteenth- and twentieth-century poetry by women from the United States, Canada, and Britain. Leading up to our week and a half on H.D., we read work by Christina Rossetti and by North American poets selected from Janet Gray's *She Wields a Pen*: Frances Ellen Watkins Harper, Emily Dickinson, Helen Hunt Jackson, Lizette Woodworth Reese, and Emily Pauline Johnson. The Dickinson selection in Gray's anthology is one entire fascicle, so we had begun to discuss how a short collection of poems might be threaded together. We had also examined idioms and strategies shared by this diverse group of writers: inherited forms engaged in interesting ways; power exerted through renunciation and refusal; recurrent motifs invoked of flowers, fruits, and gardens. During the session immediately preceding work on *Sea Garden*, I asked members of the class to compare two poems that use floral imagery: Dickinson's "Essential Oils—are wrung—" and Reese's "The Day before Spring." I then gave them a sonnet by Millay—"Say what you will, and scratch my heart to find"—to demonstrate how a modernist woman poet approaches the same metaphors through a traditional form. Before describing the next assignment, I closed with a short lecture sketching the historical changes that affected women in Britain and the United States at the beginning of the twentieth century; the rise of literary modernism; and H.D.'s place in this movement, with some biography.

One objective in asking students to create a one-page visual representation of a book is to help them come to terms with the original single-author collection as a form, to learn how brief lyrics in sequence amplify and modify each other. We were also working toward answers for the course's central questions: Do women poets share any strategies or idioms as a group? Is there a woman's way of writing poetry? How can poets perform identities through texts?

For the next meeting, I assigned the following tasks:

1. Read *Sea Garden* as reprinted in H.D.'s *Collected Poems*, in one sitting. Mark poems and phrases you'd like to go back to and jot down any elements that recur—images, sound effects, allusions, and so on.
2. Choose one of these elements and go back through the volume, noting the frequency of its appearance and thinking about its significance.

3. Create a one-page visual representation of the volume focusing on this characteristic. The end result can be a collage, graph, chart, table, map, or something else entirely, but avoid simply illustrating the book. Bring it to the next session and be prepared to explain it to the rest of the class.

I framed this task as required but low-stakes, to be graded with a check, plus, or minus.

My students responded enthusiastically to this assignment, despite its difficulty; it refreshed them by demanding skills different from those they usually apply in an English class. The routine of the class meeting also altered from group discussion in a circle to student-centered presentations. I set up the document camera and projector and then moved to the back of the room; they took turns projecting their work for the rest of the class and discussing it. (In a smaller class, the projector would not be necessary; the results could be taped to the wall or passed around.) The theater that resulted from a procession of students controlling the teaching technology transformed the conversation. Each student had mastered one small aspect of a challenging literary work, and as a result many displayed increased confidence in their own interpretive powers.

I began the class with a point from the previous session: we discussed "Sea Rose," the first piece in *Sea Garden*, in relation to other flower poems by women.[2] What aspects of this flower does H.D. describe and how? How would you describe this poem's diction, its use of line breaks? We observed the brevity of the lines, their irregularity and intensity matching the sparse-leafed sea rose; the negative vocabulary used, paradoxically, to praise; H.D.'s resistance to the traditional meanings of roses, the traditional forms of lyric poetry, and the traditional characteristics of feminine beauty; the use of apostrophe to personify the flower; why H.D. might have ended this poem on a question; the harshness of the repeated *r*, *t*, and *d* sounds; the hissing *f* and *s* sounds. The first poem in any collection obtains primacy, establishing the trends and concerns of the poems to follow.

Another focal poem in many collections is the title piece or the lyric that contains the title word or phrase. There is no poem named "Sea Garden," but "Sheltered Garden" presents the volume title's explicit antithesis. A student read the poem aloud, which helped highlight the poem's fractured rhythm, the way H.D. breaks her sentences over many lines, her urgent use of apostrophe. My leading questions here were, What does the speaker dislike about the sheltered garden? What does she want instead? The breathlessness of this poem echoes the traumatic details of H.D.'s stillborn daughter. As Aldington wrote in a letter, "the nurse said it was a beautiful child & they can't think why it didn't live. It was very strong, but wouldn't breathe" (*Autobiography* 16). Arguably "Sheltered Garden" associates mothering with smothering and seeks, in contrast, a wind-invigorated openness (see Kloepfer; Hollenberg, *H.D.: The Poetics*).

At this point, I invited my students to display their maps. Many of their collages of words and pictures highlighted the recurring colors of this collection

Addressing Flora

(associated with the sea)

1. "Sea Rose"
7. "Sea Lily"
12. "Sea Poppies"
15. "Garden" (1)
16. "Sea Violet"
24. "Sea Iris"

(associated with land)

4. "Mid-Day" (poplar)
26. "Pear Tree"

Addressing Gods
(often associated with natural forces)

3. "The Shrine"
5. "Pursuit"
8. "The Wind Sleepers"
9. "The Gift"
17. "The Cliff Temple"
18. "Orchard"
19. "Sea Gods"
20. "Acon"
25. "Hermes of the Ways"

Addressing People
(often with divine characteristics)

6. "The Contest"
8. "The Wind Sleepers"
11. "Sheltered Garden"
13. "Loss"
14. "Huntress"
22. "Prisoners"
27. "Cities"

Addressing a Natural Force
(*often as if the force is a god)*

2. "The Helmsman"
8. "The Wind Sleepers"
15. "Garden" (2)
21. "Night"
23. "Storm"

Addressing a Place
(*as if it is divinely powerful*)

3. "The Shrine"

No Addressee

10. "Evening"

Fig. 1. Mapping by addressee

At Sea (2)	The Shore (12)	Inland: Woods, Ridges, City (14)	Unclear (2)
	1. "Sea Rose"		
2. "The Helmsman"		2. "The Helmsman"*	
	3. "The Shrine"		
		4. "Mid-Day"	
		5. "Pursuit"*	
	6. "The Contest"		
	7. "Sea Lily"		
		8. "The Wind Sleepers"*	
	9. "The Gift"*	9. "The Gift"*	
		10. "Evening"	
		11. "Sheltered Garden"	
	12. "Sea Poppies"		
	13. "Loss"		
		14. "Huntress"	
		15. "Garden"	
	16. "Sea Violet"		
	17. "The Cliff Temple"		
		18. "Orchard"	
19. "Sea Gods"	19. "Sea Gods"		
		20. "Acon"	
			21. "Night"
		22. "Prisoners"	
		23. "Storm"	
	24. "Sea Iris"		
	25. "Hermes of the Ways"		
			26. "Pear Tree"
		27. "Cities"	
* The poem is set inland but mentions the sea, shore, or sand. Shifting locations are found in 2, 9, and 19.			

Fig. 2. Mapping by location

(white, violet, gold); the frequency of botanical references; and allusions to Greek myth and the Bible, especially Edenic imagery. For example, one student framed his page with forty-two tiny pictures of specific plants, flowers, and fruits; listed twenty-seven poem titles down the middle of the page; and connected those titles to photographs with a welter of multicolored lines, thereby illustrating the complexity of the book's botanical environment, populated by species from North America and Europe. Another student tracked the recurrence of certain nouns through the volume, presenting his findings in a table. He found the words "sea," "rock," and "wind" occurring most frequently, with "grass," "pears," "leaf," and "garden" also making occasional appearances. His research corroborated our initial impressions that *Sea Garden*'s diction is deliberately spare, full of resonant, concrete monosyllables, often drawn from the natural world. A third example was visually simple but high-concept: it depicted a seascape of water, sky, rock, and sand. The student, however, had manufactured this collage by using portions of her photographs out of context—sand and rock were cut from images of sunlit and nighttime clouds; the ocean was actually a field; the sky was created from an upside-down photograph of the sea. Through this strategy she highlighted the volume's dependence on paradox and surprise, as well as highlighting the permeability of H.D.'s borderline landscape.

Susan Stanford Friedman discusses the book as "a sequence of modern pastorals set in a symbolic green world removed from conventional space and time" (*Penelope's Web* 51). I intermittently asked students when and where these poems might be set (ancient Greece? Devon in the 1910s? the New Jersey beaches H.D. visited as a girl?); what besides setting unifies the volume; who is speaking in these poems and to whom; and what moods, references, and stylistic strategies predominate. We discussed the diurnal pattern some titles evoke ("Mid-Day," "Evening," "Night") and the play between highly visual imagery and hidden sound patterns. I explained my charts to them (see figs. 1 and 2); I had been surprised to realize through the process of creating them that these poems are far more pastoral than marine, as well as how consistently they employ second-person address. I parlayed the latter discovery into a discussion of spiritual questing in the volume, quoting Adalaide Morris to provoke conversation: "The poems in *Sea Garden* are thrown out as bridges to the sacred" (*How to Live* 98). If H.D. is calling to the gods throughout this book, what answers does she discover? For me, this is an open question, not fully resolvable, but it is at the heart of what *Sea Garden* means. Eileen Gregory's remarks on the "ritual intent of the whole volume" are also helpful here ("Rose" 140).

I have used this lesson plan in various upper-level undergraduate poetry courses; it works particularly well for Elizabeth Bishop's *Questions of Travel*, Gwendolyn Brooks's *A Street in Bronzeville*, and Frost's *North of Boston*, all of which possess strong spatial dimensions, like *Sea Garden*. The assignment also adapts successfully to many twenty-first-century volumes and would be an illuminating exercise in graduate-level creative writing workshops, especially if participants are planning their first collections. This strategy, however, does entail some risks and costs. It is time-intensive, especially in large classes, and a few students produce uninspired drawings or jumbles of clip art. Even hardworking mappers may invest in an unrewarding angle. In addition, because it encourages students to scout for resemblances across poems, a session spent on maps may not result in brilliant readings of individual lyrics. Yet, introduced carefully and balanced with other approaches over the course of a term, this assignment offers students a fresh, intellectually substantial, and pleasurable way of engaging H.D.'s art.

NOTES

[1] I am very grateful to all the participants in English 359 for their responses to this assignment, but particularly to Sarah Mueller, Michael Rennard, and Michael Wagoner, whose approaches I describe here.

[2] Useful sources on this subject include Friedman, *Penelope's Web* 57–58; Collecott, *H.D. and Sapphic Modernism* 211–20; and Wheeler.

Portraits of an Artist: Introducing Students to H.D.'s Poetry

Lisa Rado

At first glance, H.D.'s highly allusive, theoretically sophisticated oeuvre would seem an ill match for beginning scholars of literature. Packed with references to Egyptian and classical mythology, early-twentieth-century writers and intellectuals, and the events and relationships dominating her personal life, H.D.'s poetry and prose are further complicated by her stream of consciousness and imagistic modernist techniques. That the College Board included one of H.D.'s shorter lyric poems ("Helen," which they paired with Edgar Allan Poe's "To Helen") in the essay portion of the 1994 Advanced Placement Literature and Composition exam would thus appear a dubious choice. Yet this seeming anomaly underscored something I had discovered in my classroom: teaching H.D.'s work, particularly her poetry, to advanced high school students or early-stage undergraduates can be a very rewarding experience. Indeed, her lyrics serve as an excellent introduction to modernism and literary analysis generally as well as to the field of gender studies.

Key to my success with H.D. in the classroom has been placing her work in both historical and thematic contexts. Rather than read her oeuvre in an intellectual vacuum, I link it to central texts by other modernist writers preoccupied with the role of art and the gendered artist in a society reshaped by urbanization, secularization, world wars, and modern science. In a semester-long course I taught to advanced high school seniors, Portraits of the Artist, I paired works of aesthetic philosophy with literary texts foregrounding issues of sexuality, gender, and race by Oscar Wilde ("The Decay of Lying" and *The Picture of Dorian Gray*); H.D. (*Notes on Thought and Vision* and *Selected Poems*), James Joyce (*Portrait of the Artist as a Young Man*); Langston Hughes ("The Negro Artist and the Racial Mountain" and *Selected Poems*); and Virginia Woolf (*A Room of One's Own*, ch. 4, and *To the Lighthouse*). Reading poets like H.D. and Hughes alongside novelists whose style and content engage similar issues was particularly useful for an audience more familiar with prose narrative. Such parallels afforded new insights into poetry as argument. Moreover, approaching H.D.'s work through the issue of aesthetics enabled my students to locate a strategy of interpretation to which they could immediately relate—and from which they could confidently approach the sophisticated theme of sexual and textual politics. Because H.D.'s observations about gender derive from her struggle to define herself as a woman writer, beginning my course with an examination of her labored portraits of the artist brought my young students into her world of sexual tensions under a more familiar and accessible mantle and better prepared them for more theoretical discussions of these issues in her later lyrics.

I began my unit on H.D. with a look at her manifesto *Notes on Thought and Vision* (1919), a kind of prose poem that served as a helpful introduction to her poetry, in both structure and content, and to her struggle to articulate her complex conception of the androgynous artistic imagination. H.D.'s meditations on the anatomy of creativity (with its Freudian undertones), on the tensions between imagination and desire, and on the starkly spiritual power of "over-mind" (her term for the sublime power of imagination that connects us to a transcendent, even universal wholeness [17]) help illuminate her writerly objectives and challenges, as do her richly textured, ambiguously gendered imagery and her references to various classical and Christian deities. Beyond introducing her oeuvre's major themes, *Notes* reflects her signature reliance on such techniques as allusion and abstraction in a prose form that—while more impressionistic than discursive—is still familiar to less experienced readers of poetry.

Notes was composed on the Isles of Scilly, where H.D. sought refuge with her great friend and lover Bryher after a disastrous series of personal tragedies that included a stillbirth, the breakup of her marriage, the deaths of her father and brother, and the near death of another (unplanned) baby and herself from the flu pandemic of 1918. A visionary document, *Notes* illuminates H.D.'s efforts to use her art as a means to transcend these horrors of young adulthood, horrors she rewrites in much of her later work. Affirming the interconnectivity of body and mind, she emphasizes the importance of both physical strength and mental acuity. Most interesting, however, she posits a third category of consciousness, a transcendent over-mind that she compares to a cap with down-reaching tentacles like a jellyfish. Though H.D. initially argues that such transcendent vision can be centered in both the head and the womb, she later contradicts herself, arguing that "there is no way of arriving at the over-mind, except through the intellect" (21), and ultimately seems to view the physical as a necessary yet provisional stage of awareness. Later in the narrative, H.D. reimagines this tension using the images of the womblike thistle and the phallic serpent. Her final argument of the piece, that "Christ and his father, or as the Eleusinian mystic would have said, his mother, were one" (52), further exemplifies her subtle efforts to privilege mental experience, as H.D. associates Mary with the physical consciousness that Jesus, in his divinity, will transcend. This underlying ambiguity about the relative importance of the mind and the female body is a tension that persists in H.D.'s later poetry and prose, serving as a touchstone from which to explore her ambivalence about her identity as a female artist.

Beyond its illustration of the inherent conflict between mind and body, brain and sex, *Notes on Thought and Vision* underscores H.D.'s attraction to classical art and myth as well as to the spiritual dimension of art that again might transcend the unsettled realm of body and sex. Her references to mythological figures, which underscore her arguments about the various states of consciousness, can serve as excellent introductions to students, who can be asked to research these allusions. Moreover, that H.D. illuminates the mechanics of over-mind in lengthy descriptions of both Western and Eastern poets who employed it—Jesus, whom she describes as essentially "a great artist" (27), and the Chinese poet Lo Fu—reveals her preoccupation with the universal, spiritual, and strikingly androgynous domain of the imagination.

Notes on Thought and Vision is admittedly a difficult text for beginning students. Yet while abstract and allusion-laden, it becomes more accessible when students can penetrate its impressionistic, somewhat circular structure to see there is essentially one issue that H.D. reworks and reimagines. It is also helpful to invite students to consider, either through journal exercises or in class discussion, how they imagine the different modes of experience (physical, intellectual, artistic, or spiritual) and the relations among them. What metaphors would they use? Which, if any, states would they privilege? What texts, sights, or experiences enable them to enter into expanded states of consciousness?

Once students have at least a tentative grasp of H.D.'s experiences, interests, and gendered concerns, I move to *Selected Poems* as the primary focus of our study.[1] Written briefly prior to *Notes*, the selections from *Sea Garden* (1916) are in many ways the most immediately accessible of H.D.'s lyrics. I begin with "Sea Rose," "Sea Lily," and "Sheltered Garden," poems that establish what I call H.D.'s aesthetic of the borderline: her advocacy of a fierce, tough, resilient beauty in both content and form. These brief poems' simple, stripped-down diction and familiar imagery present no obstacles to beginning students of poetry, forcing them instead to consider the implications of the language. Beginning with "Sea Rose," students wrestle with the question of the last stanza by identifying the opposition between "sea rose" and "spice-rose" and working through the paradox of how the "marred," "meager," "thin," "sparse," "stunted," and "small" bloom could nevertheless be the speaker's preference. "Sheltered Garden" elaborates on this theme, characterizing the cultivated and refined as ironically suffocating and repetitive while affirming the speaker's determination "to find a new beauty / in some terrible / wind-tortured place" (55–57). Studying the other similarly themed poems in immediate succession enables students to gain confidence in their interpretations while developing their understanding of H.D.'s pared, modernist aesthetic whose stark, conventionally masculine appeal recalls that of the harsh images within these poems.

The repeated appeals to pantheistic or classical deities in "Orchard," "Hermes of the Ways," "Sea Gods," and the selection from "The Tribute" push students to consider H.D.'s aesthetic preferences in the context of her larger objective: a search for a new theology—uncultivated, natural, sensual, and wild—intimately connected to an androgynous artistic imagination that would transcend seemingly limited sexual categories. The nameless deity to whom the speaker in "Sea Gods" so fervently appeals recalls Hermes's elemental energy while underscoring the difficulty of imagining these seemingly forgotten presences in the modern world. Rumored to be "cut, torn, mangled, / torn by the stress and beat" of the sea (10), these ancient spirits would appear to be impotent and inaccessible, though this possibility is renounced by the speaker's insistent, commanding, yet inherently desperate directive that "you will come" (11). The excerpt from "The Tribute" builds on these themes, providing a context for the speaker's anguish that recalls the most familiar refrains of modernism in its indictment of the "[s]qualor [that] blights and makes hideous / our lives" (18). Railing against her culture's crass materialism, the speaker laments the loss of "the beat of our songs" (18) in a world of men who

> haggle and cheat,
> praise fabrics worn threadbare,
> ring false coin for silver,
> offer refuse for meat. (19)

Layering classical references within her contemporary setting, H.D. evokes the androgynous Hermes, with his "slender winged ankles" (20), as a symbol of a vital and creative energy banished by a world in thrall to violence, to "the god of the lance" (21). This poem, like "Sea Gods," ends with a desperate appeal to the divine to restore and heal her corrupt and dying culture. Here I challenge students to push beyond the obvious nostalgia for the pastoral to locate H.D.'s more immediate approach to social and cultural decline, an approach that recalls achieving the heightened experience of over-mind in *Notes on Thought and Vision*. For these poems celebrate not so much the gods as spiritual power—particularly the power to renounce an ideology of death, to embrace a healing affirmation of life, to renew and restore transcendent vision by challenging familiar, primarily gendered orthodoxies.

Later lyrics "The Mysteries" and "The Magician" echo "The Tribute" in their evocation of an ominous present whose "darkness . . . threatens the spirit / like massed hosts" ("The Mysteries" 62) while positing even more aesthetically and sexually ambiguous prophet figures whose Christ-like associations are subordinate to their imaginative, visionary powers. In "The Mysteries," a speaker variously referred to as "enchanter," "magician," and "arch-mage" (63) communicates the message to don the "enchanted armour / [that] clothes the intrepid mind" (64) and to "sanctify" the beauty of the world (65). The poem celebrates heightened vision, repeating the command "behold" to underscore the revelation possible even within a seemingly ordinary, mundane universe. Though the "I" at the end of the poem clearly alludes to Christ, the speaker also represents a more universal human potential, as the final lines of the poem suggest. Similarly, the anguished speaker of the ambiguously titled "The Magician" addresses a figure who recalls Christ yet whose advocacy of rebirth and revision alludes to the experience of over-mind H.D. affirms in *Notes* as well as to her argument in that text that Jesus was a great artist. Indeed, the power of the "Magician" is the power of imaginative vision; calling attention to such familiar objects as "a fish" or the "roots in the earth" or "an olive," he challenges his audience to ascend to a new way of seeing (74).

It is only at this point, once students are invested in H.D.'s objectives and familiar with her androgynous aesthetic, that I venture to focus more directly on the primary opposition in her poetry between art and sex, creativity and gender.

For while early on, H.D. posits the visionary potential of over-mind, her later writings simmer with anxiety over the degree to which she must imaginatively abandon or suppress her gender to access this transcendent mode of experience. Here, a close reading of such poems as "Amaranth," "Fragment 113," "Fragment 36," "Calypso," "Cassandra," "Eurydice," and "The Dancer" illuminates the triumphs and trepidations of being a female artist or seer; considering "The Poet" and "The Master" emphasizes both the attractions and tensions between the female artist and the male authority figure. Difficult questions arise during the study of these poems, such as H.D.'s presentation of the unique challenges women writers face and how her poems work through them. I have found that students who are less comfortable or familiar with gender theory can come to a greater understanding of the mechanics of sexual politics in this focused context.

I begin with several poems—"Amaranth," "Fragment 113," and "Fragment 36"—that, as in *Notes*, address the competing claims of sexual and imaginative experience, seeming to read them as mutually exclusive categories. The speaker of "Amaranth" approaches the immortalized Andromeda, the "shameless and radiant" representation of beauty and desire (28), with both adulation and resistance. On the one hand, the narrator claims to prefer the goddess over "some cold, calm god, / silent, pitiful" (26) and is seemingly in thrall to the "beauty . . . that is her wish" (27). On the other hand, she laments the failure of the goddess's gifts to sustain her lover's interest and acknowledges her willingness to resist his advances, to look for inspiration beyond the physical, outward "toward the purple ships" representative of visionary experience (28). Though Andromeda appears to defend the speaker to her recalcitrant lover at the end of the poem and even insists that the speaker is "*my poet*" (29), this testimonial is undercut by the speaker, who has confessed to distractibility even as she begs her lover to return. "Fragment 113" builds on this conflict, as the speaker rejects the sensual raptures of "the honey" and "the bee" for the ambiguously termed "strength of arm and throat" (46–47). Though not directly associated with conventional song, the final lines of the poem evoke a martial power that nevertheless transcends the physical. In both poems, H.D. portrays the realm of physical, sexual experience as exquisite and extraordinary; she also suggests that it is ultimately insufficient. The tension between these two modes of experience is most concretely articulated in the four opening lines of "Fragment 36":

> I know not what to do,
> my mind is reft;
> is song's gift best?
> is love's gift loveliest? (49)

Significantly, the question posed in those lines never gets answered, though what is affirmed in the sixth stanza is the constant opposition between the two in which, presumably, only one can claim victory.

Yet why ought the speaker find herself so torn between physical and intellectual experience? I help students understand this question by taking them through the monologue poems in which H.D. takes on representative female personae who showcase alternating expressions of frustration and empowerment. Here, students must also consider H.D.'s decision to select ancient mythic figures to dramatize such seemingly contemporary issues. Both "Calypso" and "Cassandra" paint portraits of powerful visionaries whose sex nevertheless renders them impotent in the world of men. The tragically disconnected dialogue between Calypso and Odysseus not only reveals the age-old gap between the sexes but also charts the ironic vulnerability of the goddess whose scoffing disdain for man is belied by her experience of sexual and emotional abandonment. By the end of the poem, the goddess bitterly acknowledges having been stripped of her dignity, as well as—symbolically—her creative voice by the "brute" who has taken both "my lute and my shell of crystal" (89). Likewise, H.D.'s Cassandra appears unable simultaneously to sustain physical and poetic power. The "bitter power of song"—that godlike power of vision granted by Apollo—has required the concomitant sacrifice of her sexual appeal; near the end of the poem she laments, "May I not wed / as you have wed?" (53).

Paradoxically, H.D. creates heroines in "Eurydice" and "The Dancer" who, while acknowledging gender's threat, firmly deny its power to undermine the strength and spirit of female creativity. Though bitter at the "arrogance" and "ruthlessness" (36) of her lover Orpheus, who was unable to resist glancing back at his beloved as they traveled out of Hades, H.D.'s Eurydice defiantly reclaims and reinvents her powers even as she languishes in the underworld, bragging, "[H]ell must break before I am lost" (40). Deprived of the sensuous pleasures of color and seasons, she nevertheless affirms her imaginative capacity to re-create both: "I have the flowers of myself" (40). Though Orpheus was the legendary poet, Eurydice emerges as the true artist, able to create beauty and vitality in the house of death.[2] Likewise, "The Dancer" depicts the woman-as-goddess to whom the speaker appeals for inspiration, sensation, and power. Unlike Calypso and Cassandra, who are both violated and abandoned by the male figure, the spiritual woman in this poem appears invulnerable yet strangely nameless and bodiless. In an almost defensive aside, the speaker explains this decision to her idol—"you can not betray us . . . for you are abstract" (92)—as if it is only the spiritual body of woman that is reliably empowered.

Pairing "The Master" and "The Poet" serves as an excellent finale to an investigation into these gendered tensions. Supplying students with background about H.D.'s relationships with Sigmund Freud and D. H. Lawrence (the inspirations for these works) is helpful here, as is a brief explanation of the basic principles of Freud's theories of male and female development. Both poems reveal a speaker more defiant than in the other poems though still struggling to affirm her authority as a woman and a visionary. If Freud's suggestion of H.D.'s bisexuality in "The Master" sets her "free / to prophesy" (108), his constant "talk of the man-strength" (105) prompts her to mount a defensive affirmation of female perfection. Her ambivalence toward her male mentors continues in "The Poet," where she simultaneously honors and objects to the ironical shell-like facade that shelters Lawrence from the transcendent "butterfly" consciousness she persists in seeking (113).

How is a teacher of literature to accommodate so many contradictions, especially for beginning students of poetry? H.D. wrote:

> Yes, the poems are satisfactory but unlike most poets of my acquaintance . . . I am no longer interested in a poem once it is written, projected, or materialized. There is a feeling that it is only a *part* of myself there.
> (*Tribute* 149)

That she associates her lack of interest in a finished lyric with its fragmentary quality underscores the necessity of reading her poetry as a varied oeuvre in dialogue with itself—and of insisting that students engage in these conversations by frequently grappling with her competing and often contrary perspectives in both class discussion and analytical essays on paired, thematically related poems. If the individual lyric of H.D. fails to embody her full complexity and richness, an encounter with a representative selection of her verse illuminates for students the sublime ambiguities and tensions that simmer within one of modernism's most probing minds.

NOTES

[1] All the poems by H.D. discussed and quoted here are in her *Selected Poems*.

[2] H.D.'s plans to write a companion poem, "Orpheus," were sabotaged by D. H. Lawrence, who, despite his repeated investigations into the female consciousness, discouraged her from similar imaginative leaps.

Ticking Differently: H.D.'s Time in Philadelphia

Adalaide Morris

> Now time included a new factor, a school-clock in a public-school ticked differently from the church-clock in the old town.
>
> —H.D., *The Gift*

In 1895, the nine-year-old Hilda Doolittle moved with her family from the Moravian village of Bethlehem, Pennsylvania, to the grounds of the University of Pennsylvania's Flower Observatory in Upper Darby, a trolley ride away from the city of Philadelphia, where her father, Charles Leander Doolittle, had just been named professor of astronomy and would soon become the observatory's first director. According to *MapQuest*, the distance between Bethlehem and Philadelphia can be traversed in approximately one hour sixteen minutes, but that's by our clocks in our vehicles on our roads. The purpose of this short essay is to suggest another calculus by which teachers and students can measure the distance between these two lifeworlds and in so doing better understand the interplay between H.D.'s texts and the historical and ideological contexts that at once sustain and exceed them.

I take as my gauge an array of things—clocks, paintings, photographs, and trolleys—that calibrate the distance between the village of H.D.'s childhood and the city she shared as a teenager and young adult with Ezra Pound, William Carlos Williams, Marianne Moore, and Frances Gregg. To approach H.D.'s writings through the objects, technologies, art, and architecture that surrounded her assumes with new historicism that a literary work is the product of a specific time, place, and set of circumstances, but it also opens access to moments of strangeness or opacity in which everyday things elude the explanations a culture provides for them. This moment—H.D.'s Philadelphia moment—informs not only the strangeness in her own writing but the more sweeping estrangements that generate the poetics she and her cohort carried from Philadelphia into the world.

To think about clocks or trolleys in turn-of-the-century Philadelphia takes us beyond the parameters of a particular life into a secular, social, and civic matrix shared by artists, scientists, and engineers who struggled to articulate and understand the things of everyday life in terms that superseded earlier formulations. Documents previously available to researchers only through archives and museums are now stored on the Internet, rendered searchable through powerful Web crawlers, and supplemented by maps, prints, photographs, diaries, newspapers, and even minutes of municipal meetings and blueprints of the buildings in which they were held. Unlike mid-twentieth-century New Critics, today's students of literature are only a few clicks away from information that connects a text to the matrix in which it developed. The question now is not how to cordon off a text but how to tap into the information that circulated around and through it, shaped and was in turn shaped by it.

Because it is possible to see the clocks newly installed above Philadelphia's turn-of-the-century city hall, trace the trolley tracks that ran from the city center to the station opposite the Flower Observatory, and access the serial photographs of naked running men that Eadweard Muybridge and Thomas Eakins snapped with time-rigged cameras in a makeshift lab at the university where Doolittle conducted his classes, we can explore many of the ways in which municipal, scientific, and artistic clocks tick differently from church clocks. The "thick description" of things once the province of ethnologists and anthropologists such as Clifford Geertz is now, at least in principle, in reach of anyone with a keyboard, an Internet connection, and the willingness to connect things with the language, habits, events, and representations that form around them.

This pedagogy begins with Gertrude Stein's conviction that composition is already explanation. To argue, with Stein, that "what is seen depends upon how everybody is doing everything," we must search for "what is seen when it seems to be being seen, in other words, composition and time-sense" (*Gertrude Stein* 520, 521). The different tick H.D. heard in Philadelphia is not just the quick sounds of a clock, the clack of a trolley, the click of a camera, or the stroke of a brush on canvas but also, in the distance, the poetics she and her friends would conceive by being not so much ahead of their time as in it and of it.

The terms *composition* and *time-sense* are, like so much of Stein's thinking, both very simple and very complex. If they are the patterns and pulses of the lifeworld—"so simply that anybody knows it," Stein says, "how everybody is doing everything" (*Gertrude Stein* 520)—they rise into consciousness only through a relation of nonagreement or nonidentity. Just as "time-sense" is a matter of ticking differently, for Stein "composition is the difference which makes each and all of them then different from other generations" (520). Thing theorists mark this difference through the term *thingness*, which signals, as John Frow explains, "a beyond of representation" (347). To ask students to look into how life was lived at a particular moment is to ask them to look for the lag between doing and saying and, in that lag, to identify the claims things like clocks, trolleys, cameras, and painted canvases made on the attention and actions of the people around them.

In addressing these questions, I want to try to catch the moment in what Bill Brown calls "the object/thing dialectic," when things elude interpretation, when they exceed or evade the codes by which we have understood them and present themselves instead, stubbornly if temporarily, in a seemingly irreducible thingness ("Thing Theory" 5). My two primary texts are H.D.'s memoir *The Gift* and her fictional autobiography *HERmione*, both of which capture for our attention exactly this moment. In *The Gift*, using for the most part the voice of a child-in-transition, H.D. recounts the faltering of the codes that ritualized the objects in the lifeworld of the village of Bethlehem. In *HERmione*, using for the most part the voice of a teenager-in-transition, H.D. recounts the advent of the codes that ordered the objects in the civic, social, and academic worlds of the city of Philadelphia.

To describe the object/thing dialectic, Brown makes a distinction among three terms, two of which normally overlap: *thing, idea,* and *object*. If, as Brown says, quoting Leo Stein, "[t]hings are what we encounter, ideas are what we project," objects are things so saturated by ideas that we can no longer detach them from the logical or ideological fields in which they are embedded. If we look through objects, we look at things: things are *things* because they do not yield up their meanings but "hover," in Brown's words, "over the threshold between the nameable and unnameable, the figurable and unfigurable, the identifiable and unidentifiable" (4–5).

The Gift and *HERmione* narrate a succession of shocks in which objects regain their status as things. The Moravian world of H.D.'s childhood offered a particularly dense and luminous experience of objects saturated by code: in Bethlehem every artifact of daily life had an integrated familial, communal, and sacred resonance. Turn-of-the-century Philadelphia, by contrast, was a world of things crisscrossed by competing and contested codes: civic and social rituals; academic rules, grades, and ranks; newfangled electrical, communication, and transportation technologies; manufacturing facilities for the ten-ton Baldwin steam engines that ran in and out of Broad Street Station and Reading Terminal; and such spanking new emporiums of consumer culture as Wanamaker's and the Samuel and Jacob Lit department store to which H.D. and her mother journeyed on the trolley. The distance between Bethlehem and Philadelphia is not just a difference between a church culture and a social, academic, technological, and material market culture; it is also, for H.D., the difference between a world of transparent objects and a world of opaque and resistant things. This encounter with thingness is H.D.'s Philadelphia moment: a brief but amazingly productive limbo in which her radical modernism had its origins.

In *The Gift*, H.D. struggles to describe the move's effect on the Doolittle children:

> There was something horrible about the school. We took lunch in a basket and did not get back until four. . . . There were hours which were torture, it was too far to walk home in that noon-hour and back. There was twelve to one for lunch. Now time included a new factor, a school-clock in a public-school ticked differently from the church-clock in the old town. There was no doubt about it. . . .
>
> . . . We go to a public-school; that is not what is wrong. It isn't that the room *smells* differently, it's the way the clock ticks on the wall. (91)[1]

In Bethlehem bells rang from the church to partition the day. From the house in which H.D. was born, she could see the church cupola from which the trombone choir played to mark the deaths of members of the community, the births of babies, and the rebirth of the year when, H.D. relates in *The Gift*, "at the Easter services in the old grave-yard . . . we went out and said *the Lord is risen indeed* and watched the sun come up over the graves" (36). This cyclic, sacred time-keeping chimed not only over the town but also through the house, in harmony with a grandfather clock made, the children were proud to say, by the same great-grandfather who played in the trombone choir for fifty years.

The clock that ticked on the wall of the Doolittle children's public school administrated a different kind of time: "you can't go home for lunch," it said; "you can open your lunch basket"; "you *must* return to class." The tick of a public clock is regulative: it controls, governs, or directs at the discretion of boards, councils, and other administrative agencies. A clock in a public school does not track the rising and setting of the year, the births and deaths in a community, or the narratives marked by sacred rituals but ticks along with the start and stop of the working day. Public clocks are elements of civic design: Philadelphia's timekeepers could be found in the tower above Wanamaker's to mark the opening and closing of commerce; on the street corners and in the halls of Reading Terminal to signal the arrival and departure of trains; at the Philadelphia Stock Exchange to regulate the trading of shares; and, most grand, on the tower above Philadelphia's city hall, where courts, councils, and caucuses set the permissions and prohibitions that organized civic life.

Constructed between 1871 and 1901, Philadelphia's city hall still has the distinction of being the world's largest stack of bricks: 88 million bricks, to be precise. Its walls are 27 feet thick and 650 feet long, and they enclose a total of 651 rooms. Rising to a height of 510 feet at the exact geographical center of William Penn's original plan for Philadelphia, its spire is topped by a 27-ton statue of William Penn, surrounded, on a second tier, by statues of a Native American warrior, a Native American woman and child, a male settler, a female settler and child, and, perched above each of the tower's clock faces, four 7,000-pound bronze eagles arching their 12-foot wingspans over the progression of civic time.

City hall stands to the city of Philadelphia as the Central Moravian church stood to the village of Bethlehem. In a tinted view from 1908, the building looms over empty streets against a huge and vacant sky. In contrast to the hominess of Bethlehem's architecture, it is as forbidding as it is aloof. With its high, sloping, double-sided, boxy roofs and monumental statuary, Philadelphia's city hall has been called, perhaps justly, America's finest example of French Second Empire architecture (Van Zanten 9), but Walt Whitman described it best: "silent, weird, beautiful" ("Exposition Building").

To be "weird" is to be *unheimlich*, out of the ordinary, neither familiar nor familial. City hall is not exactly uncanny—it would not be something the Doolittle children had known and then repressed, but they would not know their way around or through it. The codes its architecture so diligently replicates would have been, like the codes of the public school, alien and opaque. To return to Brown's distinction, the clocks on its tower would not be objects to be looked through but things to be looked at; the time they told ticked differently.

As she tells her story in *HERmione*, H.D., at twenty-three, was neither here nor there. "Everything was something to everyone," she reports, ringing the changes on the word *thing*, "but nothing was anything to Her" (29). In the family but not of it, a creature that flailed at Bryn Mawr's "Anglo-saccharine" tea parties (129), failed in Bryn Mawr's Anglo-Saxon literature and science curriculums, was engaged to Pound but in love with Gregg, she had returned to the observatory grounds to drift: similar to the way Brown describes the moment in which objects collapse back into things, she hovers, in her Philadelphia moment: "Nothing held her, she was nothing holding to this thing" (4).

But isn't this delirium the condition known as adolescence? *HERmione*'s narrator ticks off a list of diagnoses that had not yet, in 1909, been codified: "failure complex," "compensation reflex," "arrested development" (3); "Oedipus complex, inferiority complex, claustrophobia" (15). None of these labels sticks. This hovering on the threshold between the nameable and unnameable is not easily—or importantly—pathologized because it is also a moment of generativity. If it begins with H.D.'s move from Bethlehem to Philadelphia, it concludes for her as it did for Pound, Williams, Moore, and Gregg in a migration from Philadelphia to and through cities—New York, London, Paris, Berlin—where they and other artists began to practice another form of thinking. What did they take from this Philadelphia moment that helped them think and be thought by modernist poetics?

To begin to address this question, students might look at the dialectic of things and objects through the lens of the imagist poetics H.D., Pound, and their cohort developed in pre–World War I London. The enemy of imagism was the tyranny of concepts—theological, social, civic, or academic—that transformed things into code-saturated objects. Their aim was to learn to look not through but at things to discern not ideas but, in Ernest Fenollosa's words, "the actual and entangled lines of forces as they pulse through things" (12). Crafted to thwart the projection of concepts, the imagist poem set out to capture, if only for a moment, the tick or flicker of the thing. This tick or flicker is the moment in which, as Fenollosa put it, "[t]hinking is thinging" (qtd. in Chisolm 168), the moment in which, in Williams's famous formulation, there are "[n]o ideas / but in things" ("A Sort" 47).

Two paintings prominently displayed in the Doolittle residence (see H.D., Gift 90)—one associated with Bethlehem, the other with Philadelphia—suggest the art H.D. and Pound dismissed as representations of abstractions or "concepts drawn out of things by a sifting process" (Fenollosa 12). *The Power of the Gospel*, painted by Christian Schussele in 1862, portrays the Moravian missionary David Zeisberger bringing the light of the Lord to Pennsylvania's Native Americans; *The Horse Fair*, completed by Rosa Bonheur in 1855, portrays animals on display in a Parisian horse market.

Schussele, Eakins's predecessor as professor of drawing and painting at the Pennsylvania Academy of Fine Arts, was a thoroughly schooled exponent of the academic tradition in France, a genre and historical painter. *Power of the Gospel* portrays one of Bethlehem's luminaries "coaxing his flock," as the art historian William H. Truettner puts it, "out of the dark forest and into the light of salvation, symbolized by the campfire around which the Indians have gathered" (17–18). No thing in this painting—rock, grass, fire, forest, or mist—eludes capture as a sign of the spirituality that suffused H.D.'s birthplace and organized her childhood world. By contrast, Bonheur's muscular horses possess the gleam of goods on display in a market. As they cavort in stately defiance of gravity, they exist as matter in motion, material in a cycle of exchange, commodities that were sold, purchased, accumulated, or traded in a site of commerce few women frequented. Dressed as a man to blend into the fair she attended twice a week for a year and a half to paint from life, Bonheur gives her subjects the allure of merchandise in a retail world that, by the turn of the century, had expanded from fairs, street markets, and small shops to mail-order houses, chain stores, and emporiums like Philadelphia's Wanamaker's and Samuel and Jacob Lit. In their circular parade, her horses are neither spiritual signs nor objects of use but robust participants in a market-driven spectacle of desire.

If the paintings of Schussele and Bonheur depict alternate object worlds—one spiritual, the other material; one ethereal, the other economic—what strategies might an imagist use to capture, if only for a moment, the tick of things as things? Pound, in exhorting would-be imagists to "[c]onsider the way of the scientists rather than the way of an advertising agent for a new soap" (*Literary Essays* 6), tapped into yet another Philadelphia tradition: the ingenuity of citizen-scientists, philosophers, and tinkerers like Benjamin Franklin; the versatility of artist-inventors like Eakins, who studied logarithms for fun, constructed his own cameras, and designed elaborate gymnastic devices to demonstrate the muscular actions of the human body; and the skill of artist-technicians like Muybridge, who, with Eakins's assistance, rigged up a series of elaborate electromagnetically triggered cameras in the University of Pennsylvania's veterinary labs to capture precise images of bodies in motion.

Just as the telescope used by H.D.'s father brought into view the transit of celestial bodies and the microscope used by H.D.'s grandfather, the botanist Francis Wolle, made visible the cellular structures of freshwater algae, Muybridge's photographs of galloping horses captured elements of action beyond the range of the unaided eye (see Morris, *How to Live* 155–59; Mandel, "Magical Lenses"). Bonheur's horses, painted from life, have the sprightly stolidity of Paolo Uccello's steeds: their prancing is an idea of prancing at play in painting since the Italian Renaissance. In contrast, Muybridge's photographs of horses in action are engineered to capture not the idea of galloping but galloping itself. Photographed against an array of numbered spatial markers by cameras set to release at equal intervals, Muybridge's parsing of the successive ticks of a gallop was published in *Muybridge's Complete Human and Animal Locomotion*, a compendium of 781 plates including more than twenty thousand individual exposures, each documenting a component of the dynamics of complex human and animal behaviors (see Kirkpatrick 306–09; Prodger; Gunning).

Conceived, like imagism, at the crossroads of science and art, Muybridge's photos of horses trotting, men leapfrogging, women curtseying, and naked toddlers climbing stairs aspired to an ideal of thingness—a beyond of representational conventions—analogous to the idealized directness Fenollosa imagined in the Chinese written character and Pound appropriated for imagist and vorticist poetics. For the photographer, linguist, and poet-theorist alike, these semiotic sequences were, in Fenollosa's formulation, "something much more than arbitrary symbols": not conventional representations but "vivid shorthand picture[s] of the operations of nature" (8). Although always and inevitably saturated by late-nineteenth-century notions of gender, race, and class, Muybridge's photos, like Fenollosa's treatise and H.D.'s and Pound's imagist poems, aspired to make visible "the actual and entangled lines of forces as they pulse through things," and their creators believed themselves to be "watching *things* work out their own fate" (Fenollosa 12, 9).

The terms *forces, pulse*, and *work* imply a physics of thingness that links the experimental aesthetics of the Chinese written character, Muybridge's photographic plates, and H.D.'s and Pound's poems in a common project that Gertrude Stein would situate at the intersection of composition and explanation. In these artistic experiments, semiotic units are engineered to capture an energy that exceeds conventional categories. Muybridge's frames, Fenollosa's ideograms, H.D.'s and Pound's images all function as both states and actions, nouns and verbs, stills and sequences. In this sense, they initiate an interstitial flow or transfer of power, unit to unit, that gives them "something of the quality of a continuous moving picture" (Fenollosa 9), an effect Muybridge, in his turn, realized by projecting his frames through the zoopraxiscope he invented to animate and exhibit them (Prodger 154–61).

The connection among clocks, trolleys, and cameras; imagism and motion pictures; Doolittle, Eakins, and Muybridge; Pound, Gregg, Williams, and H.D. runs through a circuit of everyday life in Philadelphia in the decades flanking the turn of the century. To listen to the ticking of those decades is to understand the ways in which changes in perception theorized by modernism were also and initially produced and pronounced in daily life. As Stein would say, "[E]verybody knows it because everybody says it" (*Gertrude Stein* 520)—everybody, that is, that rode a trolley from here to there and back again, thinking all the while, as H.D., Williams, Pound, Moore, and Gregg did, about how to put words to the world to capture the velocity and linearity of its energies.

NOTE

[1] All quotations from *The Gift* are from Jane Augustine's edition.

MYTH, RELIGION, PSYCHOANALYSIS

Teaching H.D. and Spirituality

Jane Augustine

The writings of H.D. are deeply imbued with her need to illuminate spiritual truth and dense with references to institutionalized religious histories, cultural traditions, and theological ideas that can be difficult for students. At the core of her unsystematic spirituality is her belief that the artist, someone said to be "gifted" or "inspired by the muse," has a conduit to the divine. H.D. believed that she had a special sensitivity and a gift of this kind. In this view, derived from Romanticism, beauty in any form speaks of divinity. The beautiful work of art conveys an aspect of the eternal ideal world that exists above all expressions of it in earthly religions. The creative artist has the power of a priest or prophet to mediate and bring transcendent visions to the secular world. This essay offers an overview of the development of H.D.'s spiritual beliefs and how they are incorporated into her poetry and prose throughout her life.

H.D.'s first intuitions of the artist's power came to her through her fascination with Bible stories, Greek myths, and fairy tales that she read as a child in Bethlehem, Pennsylvania. The benign patriarchy of a typical nineteenth-century American family surrounded her. Her father, Charles Doolittle, whom she invariably referred to as "my father the astronomer" (Guest 14), gazed at the heavens nightly, and her mother, Helen Wolle Doolittle, who had been a painter and accomplished pianist, devoted her energies to her large family rather than to art. They lived on Church Street, next door to Helen's brother, Hartley Wolle, and H.D.'s grandparents, about a block or so from the Central Moravian church where Hilda went to parochial school with her brothers and many cousins, all boys. Around them lay a town exceptionally suffused by a warmhearted, musically oriented form of Protestantism brought to Pennsylvania 150 years earlier by Count Nicholas von Zinzendorf (1700–60) and his followers in the Unitas Fratrum, Unity of Brethren, popularly called the Moravian Church.

This name for the Old Church of Bohemia, the nationalist church of Jan Hus, came about because its remnant, persecuted in Roman Catholic Moravia, escaped in 1722 over the mountains into Protestant Saxony and found refuge on Zinzendorf's estate—a history that H.D. recounts in *The Gift* (227, 234–35).[1] These refugees formed Herrnhut ("The Lord's Watch"), a community that expanded ecumenically as German Lutheran and Dutch Reformed church members joined it and later went out as missionaries to all parts of the world, preaching Zinzendorf's Pietist-influenced nonsectarian "heart religion" (Gift 11; *Mystery* xxx, 100). The count traveled frequently to oversee these settlements, and on Christmas Eve 1741, he gave the town of Bethlehem its name (Gift 235–36; *Mystery* 9, 118). In 1742 a large group from Europe arrived, most of whom were ethnically German, including H.D.'s ancestors, and brought with them the German high culture of music, art, language, and literature (Gift 228–29).

Legends of Zinzendorf abounded in Bethlehem, describing his frequent visits, his courage and exuberance, his miraculous escapes from death, his decision making by drawing lots, his rapport with Native Americans, and his literary gifts (Gift 243–47). His confidence in his closeness to God inspired him to write more than twelve hundred sermons and hymns and to create the unique Moravian liturgies at Easter and Christmas. H.D. especially loved the Christmas Eve candlelight service that commemorated the historic 1741 Christmas Eve as well as the birth of Christ. She absorbed these legends in the same way that she absorbed Grimms' fairy tales, Greek myths, and the scriptural narratives whose power increased as she read them next to the Gustave Doré illustrations in the family Bible. Through her reading she lived the lives of heroes, prophets, Moses, and David, as well as Jesus, who worked miracles, healed people, and brought them back to life and who, above all, loved the world and gave his life to save it, as was constantly taught in church. By the time H.D. reached young adulthood, however, she had expanded her beliefs. For her, the Christian myth was one among many; Christ was one of many gods who died and rose again in the mystery religions, as in J. G. Frazer's *The Golden Bough*, published in 1890 and immediately influential.

The influence of these multiplied mythologies, especially the Greek, is clear in H.D.'s early work. In 1910 H.D. became romantically involved with Frances Gregg. Their closeness became erotic, fusing spiritual communion with poetry and sex enhanced by their reading together the overlush sensuality of A. C. Swinburne's poems, especially "Itylus" and "Faustine." "*[L]ips long since half kissed away*" became a leitmotif in H.D.'s 1920s fictional autobiography *HERmione* (163). H.D. was already immersed in the classical world and in mythologizing herself, the technique she would use in her imagist poems and later novels. Gregg, in a memoir, recalls that the young Hilda frequently proclaimed herself as "one, or another, youthful god" (66). This affair opened up a new dimension of religious experience to H.D.: ecstasy. She thought it could belong only to the gods. She associated it with the Dionysian excesses of wine, song, and dance meant to achieve the union of initiate and deity as well as with the fertility religions of Egypt and the Middle East that celebrated sexual union as a natural force. The myth of Isis and Osiris became particularly compelling. H.D. saw the forces of nature as depicting intense human emotion, as in *Sea Garden*, when storms "swirl and crash," wind "whips round [her] ankles," the rose "drip[s] acrid fragrance" (*Collected Poems* 36, 38, 5). She saw the natural world's energies as inherently sexual, creative, and sacred, reflective of the transcendent loves of goddesses and gods. Through her clean, precise imagist language, she hoped to transmit the erotic charge she felt from the beauty of Greek art and landscape.

The connection of art and Eros was strengthened in summer 1919 when H.D. had a vision on her "honeymoon" in the Isles of Scilly with Bryher. The two women had pledged lifetime loyalty to each other after the birth of Perdita, H.D.'s daughter, on 31 March 1919. As H.D. rested in the beauty and warmth of the Scillies, assured of Bryher's love and support of her literary gift, a "supernormal" episode came to her that she called the "jelly-fish" experience. She wrote of it immediately afterward in *Notes on Thought and Vision*, which remained unpublished until 1982. Artists, she wrote, need "certain definite physical relationships" to develop their talents (17). These relationships, allied with the artist's commitment to creative work, produce an "over-mind," or superconsciousness, that she visualized as a "cap" over her head, "transparent, fluid," somewhat "like a closed sea-plant, jelly-fish or anemone" in which thoughts are "visible like fish swimming under clear water" (18–19). This over-mind, she said, is also "centered in the love-region of the body or placed like a foetus in the body" (19). The over-mind and "womb-mind" are "capable of thought. This thought is vision" (22). Certain works of art, she felt, such as "words and lines of Attic choruses, any scrap of da Vinci's drawings, the Delphic charioteer, . . . are straight, clear entrances, to me, to over-world consciousness" (24). They are like jellyfish with far-reaching tentacles or like seeds that, "as it takes a man and woman to create another life," are needed "to make a new spiritual birth" (50). The jellyfish of spiritual energy transforms into a concentrated light, a pearl, in her forehead and leads to *Notes*'s ending in a multimythic fusion: "Christ and his father, or as the Eleusinian mystic would have said, his mother, were one. . . . He was the body of nature, the vine, the Dionysus, as he was the soul of nature" (52–53). After this experience, H.D. felt more strongly the sense of being a gifted artist touched by the divine.

In 1929, her consciousness of universal male dominance sanctified by organized religion led H.D. to revisit in her novel *Pilate's Wife* the accounts of Jesus's crucifixion and the nonbiblical legend that he did not really die on the cross. Two problems troubled her: the absence of powerful women in the Christian story and the ugliness of the church's centrally displayed icon, the mutilated body of Christ on the cross. For her Christians were death worshippers, only looking to future life and ignoring life now. In her rewriting of the story, she adopted the persona of the wife of Pontius Pilate, whom she names Veronica (from the Latin words meaning "true image") after the legendary woman who, in pity for Jesus's suffering on the road to Calvary, wiped his bloody face and found afterward its image imprinted on her veil (vii). That woman had tried unsuccessfully to intervene; this Veronica will succeed. She arranges with her Roman centurion lover Fabius, a follower of Mithra, to save Jesus because "she loved this manifestation of her old gods; the young man was beautiful" (104). She then begins a meditation that expresses H.D.'s syncretization of Greco-Roman, Egyptian, Christian, and occult religions into a single revelation that the divine exists in all human beings, equally in women and men (106). Fabius comes back to tell Veronica that Jesus is safe, and they drink wine together, a Dionysian moment of union. Fabius also links the spiritual with art, remembering Jesus's teachings and thinking of him as a poet:

> Poetry . . . is living. Jesus had taught that. . . . O, if only that Prophet . . . could really found a new religion! . . . [W]hat an inheritance; to have all the past to draw on . . . blending with an actual re-created present. (134)

The two speak aloud their joint thought: "'If,' said Fabius, 'we could combine this Jesus with these others—' Veronica said, '—so I was thinking'" (135).

The idea of founding a new religion appeared in what H.D. came to call her "Princess Dream" during her psychoanalysis with Freud, which ended in 1934 (Gift 7), the year in which she finished revising *Pilate's Wife*. In *Tribute to Freud*, H.D. writes that this dream, reminiscent of Pharaoh's daughter's discovering the baby Moses in a basket in the bulrushes—a Doré illustration—led Freud to suggest that H.D. was the baby and to ask her if she wanted to be "the 'founder of a new religion'" (119). She internalized this wish and did not forget it (36–37), although Freud thought it bore "a suppressed desire to be a Prophetess, to be important anyway, megalomania they call it" (51) as well as her desire for "union" with her mother (44).

Seven years later, after she lived through the Battle of Britain and the Blitz, Freud's suggestion took on decisive power for H.D. In early December 1941 in war-torn London, her mother appeared to her during a spiritualist séance, as fictionalized in *The Sword Went Out to Sea*. Just as the narrator, Delia Alton, is leaving her first private session with the medium Ben Manisi, he says, "There is a lady here. . . . I thought this lady was your mother, but she calls you sister" (7, 8). Delia recalls that her mother had called her "sister"—she was the only girl among brothers and cousins—but "Sister" was also the common form of address among Moravian women. This moment fused psychoanalysis, spiritualism, Moravian religion, and artistic inspiration for H.D. It told her definitively that she had an inseparable poetic and psychic gift, her inheritance from her Moravian women ancestors and the mystic Zinzendorf. It explained her supernormal visions, her skill at interpreting dreams, and her survival of the Blitz. She considered that she had been miraculously saved to use her gift to help end the war, and a creative outpouring ensued over the next four years.

In early 1942, within a few weeks of her mother's appearance to her, H.D. resumed work on *The Gift*, begun in 1940 during the Battle of Britain as a "series of family-portraits" ("H.D." 188). This project revived her interest in the Moravianism of her childhood, and she conducted extensive research, not simply relying on her memories. During her researches, she learned facts she had never heard in childhood about the scandals of the "Sifting Time" (c. 1745 to 1750), when Zinzendorf overzealously preached his "Blood and Wounds" theology, and his followers fell into devotional extravagances, even orgies, that brought disrepute on the church. Virulent attacks by members of the Protestant clergy ensued (Gift 155, 268). They were offended by the count's preaching in explicit language that sexual union in marriage enacts the union of Christ with his church (263).

Most offensive to the Protestant clergy, however, and in their view heretical, was Zinzendorf's elevation of the feminine principle in his description of the Holy Spirit as female, a "Mother," and the "Comforter" promised by the risen Christ (Gift 9, 22; *Mystery* 215–17). Zinzendorf replaced the creedal Father, Son, and Holy Ghost with a family-model Trinity: God is the father, the Holy Spirit is the mother and bride of God, and Christ is their child (Gift 9–11, 155). This view was expunged from the church after Zinzendorf's death in 1760, but H.D. was delighted to learn of it late in life. It strengthened her sense of having a gift and permitted her to invent the scene in *The Gift* in which her grandmother has a vision. She sees, as if in a séance trance, a group of eighteenth-century Moravian churchmen and Native American leaders meeting to make peace through a conjoined Christian-magical ritual that invokes their common god, the Great Spirit (162–68). This vision leads into *The Gift*'s final scene, in which H.D. imagines that the Moravian Anna von Pahlen and Chief Paxnous's wife exchange names and become members of each other's religions and nations (213, 223). Their spiritual union represents the peace between Germany and America that H.D. hoped her writing could help to bring about.

The feminine Holy Spirit also manifests in the Lady who appears in section 25 of *Tribute to the Angels* in *Trilogy*, as if summoned by the ritual alchemical magic of section 8. She is invoked as "mère, mater, Maia, Mary, // Star of the Sea, / Mother," but H.D. says the Lady is not the Virgin Mary (71). She carries in her arms not a baby but the "unwritten volume of the new" (103). H.D. links her as well "with Venus-Annael, with the Moon, with the pre-Christian Roman Bona Dea, with the Byzantine Greek church Santa Sophia and the SS of the Spiritus Sanctus" (Gift 13). The name Venus-Annael links "Anna, Hannah or Grace" to the Christian Anna von Pahlen of *The Gift*. In section 32 of *Tribute to Angels*, H.D. speaks of the Lady in the biblical terms of Jesus's transfiguration: "her veils were *white as snow, // so as no fuller on earth / can white them*" (97). The veils melt into light, "all-colour," in union with music (109), the "deep-deep bell" of "Zeus-pater or Theus-pater, // *Theus*, God; God-the-father" (108).

This passage parallels an episode in *The Gift*, in which H.D. wakes from a bad dream and prays for the "nightmare" of war to end (113). Here again alchemical wordplay—"Mary, Maia, Miriam, Mut, Madre, Mère, Mother"—invokes the goddess: "This is Gaia, this is the beginning. This is the end" (114). The father god is variously "Zeus, . . . Jupiter, . . . Zeu-pater or Theus-pater or God-the-father," and his temple hides "the dark cave or grotto or inner hall or cella to Mary, mère, Mut, Mutter" (114). The cella suggests both the womb and the holy of holies, the empty and most sacred space at the center of Jewish temples. H.D. is asserting that the dark earth forces control the life cycle of birth and death far more powerfully than the gods of patriarchy. The link to the Lady implies a supreme transcendence of the feminine principle over the dichotomies of good versus evil in the Adam and Eve myth. This dark, or phallic, earth mother is also the Holy Spirit, fully God, who, in the beauty of poetry, unites with the goddess figures of light, heaven, and creative inspiration. The séance, having replaced the psychoanalytic hour as the site of H.D.'s spiritual work, made it possible for her to convert her war fears into hope-filled visions of resurrection and new life. As the war went on, these visions became her reality, "more real, hav[ing] proved more enduring than all the high explosives and the sirens" (*Sword* 12).

That reality fell apart in February 1946 when Lord Hugh Dowding, retired Royal Air Force commander and spiritualist lecturer, rejected her séance messages predicting World War III. He implicitly impugned her gift, and she had a nervous breakdown. Bryher took her to Switzerland for treatment. H.D. had been corresponding with Dowding since October 1943, when a séance vision convinced her they had been linked in previous lives and were to work together in this one. He came to tea in her flat but remained unconvinced. Her letters to him in November 1943 appear almost verbatim as part 1 of her novel *Majic Ring*, with only the names changed to "Delia Alton" and "Lord Howell." As her recovery in a Swiss clinic progressed from 1946 to 1948, she kept her sense of her medium's gift as Delia and wrote two long novels, *The Sword Went Out to Sea*, explaining Dowding's rejection as part of an eternal pattern of near misses between destined lovers, and *White Rose and the Red*, drawing parallels between herself and Elizabeth Siddall, the Victorian beauty and rejected wife of Dante Gabriel Rossetti.

Perhaps because Siddall had committed suicide, H.D. could not finish the novel, but soon her Moravian heritage came to her rescue. In 1950 she wrote to Norman Holmes Pearson in "H.D. by Delia Alton" that she had begun "to live or to 'see' another story," making use of the notes she had assembled for *The Gift*:

> I had become very devoted to the Zinzendorf legend and suddenly one of his grand-daughters, another Elizabeth, steps as it were, out of history to take the place of the (as yet) vaguely questing Elizabeth Siddall Rossetti. . . . I have a title for the new story. It is called *The Mystery*. (200)

In its fictional construction, she reverses the roles she and Dowding had played as rejectee and rejecter. Her central male character, taken from a historical figure, a magician known as Count Louis Saint-Germain, is deceived by fraudulent religion and has a nervous breakdown. The Moravian Countess Elizabeth de Watteville—a palimpsest of Anna von Pahlen, H.D.'s grandmother, her mother, and herself—embodies true religion inseparable from true or "white" magic. As

Zinzendorf's feminine Holy Spirit, described by Zinzendorf as the "mother" and "Comforter," Elizabeth cures Saint-Germain by using the Native Americans' herbal remedies. Like the Lady of *Trilogy*, she is the *midons*, the unattainable object of the medieval poet's adoration, the Beatrice of Dante, and the madonna of the "'lost' Church of Provence, the Church of Love" of which, in H.D.'s mind, the Moravian countess is a later manifestation ("H.D." 202). Elizabeth is the instrument of this transcendent church and, as Saint-Germain's spirit guide, makes possible Zinzendorf's appearance to him as a spiritual presence in the novel's final scene. The presence induces Saint-Germain to reverse his mistaken religious course and take up his true vocation as worshipful lover of the Lady, although it will cost him his life (*Mystery* 85–88). By symbolic means, H.D. accomplished her desire: spiritual union with the eternal lover, a union of feminine and masculine principles inseparable in the new religion she had long envisioned.

With this novel H.D. ended her spiritualist involvement decisively and with it the need to summon her mother's Moravian religion in support of her gift. On *The Mystery*'s manuscript title page, she crossed out "Delia Alton" and wrote firmly "H.D." Her mediumistic self had been fully assimilated into her as the Holy Spirit, which was no longer external. In effect she had become her mother, Helen, and in 1952 began to write *Helen in Egypt*, redacting the patriarchal myth of the *Iliad* from the woman's point of view. At the same time, well cared for in Swiss clinics and residential hotels, she continued her path of meditative and literary religious practices that combined hermeticism and Christianity. Her three long poems in *Hermetic Definition*, written between 1957 and 1960, are almost diaries of her daily life and the elaborate rituals she engaged in to commune with the angels whose names she found in Robert Ambelain's *La Kabbale pratique* and in Athanasius Kircher's three-volume *Oedipus Aegyptiacus* (*Hermetic Definition* 63, 66). The names of Arabic or Hebrew origin are incantatory, sounding as musical mantras in counterpoint to Ambelain's lines of French. Mixed among the invocations of the spirits are poems recording her love longings, erotic desires as strong in old age as in youth. Her quest for ecstasy—perfect union of sexual and spiritual love—remained undiminished. In *Notes on Thought and Vision* in 1919, H.D. had written: "We must be 'in love' before we can understand the mysteries of vision" (22). In art and religion, she understood that the path is the goal.

NOTE

[1] All quotations from *The Gift* are from Jane Augustine's edition.

God or Goods? Teaching *Tribute to Freud* in an Undergraduate Course on Critical Theory

Elizabeth Hirsh

H.D.'s *Tribute to Freud* is at once a gem of modernist narrative and a fascinating document in the history of psychoanalysis. I have found that it is also a wonderful teaching tool in the undergraduate theory classroom. H.D. sought treatment with Sigmund Freud in the 1930s while suffering from writer's block and a paralyzing sense of anxiety triggered by personal losses and the ominous political events of the day. For a period of three months in 1933 (1 March to 12 June) and for an additional five weeks in 1934 (30 October to 2 December), she worked with him in his famous consulting room at Berggasse 19 in Vienna. This experience was intense; the two met six times a week from 5:00 to 6:00 p.m.—a time of day H.D. particularly liked, as she wrote to her longtime companion Bryher (qtd. in Friedman, *Analyzing* 107)—as the signs of impending disaster gathered in the streets outside. An engaging record of this encounter can be found in *Analyzing Freud*, Susan Stanford Friedman's richly glossed edition of the letters exchanged during this period among Freud, H.D., Bryher, and their circle; Friedman's groundbreaking *Psyche Reborn* is also essential reading for those wishing to explore the relationship between H.D. and Freud.

In my experience, *Tribute to Freud* can effectively supplement the case study method in an undergraduate course on critical theory. The case study approach seems inevitable but can also feel mechanical, positing each critical method and the literary text to which the method is applied in a relation of simple exteriority—which in turn tends to become a hierarchy where one text is seen as mastering the other. Either the theory is showing what the text "really means," or (more common among the students I teach) the literary text is exposing the pretensions of the critical method, thereby preserving its transcendent status as a work of art. I try to suggest a more dynamic relation between theoretical and literary texts, a mutually illuminating (sometimes mutually contestatory) relation that makes literary and cultural theory interesting. Because *Tribute to Freud* can be called both a literary work and a theoretical intervention, it models the kind of reading I try to foster, an engagement with theory that goes beyond the logic of method and application.

Many English majors delay fulfilling the critical theory requirement because they approach all things theoretical with trepidation, if not suspicion. As a group they are most confident reading literary texts formalistically, biographically, or as (critical) mirrors of their historical context. The hybridity of *Tribute to Freud* as both lyrical and critical can draw in students who will tackle a challenging literary text more willingly than a challenging work of theory. Fostering reading literature in dialogue with theory, *Tribute to Freud* can also illuminate specific concepts in terms of a poetically rendered human drama that undergraduates find compelling: the personal and hermeneutic struggle between H.D. and Freud. That the central scene of this struggle plays out in the heart of modern Europe during one of the worst crises of its history further heightens student interest.

I teach critical theory using a "problems" format, not as a survey of periods or schools. Helping students cultivate a new literacy rather than master a new body of content is my aim, though the former implies the latter to an important degree. Integrating old classics (Plato, Sidney, Shelley) with newer classics (Beauvoir, Fish, Foucault), we ask, What is literature? What is an author? In tandem with a historical anthology of theoretical pieces, a critical case study informs students about specific idioms and schools like reader response and new historicism, but, in keeping with the literacy approach, this material is subordinated to the topic questions that structure our process.

Tribute to Freud adds a dramatic third dimension. I assign it about two-thirds of the way through the semester, when the students have been exposed to some basic tenets of poststructuralism, psychoanalysis, and feminism, idioms foundational to more recent work in postcoloniality, trauma studies, queer theory, and ecocriticism. Specifically, students will have read and discussed basic background materials. For poststructuralism, they read excerpts from Ferdinand de Saussure's *Course in General Linguistics* concerning the arbitrary and differential nature of the linguistic sign and Roland Barthes's "The Death of the Author" concerning the play of the signifier and the productive role of the reader. For psychoanalysis, they are assigned excerpts from Freud's *The Interpretation of Dreams* and his essay "Femininity" (from *The Standard Edition* [22: 136–57]), as well as Jacques Lacan on the mirror stage and a brief excerpt from "The Instance of the Letter in the Unconscious," the famous anecdote about a young sister and brother arriving at a train station and mutually mistaking its marked restroom doors for the proper name of the destination they've reached. The accompanying graphic, contrasting Saussure's model of the sign (Tree/[tree]) with the juxtaposed restroom doors (GENTLEMEN/LADIES) illustrates Lacan's precept that "the Signifier enters the signified" by virtue of its materiality and specifically with reference to sexual difference (151). (This graphic provides an effective stimulus to discussion of the relation of culture, language, and nature in Lacan.) For feminism, students read Virginia Woolf on the culturally constructed conflict between the female body and artistic creativity (from *A Room of One's Own*), Sandra M. Gilbert and Susan Gubar on the pen/penis equation in Western tradition (from *The Madwoman in the Attic*), and Hélène Cixous's anarchic send-up of masculinist theory, "The Laugh of the Medusa." Working through *Tribute to Freud* in connection with theories introduced earlier affords an opportunity for students to consolidate what they've begun to learn. The fresh context provided by H.D. allows some students to begin understanding earlier topics for the first time, while others deepen or extend their previous understanding. *Tribute to Freud* is a difficult text, and the process of working through it promises not to make theory easy but to make it vivid and help show why it matters.

My approach has three stages: help students establish a connection with H.D.'s text, articulate her text with the relevant theoretical material, and consider how these discourses mutually illuminate or interrogate one another.

Since New Directions typically publishes its texts without gloss, to help students negotiate H.D.'s dense palimpsest I provide in advance a reading aid that lays out the basic chronology of *Tribute to Freud*:

[1889, 1891]	Childhood scenes with father and brother (H.D. age 3 and 5)
1910	Meets Frances Josepha; vision of serpent and thistle
1911	To Europe
1915	Stillbirth of first child during WWI
1919	Learns of father's and brother's deaths; pregnant; influenza
1920	In Corfu with Bryher: sees writing on the wall
1933–34	In Vienna with Freud during rise of National Socialism
1938	Freud exiled in London
1944	Writes *Tribute to Freud* in London during World War II

The reading aid also identifies some important intertexts, figures, and motifs of the text:

Images	Rembrandt's *The Anatomy Lesson of Dr. Nicolaes Tulp* (1632)
	Landseer's *Stag at Bay* (1846)
	Doré's *Finding of Moses* (1866)
	Winged and wingless Nikes
Visual motifs	The signet ring
	The Princess dream
	The writing on the wall
Texts	Shakespeare's *The Merchant of Venice* and *As You Like It*
	The Old Testament's Daniel 6.1–28 (in the lions' den) and Exodus 2.1–8 (baby Moses rescued by Miriam)
	Poe's "To Helen"
Historical figures	Princess Marie Bonaparte, Walter Schmideberg, Charcot and the Salpêtrière, Mary Carmichael, Hanns Sachs, Helen Wolle, Ezra Pound, Caesar, Hannibal
Mythic figures	Prometheus, Perseus, Askelepios, Phoebus Apollo, Athena/Nike, Castor and Pollux, Helen and Clytemnestra

I post this material online and distribute it in class, to be sure students are not overwhelmed by the text's rapidly shifting scenes and dense allusiveness.

So armed, students must actively engage the text when I ask them to reconstruct in detail the specific scenes of H.D.'s palimpsest, in small groups, either in class or as homework. Different groups are responsible for reconstructing different scenes and then reporting back to the whole class, using the board to display their findings. The important thing is to disarticulate as clearly as possible the major elements of the palimpsest to better grasp how they relate to one another. One group may be assigned to re-create H.D.'s 1933 meeting with Freud in Vienna: I elicit detailed descriptions of the scene outside Freud's home (secs. 43–46); the staircase leading to his office on which she encounters Gerardus van der Leeuw, "the Flying Dutchman"; the encounter with Yofi, "the little lioness" (sec. 95); the office, with its couch, stove, rug, and ancient figurines; and the behaviors of H.D. and Freud during their sessions. (I direct students to review sections 1, 10–11, 13, 15, and 51 in addition to those already indicated.) Another group may be asked to re-create scenes from H.D.'s childhood in Pennsylvania: her father's office (secs. 13, 23, and 26) and the scenes in which her brother uncovers hidden life beneath a log, "plays with fire" (secs. 14–15, 17–18), and publicly defies their mother (sec. 20). A third group may re-create the 1920 scene of "writing on the wall" in Corfu, with its ladder, flies, goblet, tripod/washstand, question marks, tents, male and female twins, and "sun-disk" (secs. 29, 32–34, and 38–41 are most relevant here).

With these scenes arrayed before us we begin as a class to trace the mutating motifs that connect them: the ladder/staircase and themes of transcendence or flight; the father's and doctor's studies as bastions of authority and comfort; family configurations of parents, children, and siblings and the theme of return or repetition; the seizing of fire from heaven and defiance of authority by Titans, children, Jews, and women; the effect of doubling or twinning in which disparate elements are identified, made literal in the figures of Castor and Pollux, Helen and Clytemnestra. The reading aid can help to further elaborate the logic of the palimpsest. I display the images by Rembrandt, Edwin Henry Landseer, and Gustave Doré as well as examples of Nike winged and wingless (readily available online). We discuss their relevance to themes of illness and healing; science, religion, and art; violence and predation; heroism and megalomania; triumph and loss. We map Doré's illustration with H.D.'s "Princess dream" and her imaginary rivals, Marie Bonaparte and Mary Chadwick, and explore her feelings toward Freud—rivalry, reverence, protectiveness, and anger.

This exercise fills one meeting of a biweekly class or the first half of a longer, weekly class. Building on their textual knowledge, students can then connect what they have learned with specific theories studied earlier. Students quickly grasp the relevance of free association, castration, feminine lack, and the Oedipus complex and make connections with Woolf and with Gilbert and Gubar. My main concern now is to have them consider the hermeneutic struggle between H.D. and Freud in terms of the play and politics of the signifier that they have encountered through reading Saussure, Barthes, Lacan, and Cixous. I draw attention to the way H.D.'s fascination with puns and homonyms underscores the materiality of the signifier, its status as a perceptible mark or sound, and how this materiality constitutes the basis of figurative language. H.D. puns on *matches* in the fire anecdote involving her relationship with her rebellious brother (24), whom she matches with Prometheus, and puns in a similar vein on the homonym *pairs/pears* (20). Earlier in the text she writes that she and van der Leeuw exchanged "hours" (8), meaning both a slot in Freud's daily schedule and fate or doom, as in "the hour of one's death." Like *matches* and *pairs/pears*, the signifier *hours* participates in more than one signifying chain, and the metaphoric sense of *hours* constitutes a second-order signification (a new sign) that depends on the first one, both preserving and canceling (sublating) the literal sense of *hours*. I emphasize that from a poststructuralist perspective the capacity of a signifier to diverge, wander, or be diverted from its primary, proper locus proceeds from the instability or arbitrariness of the link between signifier and signified that Saussure identified (but the full implications of which he had not appreciated). This divergence also accounts for existing signifiers' being purloined to new significations, as Cixous does with Medusa and H.D. with Nike, ancient figures of feminine excess and lack, respectively.

In this context H.D.'s text, like Cixous's, posits language not as an abstract, ideal order of authorized meanings but as a kind of manufactory where meaning is actively generated through the collision of heterogeneous intentions and conflicting interests. We recall that Lacan's mapping of Saussure and Freud—of linguistic difference and sexual difference—reinterpreted *castration* as the fall into language, the subject's constitutive splitting by the signifier. But if Lacanians often stress the imperatives of language as law, Barthes and Cixous celebrate the deauthorization of the signified in favor of the play of chance, readerly invention, and the potential for subversion at the site of language. Similarly, when H.D. writes that "thoughts are things" that can be "collected, collated, analyzed, shelved" (14), she alludes to Freud's collection of artifacts, including the Nike figurine that the analyst interprets as lacking, and suggests that the process of psychoanalytic interpretation consists in the pursuit and (re)arrangement of these thoughts or things. In fact, H.D.'s encounter with Freud reveals how thoughts depend on things, as signifieds depend on the signifiers with which they are yoked in the signifying process. Without material figures like Nike, Western tradition could not produce (the meaning of) woman as lacking, just as in Lacan's train station anecdote the production of (the meaning of) man and woman as opposites—one "having," the other "being" ("lacking")—depends on the concrete practice of "urinary segregation" enforced by the opposing doors (151): the primal scene of linguistic difference. H.D.'s formula, "thoughts are things," underscores the materiality of psychoanalytic reading, its intense focus on the vicissitudes of the signifier, and might be translated as "signifieds are signifiers"—or, more aptly, "signifiers enter into the constitution of signifieds." In Freud's culturally authorized reading of Nike, the signifier again enters the signified—but by the same token H.D.'s text works to deauthorize this signification by purloining its signifier(s).

The signifier's propensity to wander from its proper course produces not only puns but also the kinds of linguistic slip that Freud made famous. Early in the text H.D. quotes Freud's note of November 1938, acknowledging her gift of gardenias and salutation, "to greet the return of the Gods" (a comment again referring to Freud's collection of artifacts, recently arrived at his place of exile in London). Freud's return note wryly comments: "(other people read: Goods)" (11). This amusing exchange recapitulates H.D.'s argument with Freud in that, by her account, Freud's diagnosis of her experience was based on his underlying moral pessimism and philosophical materialism (goods), while her understanding reflected a basically hopeful and spiritual worldview (gods). Whether this error resides in a slip of H.D.'s pen or a misreading of her words by "other people," it again focuses attention on the waywardness of the signifier, its susceptibility to the play of chance and the alien intention of the other. For H.D. this seemingly trivial accident in fact expresses an important truth: there are no accidents. To her, this revelation implies cosmic design; to Freud, scientific determinism. Nonetheless, her ability to discern this truth in a trivial slip was learned from Freud. In this way, as in others, *Tribute to Freud* is indeed a tribute as well as a challenge to Freud's cultural authority.

Having linked the materiality of the signifier with Freud's insight (as reframed by H.D.) that thoughts are things, we now link their father/daughter drama to the historical scene of its production, 1933 and 1944. Our consideration of the textual politics of identity expands to include ethnicity and religion. H.D. notes that Freud "refused" the imputation of Jewish inferiority (78), and as a feminist she recapitulates this gesture in refusing the imputation of feminine inferiority epitomized in Freud's interpretation of Nike. Relating Freud's hermeneutic genius to a materialistic cast of mind, H.D. alludes to *The Merchant of Venice*, identifying Freud with Shylock when she writes of their dispute over the value or meaning of the Nike figurine:

> He was speaking in a double sense, it is true, but he was speaking of value, the actual intrinsic value of the piece; like a Jew, he was assessing its worth. . . . He knew his material pound, his pound of flesh, if you will, but this pound of flesh was a *pound of spirit* between us. (70)

Suggesting that the insights of psychoanalysis reflect Jewish literal mindedness, H.D. affirms a cultural stereotype even in the act of revalorizing it as positive. Some students see at once that this move poses problems, especially given the setting of H.D.'s drama.

I point out that H.D. challenges Freud's gender theory specifically by positing her identity as a rival of his. She demands to be his equal, staking her vindication of woman on the ground of the ego, and this assertion seems to involve her in a negation of Freud as Jew, as other. For Lacan the misrecognition that founds the ego entails both love and hatred, both erotic fascination and murderous rivalry, toward the imaginary other. In keeping with imaginary logic, *Tribute to Freud* represents Freud and H.D. as opposites (male/female, scientist/poet, Jew/gentile) in need of reconciliation but also identifies the two as both seeing and casting themselves as heroes or prophets. Freud's childhood adoration of Hannibal presages his towering ambition (79); H.D.'s ambition is particularly invested in seeing the writing on the wall, an experience that marks her as different. This experience identifies H.D. with both Miriam and Moses of the Princess dream or the Doré print (37) and with Daniel, the Old Testament seer whose chosen status protects him in the lions' den. Amplifying her defense of Nike/woman, the prophet H.D. now posits herself as perfect, lacking nothing. This stance sets the two prophets' visions on a collision course. Freud negates H.D.'s self-image when he reads the Corfu experience as a psychotic episode (he interprets the writing on the wall as a hallucination signaling a suicidal wish for a return to the womb, that is, to H.D.'s mother, Helen, whom she identified with Hellas/Corfu). He thus places her on a par with the grandiose inmates of the Salpêtrière, who also misrecognize themselves as heroes like Caesar (37). H.D. in turn negates Freud when she attempts to "de-Judaize" him, "to generalize and dilute those aspects of his work she finds related to his Jewishness" (Spiro 617). Just as Freud's "pound of flesh" becomes H.D.'s "pound of spirit," the (Jewish) insight that thoughts are things gives way to a Christian emphasis on the spirit of the law. H.D. even exploits the play of the signifier to identify the father of psychoanalysis with Jesus: "there was another Jew who said, the kingdom of heaven is within you" (*Tribute* 104). Here the word *Jew* acts as a switchpoint between Freud and Jesus, between the old dispensation and the new one that—from a Christian point of view—supersedes it. Set apart near the end of H.D.'s text, this gesture displaces any emphasis on the materiality of reading and writing. Privileging spirit, it puts an end to play, reasserting the authority of the signified. Joanna Spiro reads H.D.'s gesture as a posthumous "conversion" of Freud akin to the forced conversion of Shylock. Spiro's reading, too, puts an end to play, calling for a decision on the part of the reader—but one that aligns itself with Freud, not H.D.

During the kind of violent crisis in which H.D.'s text is set, definitive answers are often demanded. But the demand for final answers may itself imply violence. If we elect to take sides with Freud, against H.D., closing the play of the signifier, do we betray his insight by returning to the logic of idealism from which, as a Jew, he dissented? Or, to the extent that H.D.'s subversion of patriarchal authority depends on the play of the signifier, if we take sides with H.D., against Freud, does the same question apply? I do not ask my students to answer these questions, but I do ask them to weigh the relative claims of free play and commitment in reading *Tribute to Freud* (or any other text). This exercise requires students to give close attention to the specificities of text, intertext, and context; to issues of cultural authority always at work in reading; and to the potential for violence inherent in any interpretive decision.

Excavating H.D.'s Egypt

Marsha Bryant and Mary Ann Eaverly

Although anthology selections tend to emphasize the influence of Greek mythology on H.D.'s early poetry, ancient Egyptian culture was crucial to her emergence as a major writer of long poems. Archaeological sites such as Karnak influenced her portrayal of an Egypt that is both material and mythic, lending imagist precision to the epic sweep of *Trilogy* and *Helen in Egypt.* Most discussions of this topic combine Freudian and feminist lenses so that Egypt's ancient past represents a repressed maternal unconscious (see Friedman, *Psyche*; Edmunds; Chisholm). While psychoanalytic approaches lend valuable insights to much of H.D.'s writing, they do not show the extent to which her most ambitious poems relied on Egyptian architecture and art. Why does "*for Karnak* 1923" appear in the dedication to the first part of *Trilogy*? Why does the Amun temple frame the reader's entry to both *Trilogy* and *Helen in Egypt*? How do sculptures of Egyptian pharaohs shape H.D.'s fluid conceptions of gender? Our archaeological approach to teaching *Trilogy* highlights H.D.'s use of Egyptian monuments to reroute cultural origins and reconfigure gender roles.

H.D. had more than a museum visitor's knowledge of ancient Egyptian artifacts. The library she shared with her longtime companion Bryher contained several books on Egyptology, including *A Concise Dictionary of Egyptian Archaeology*, James Henry Breasted's *A History of Egypt*, Arthur E. P. Weigall's *A Guide to the Antiquities of Upper Egypt*, Margaret Alice Murray's *Egyptian Sculpture*, and A. Lucas's *Ancient Egyptian Materials* (Smyers 17, 21). H.D. toured Egypt in February 1923, three months after the discovery of Tutankhamun's tomb. In addition to the Valley of the Kings and the Egyptian Museum in Cairo, her itinerary included Hatshepsut's temple at Deir el-Bahri, the Temple of Edfu, the Temple of Luxor, and the Amun temple complex at Karnak (Silverstein, pt. 3).

Of all the sites H.D. visited in Egypt, Karnak made the most impact. She saw it on four occasions, reworking some of these experiences into the culminating section of *Palimpsest*, "Secret Name: Excavator's Egypt." In teaching H.D., we find that Karnak and its monuments best distill ancient Egypt's pivotal position in H.D.'s move to the long poem. Even before King Tut engaged the popular imagination, Karnak was a much studied and excavated site. Jean-François Champollion, the first scholar to decipher hieroglyphic writing, visited Karnak in 1828. His translations of the inscriptions that covered the walls and columns revealed Karnak as the site of Egypt's most important god—Amun, who was the king of the gods and was also referred to by the Egyptians as the hidden one (Tobin 82). (In *Helen in Egypt* the protagonist seeks to decode these inscriptions, which she calls "the Amen-script" [21].) Combined with the sun god Re, Amun was the major deity of the Egyptian state and the staunch support of pharaonic rule. Karnak served as the main site of Amun worship, a place where ceremonies and festivals would be celebrated in his and the pharaoh's honor. Systematic excavations of Karnak began in 1858, and the early twentieth century proved to be a particularly fruitful period. In 1903 archaeologists found hundreds of buried statues of pharaohs from a wide range of periods. Especially exciting was the 1923–25 discovery of colossal statues of the pharaoh Akhenaten, most of whose statuary had been destroyed by his successors in protest of his radical religious beliefs. Every ancient Egyptian pharaoh from the Middle Kingdom (c. 2000 BCE) until the Ptolemaic period (c. 330 BCE) made additions to Karnak, so the site manifests the great sweep of Egyptian history.

Karnak's extent is also vast—it includes the temple of Amun, gateways, hypostyle halls (multicolumned rooms), obelisks, and smaller temples—and the scale of its individual monuments is enormous. One of Karnak's most majestic buildings, the Great Hypostyle Hall, contains still-standing columns that are 72 feet high. Some of its entrance gateways are over 100 feet high, and 100 standing people could fit on each column capital. In *Palimpsest* H.D. notes that these "enormously uplifted columns still held some cross-beam of the original massive ceiling" (207). The story's main character, Helen Fairwood, is struck by the way Karnak's scale reflects divine rather than human standards of measurement:

> It seemed natural that they should be dwarfed. In Greece, even in so late a building as the Italian Paestum [the "Temple of Neptune" at Paestum] there was that strange insistence upon human achievement. . . . Here was magnificence of another order. (208)

She also remarks that "the Parthenon itself" would fit into one of Karnak's courtyards (214). Classical Greek temples are no match for Egypt's architectural grandeur. The columns of Paestum, one of the three best-preserved temples on the European mainland, are 29.5 feet tall, less than half the size of those in Karnak's Hypostyle Hall. By the time H.D. writes *Helen in Egypt,* she expands Karnak's Amun temple to cosmic proportions: "*It is the same Amen-temple, at all times, in all places, on all planes of existence*" (212). Karnak's colossal size, combined with its reflection of divinity, offered H.D. a potent source for spiritual renewal during World War II.

In the first section of *The Walls Do Not Fall,* the first part of *Trilogy,* H.D. situates Karnak within three temporal layers that reveal the endurance of ancient Egypt within an unstable modern world: World War II (London, "here"), the classical era (Pompeii), and Egypt's New Kingdom (Karnak, "there"). While all three planes show signs of destruction, Egyptian sacred architecture has a degree of "sheer permanence" and "cryptic power" that the other planes lack, as H.D. writes in *Palimpsest* (182). H.D. bids readers to "enter" the remains of sacred sites, revealing Karnak's Amun temple as spiritual predecessor to the now damaged Saint Paul's Cathedral (*Trilogy* 3). If Karnak's ruins offer a parallel to modern London, their longevity and stability offer a striking contrast. H.D.

notes that while the railing from London's "old town square" has been removed to make guns, the hieroglyphic inscriptions on Karnak's temples still "pursue unalterable purpose" in a place where "eternity endures" (*Trilogy* 3).

The ancient Roman city of Pompeii, which represents H.D.'s classical plane, was destroyed by the eruption of Mount Vesuvius in 79 CE, leaving behind a time capsule of Roman life that included bodies of victims, household equipment, and even carbonized loaves of bread. H.D. alludes to "poor utensils" that appear "like rare objects in a museum" (*Trilogy* 4). Although the popular imagination tends to consider Pompeii completely preserved, the weight of the eruption's ash and stone crushed walls and collapsed roofs. Built of plaster, stone, brick, and wood like London, Pompeii reflects neither the durability nor the longevity of Karnak, which was built of large blocks of stone and spans millennia; as H.D. writes in *Helen in Egypt*, "it is stone and heavily built; / it was built to last forever" (65). Moreover, the livable scale of Pompeii's architecture reflects human rather than divine habitation. Consequently, H.D. writes that "Pompeii has nothing to teach us" now that modern Londoners know the terrors of airborne destruction (*Trilogy* 4).

Recalling Karnak during the Blitz renewed H.D.'s faith in the power of writing, so that *Trilogy* in part becomes a defense of poetry in wartime. As Adalaide Morris points out, H.D. and Bryher lived "only blocks from the anti-aircraft batteries in Hyde Park," so that they—and their manuscripts—were "in priority range for incoming bombers" ("Signaling" 123). Book burnings and paper shortages also brought home to H.D. the physical vulnerability of her writing. If the war makes poetry appear useless and dispensable to the unappreciative, Karnak's preservation of ancient writing functions as a "stone papyrus" that will "continue to prophesy" in the face of destruction (*Trilogy* 3). Hieroglyphic inscriptions carved into its columns and walls record the deeds of the many rulers who contributed to the site, a permanent chronicle not found in classical sites. These inscriptions reflect the importance of writing as a component of the divine in ancient Egyptian culture. H.D. uncovers the ancient meaning of *cartouche*—the oblong shape enclosing a pharaoh's name—beneath its modern meaning of cartridge casing. Significantly, the poet chooses Hatshepsut's cartouche because the name of this female pharaoh survived her successors' attempts to erase her from history. Many of Hatshepsut's monuments were destroyed or covered over by her successors. Although today's scholars disagree about specific cases, citing an Egyptian tradition of recycling monuments, during H.D.'s time it was widely believed that Hatshepsut's obelisk at Karnak was deliberately defaced with a masonry cover by Thutmose III. By the nineteenth century the cover had collapsed, revealing her inscriptions.

In ancient Egypt the rule of the god-king, pharaoh, was supported by a large bureaucracy of scribes, whose profession was considered one of the most noble. The ancient Egyptians associated writing and the scribal tradition with the god Thoth. As a messenger god, Thoth was equated with the later Greek god Hermes and the Roman god Mercury; H.D. fashions this spiritual genealogy into an artist's holy trinity: "Mercury, Hermes, Thoth / invented the script, letters, palette" (*Trilogy* 17). (Thoth returns as Hermes Trismegistus to anchor the next part of *Trilogy, Tribute to the Angels*.) Viewing herself and her peer poets as modern scribes, H.D. clothes these "bearers of the secret wisdom" with the headdresses that adorned Egyptian gods and pharaohs (14). Isis wore the "twin-horns" and disk, Amun wore the two-feathered crown ("double-plume") and pharaohs wore the cobra ("erect serpent") (14). Excavating the ancient Egyptian source of her profession, H.D. asserts that the poet-scribe's words are "magic, indelibly stamped" and that the scribe "takes precedence of the priest, / stands second only to the Pharoah [*sic*]" (17, 15). Although Egyptian scribes were male, H.D. finds them a more empowering precedent than the classical reliance on woman as muse.

Egypt offered an alternative foundational mythology for H.D.'s long poems. Unlike the classical tradition, Egypt's does not have epic cycles of heroic human deeds such as the *Iliad* and *Odyssey*. Moreover, Egyptian mythology does not emphasize its deities' humanlike escapades but focuses on their struggle to maintain the ancient Egyptians' greatest desire, order—a concept personified by the goddess Maat. Thus Egyptian mythology stresses that the life cycle will continue, chaos will be defeated, and order will prevail; both the gods and divine pharaoh guarantee the correct functioning of the universe. In addition to mythic cycles that deal with creation, the most important guarantor of order—the Isis-Osiris myth—holds the promise of eternal life. The goddess Isis restores Osiris to life and creates a son, Horus, with him; Horus in turn triumphs over the forces of chaos represented by the god Seth. Overall, the optimistic view of Egyptian mythology contrasts with the more pessimistic view of the Greeks, for whom the gods were not especially interested in the welfare of human beings.

Most critics who discuss H.D.'s engagement with Egyptian mythology focus on Isis, whose worship extended into the Roman Empire. Although Isis's appearances in *Trilogy* are not as numerous as Amun's, they are important in establishing an "original great-mother" to counterbalance Amun's role as "world-father," thus mirroring the cosmic unity of the Isis-Osiris myth (47, 25). Alluding to Isis also furthers H.D.'s agenda of revealing the Egyptian sources of Western culture. In *The Walls Do Not Fall,* Isis unites the poem's goddesses into a feminine force; Susan Gubar asserts that Isis also "links humanity to the ancient wisdom" (304), which H.D. calls "the one-truth" and "the secret of Isis" (*Trilogy* 48, 54). The goddess appears early in the poem, anchoring a trinity that includes her Egyptian name (Aset, also Eset) and the Phoenician fertility goddess, Astarte. Later in the poem H.D. joins Isis/Aset with Hestia, Greek goddess of the hearth (abbreviated as Hest in the poem), and Serqet (also Selket), the Egyptian goddess of scorpions and magic (5, 47). While Hestia's sustaining fire counters the incendiary bombs of the Blitz, Serqet's magical powers complement Isis's status as great magician.

If Isis and Thoth help H.D. move across ancient Mediterranean cultures, Amun enables her to move across gender boundaries. (H.D. spells his name

"Amen" in her long poems, a device that connects Egyptian and Christian religion in *Trilogy*.) When Amun merges with Ra and Osiris as "the world-father," he anticipates the androgyny that H.D. will develop further: this initial Amun is "beardless" and "slender" (*Trilogy* 25). In his more extended incarnation as the Amen-Ra figure who takes the speaker "home" to Egypt, Amun manifests divine androgyny by combining a ram's horns with a "curled fleece" and nurturing womb (the "warm . . . belly" [31]); he is a spiritual "Father" through whom the speaker is "mothered again" (31, 30). Although the ancient Egyptians considered Amun imperceptible, they usually depicted him in human form with a tall feathered crown. Yet he could also be shown as a ram or a goose. H.D. uses the goose figure to link the first and final components of *Trilogy*. Susan Schweik notes that "Christ is a wild goose" in *The Flowering of the Rod* (254), a mirror image of H.D.'s earlier assertion that "*Amen* is our Christos" (*Trilogy* 27). Unlike Greek gods, who can transform themselves into animals yet are almost always shown in human form, Egyptian gods can be depicted either as animals or as hybrid forms that combine an animal head with a human body. Amun bridges animal and human forms in H.D.'s memoir *The Gift*, appearing first as "our old friend Ammon-Ra," "*Amen forever and ever*," and then shifting into a Saint Bernard, "the Lion of Saint Mark's or the Lion of Saint Jerome," and finally "Aries, our gold-fleece Ram" (Gift 84). In *Helen in Egypt*, Amun shifts across a plethora of identities; he is "*the Absolute, the King of Egypt, Proteus or Amen, 'the Nameless-of-many-Names'*" (105). Indeed, Amun proves the most protean mythic figure in H.D.'s long poems, reflecting her sense that the Egyptian myth system and artistic repertoire offered her a more heterogeneous source than the classical tradition.

Depictions of the pharaoh appear to cross male and female boundaries in two periods of Egyptian art. During the eighteenth dynasty of the New Kingdom (1550–1168 BCE), Hatshepsut was pharaoh, which, with a few brief exceptions, was a male role. Thus in some statues she is shown as a woman, but with the beard and headdress that are symbolic of her office, and in others she is completely male except for the inscriptions in the feminine grammatical form. While ancient artists wrestled with this contradiction, H.D. reveled in the gender fluidity that she perceived in such images. As Susan Edmunds points out, H.D.'s allusion to Hatshepsut serves as "the poem's first evocation of a doubly sexed god" (42); in a letter to Bryher from 1939, the poet wrote that "Queen Hatshepsut pretended to be a man" (qtd. in Edmunds 42). Statues of Akhenaten, another New Kingdom pharaoh, go beyond Hatshepsut's, showing a male figure with the rounded hips and stomach usually characteristic of females. When the statues were first discovered at Karnak, scholars considered them so bizarre that they postulated various physiological conditions as the source of his atypical features. H.D. was familiar with some of these controversies, having read James Strachey's "Preliminary Notes upon the Problem of Akhenaten" in the *International Journal of Psycho-analysis*. Some scholars today believe that Akhenaten's physical attributes in his statuary may indicate his desire to suggest the all-encompassing, complete nature of the sun and thus reflect his allegiance to the sun god, Aten. Although H.D. does not refer explicitly to Akhenaten in *Trilogy*, her image of "the sun-disk, / the re-born Sun" alludes to the pharaoh's new solar religion (31). As with Hatshepsut's, Akhenaten's name and images survived subsequent attempts to efface them. Some of Karnak's most significant pharaonic sculptures give students a clearer sense of how H.D. reconfigures gender in *Trilogy* so that she can move beyond biological and other essentialist constructions. Drawing on these sources from the Egyptian artistic repertoire surely enabled the poet's depiction of the unconventional goddess figure who appears later in *Tribute to the Angels*: the Lady who does not need traditional feminine attributes to assume her divine role. For H.D., Hatshepsut and Akhenaten proved more significant figures than Tutankhamun, whose treasures created a sensation during the modernist era.

Because students tend to have more knowledge of classical and biblical cultures than of ancient Egyptian culture, visual contexts help them understand H.D.'s strategy of "drawing upon alternative sources of authority and authenticity," as Helen Sword writes of *Trilogy* (*Engendering* 120). In our interdisciplinary teaching, we show images of Karnak, its monuments, and Egyptian deities to distill H.D.'s parallel journeys to Egypt and the long poem. Our sample slide show keyed to *Google Images* offers one possible scenario for providing these contexts in the classroom (see fig. 1, opposite).[1]

As a woman writer, H.D. found in Egyptian mythology and art more fluid gender delineations than those of the classical tradition. Egyptian mythology also offered her more maneuvering room than the manly heroics and warrior band narratives of its Greek and Roman counterparts. The quality of permanence that hieroglyphs, literally sacred carvings written in stone, gave to Egyptian writing prompted her to envision her calling as sacred scribe and to reenvision divinity beyond classical and biblical frameworks. As a Londoner, H.D. found in Egyptian monuments a sharp contrast to the seemingly ephemeral buildings destroyed by the Blitz. Recalling that "eternity endures" in Karnak's temples, she drew strength to endure a place where doors are "*twisted on hinges*" and "*the floor sags*" (*Trilogy* 3, 58–59). The need for a regenerative past became more urgent in the face of global war. H.D.'s stance of "Egypto-modernism," as we have termed it, distinguishes her long poems from those of her peers, because H.D. turned to Egypt rather than Greece as Western culture's source (Bryant and Eaverly 437). Excavating H.D.'s Egypt in the classroom gives students a sense of how ancient cultures shaped her artistic sensibility.

NOTE

[1] For images of major Egyptian gods, including Amun, Thoth, and Isis, see Wilkinson; for information on Egyptian sculpture, painting, and architecture, see Malek, Robins.

Slide Show for *Trilogy*	***Google Images* Search Terms**
Part 1: Temporal Layers	
Modern	
London Blitz	London Blitz
Cecil Beaton's photos of St. Paul's Cathedral	Beaton, St. Paul's
Classical	
Pompeii aerial and street views	Pompeii destruction, Pompeii street
Paestum	Temple of Neptune, Paestum
Egyptian	
Karnak site and Amun temple complex	Karnak, Karnak aerial
Hypostyle Hall	Hypostyle Hall Karnak
Hieroglyphs at Karnak	Karnak inscriptions
Part 2: Scribes, Deities, and Pharaohs	
Statue of Kai as a scribe from his tomb at Saqqara (Old Kingdom, Louvre, Paris) and similar statues	Egyptian scribe
Relief of Ibis-headed Thoth from Luxor temple	Thoth Luxor
Amun statues and reliefs that show his double-plumed crown	Amun Ra Karnak
Akhenaten statue from the Temple of the Aten, Karnak (New Kingdom, Egyptian Museum, Cairo), other statues and reliefs	Akhenaten, Egyptian Museum Cairo
Head of Hatshepsut with beard and seated granite statue of Hatshepsut as female wearing male headdress (New Kingdom, Metropolitan Museum of Art, New York)	Metropolitan Museum, Hatshepsut

Fig. 1. Sample slide show

Approaches to Teaching *Helen in Egypt*

Cyrena N. Pondrom

H.D. in *Helen in Egypt* immerses us in the multiple Greek narratives of the events claiming to be the story of Helen of Troy. As this fictive Helen struggles to understand and tell her story, the reader too struggles to sort out the interconnecting, fragmentary, partially contradictory narratives. The text thus forces the reader to perform its central questions: What is real, what is vision, what is dream, what is illusion, what is fact? Are vision and dream any less real than fact? Who is Helen—and what are identity and the human quest? How does H.D. ask us to reexamine (from Helen's viewpoint) the narratives and interpretations that have naturalized the values and established practices of patriarchal culture?

Such a text may be difficult for students to read and challenging for instructors to teach—but these hurdles can be overcome, if the instructor provides three things. First, an introduction to the materials of the poem—which include background material and contexts, mythic content (including the identification of characters), structural concept and narrative method, and central symbols—is necessary. Second, the instructor can give students a set of pointed questions to answer (in oral presentation and class discussion, informal writing, or e-mail postings), so that each student can propose and defend by citations important interpretive hypotheses. Third, the instructor can provide theoretical frameworks from poststructuralist criticism that enable students to see the implications of the narrative method and symbolic practice H.D. utilizes. These strategies are useful both in advanced undergraduate and beginning graduate classes. (This text is probably not the best choice for an introductory class.) The primary distinction between these two levels is information supplied by the instructor and that supplied by students. In the description of materials that follows, I assume the instructor's presentation to undergraduates. In graduate classes, students may be asked to use resources named in the syllabus to provide background information to the class.

Materials of the Poem

Background Material and Contexts

One may begin with information on H.D.'s biography, including relationships in her life that inform *Helen*, and continue with a brief description of the epic, a genre *Helen* invokes. Readily available sources like the *New Princeton Encyclopedia of Poetry and Poetics* (Preminger, Brogan, and Warnke) summarize the characteristics of epic. I stress the function of epic to display the actions of (male) heroes, whose stalwart and usually violent actions illustrate for the benefit of the community characteristics of courage, skill, strength in battle, and loyalty to the tribe or national group and who also display the consequences of overreaching or betraying these ethics and of succumbing to seduction by a dangerous but enchanting female. These qualities describe Homer's *Iliad*, the narrative of the Trojan War from which H.D. (invoking the fragments of Stesichorus and plays of the later Euripides) diverges by installing a woman hero and a quest, not for possession of the female, success in battle, or the Golden Fleece, but for a visionary understanding of the self and reality. Moreover, this narrative challenges the myth of female guilt for the falling of civilizations by questioning whether Helen was ever in Troy. In a modernist context, the epic may be a narrative in which a questing poet-hero confronts the paradigms of many cultures across time and conquers the temptations of Aphrodite and her siblings to demonstrate for the community the meaning of right action in history—a cursory account of the *Cantos* of Ezra Pound. It is important for H.D.'s woman's epic to be as much understood in the light of its status as a dialogue with Pound's *Pisan Cantos* as it is as a dialogue with the masculine epic traditions of the Western tradition inherited from Homer.[1]

The quality of revising traditional male myth, whether of Homer or Pound, informs the title of the first section of *Helen in Egypt*, "Pallinode." A *palinode* is a poetic genre of recantation, of reversal and apology, and it is the name given to fragment 192 of the sixth-century BCE poet Stesichorus, whose work, highly regarded in the time of ancient Greece, we have only in scattered fragments. The retraction and retelling of the story of Helen in Troy opens in "Pallinode" in Egypt, where Helen resides in the Amen temple overlooking the beach, and at the end of book 1, canto 8, she confronts the figure of Achilles on the shore in an electrifying scene of violence dissolving into passion (16–17).

"Pallinode" is followed by "Leuké," or "L'isle blanche," an island near Crete, unoccupied since the early Christian era and hence the repository of unusually well-preserved structures dating as far back as the Early Minoan Period. In this narrative, Egypt is the site of the mystical and timeless, Greece (i.e., Crete/Leuké) the setting of the rational and historical. Dream is the mode of Egypt; memory the mode of Leuké.

The third section is entitled "Eidolon," from the Greek εἴδωλον—image, spectre, phantom ("Eidolon"), a term used in theosophy to refer to the astral double of a living being. In *Helen* the term refers first to the "wooden doll" or image of Thetis, Achilles's mother, left with the child in Chiron's cave (284) and later carved on the prow of Achilles's ship (244, 256–57, 291, 295); second to the double Helen and Thetis become (261); and ultimately to a symbol of the eternal, cyclic, and universal human quest for love and regeneration. Such a quest is given mythic expression in the narratives of Oedipus and of Isis, Osiris, and Horus, repeatedly invoked in *Helen*, and is symbolized by the child of Achilles and Helen, "Euphorion/Paris," whose "*Eidolon*" forms the final poem in the book (304). In addition, the identity of the real is subject to question since it is not always clear if the character speaking is flesh and blood or an astral double (208). If the first section is the realm of the mystical and timeless and the second of the intellectual and diachronic, we might think of the third as the domain of the ethical, for here Helen seeks *"the human content of the drama"* (255), and it takes the form of the repressed pursuit of the absolute union that is at once love and death (303).

Mythic Content and Identification of Characters

Because so many mythic figures are referred to in this text, it is useful to provide students with a map of the relationship of these figures, such as may be found in Edith Hamilton's *Mythology*. Of particular importance are the genealogies of the houses of Thebes and Atreus and the ancestries of Helen and Achilles. It is useful to describe the myths associated specifically with Helen, including her birth to Leda and Zeus / the Swan, the judgment of Paris, the brief outlines of the *Iliad*, and the variant accounts by the fragments of Stesichorus and by Euripides's comedy *Helen*. Helen's three lovers are all present here—Theseus, who carried her off to Attica as a girl; Paris, who was awarded her, because she was the most beautiful woman in the world; and through an alternative tradition, Achilles, to whom she bore a son on the island of Leuké. One driving force behind many of H.D.'s narratives is the attempt to impose or intuit a meaningful pattern ordering the memories of her life, particularly of her intense emotional relationships with several men. Thus some major characters correlate with figures in H.D.'s life: Theseus with Sigmund Freud; Paris with Erich Heydt, an analyst she met in Küsnacht in 1953; and Achilles with the Royal Air Force marshall Hugh Dowding, with whom she sought (and ultimately failed) to share the communications from pilots she felt she received in her spiritualist séances during World War II. H.D., of course, is figured by Helen, but as the text progresses, doubles of Helen also refer to H.D.'s mother, Helen Wolle Doolittle (Edmunds 95; Friedman, *Psyche* 20–21, 60, 83, 187–88). If time allows, brief summaries of the myths surrounding related characters in the text, including Theseus, Clytemnestra, Thetis, and Oedipus are also helpful. In addition to classical mythology, students should be introduced briefly to the Egyptian myth of the mother-god Isis, along with her brother-husband, Osiris, and son, Horus, for in the crucial moment of violence on the beach, the touchstone for the entire narrative, Achilles conflates the figures of Helen and Isis (17), who serves in part as symbolic agent of endless regeneration.

Structural Concept and Narrative Method

An important structuring concept in *Helen in Egypt* is palimpsest, the inscription of a new text or image over an old one, obscuring it but letting elements of the previous text show through. H.D. regarded human experience in its fundamentals (though not in its details) as repetitive and roughly cyclic. Structurally similar narratives and motifs abound in this text, and by the intermingling of dream, vision, and memory, they are superimposed on one another, often in ways that alter chronology. The first palimpsest we might identify is the

	Isis	**Helen**	**Mary**
Partner or Partner/Brother	Osiris	Achilles	Joseph
Son or Partner/Son	Horus	Euphorion/Paris	Jesus
Supreme Deity	Amen	Zeus	God
Agent of Destruction	Set	Typhon	Devil/Serpent
Source	Egypt	Greece	Christian

Fig. 1

superimposed narratives of Helen's attraction to and love affairs with Theseus, Paris, and Achilles. Each of these quests for union is truncated or thwarted and rises again in a different form.[2]

Next we should note that the quest for union and understanding of reality is repeated in each of the three titled sections, in different spheres: the mystical or dream vision in "Pallinode"; the empirical, historical, and remembered in "Leuké"; and in "Eidolon" the human and psychoanalytic, which is represented as in Egypt but blends the characteristics of the first two and is referred to as "*waking-dream or day-dream*" (222). H.D. traces the quests in her narrative along the trajectory taken by previous mythic narratives of quest, destruction, and regeneration, and the frequent shifts in allusion among these myths make a palimpsest of the previous narratives. Here are three of the most prominent ones (see fig. 1).

In addition, H.D. uses the Oedipus story, and the Freudian use of that story in psychoanalysis, as the interpretive framework for crucial elements of the love relationships. It is the magic word "Thetis," the name of Achilles's mother, that Helen breathes as she unintentionally sets off the touchstone act of violence dissolving into love on the beach (13–17). Achilles quite literally follows his mother into war, since her image, or eidolon, is carved on the prow of the ship he takes into battle (240). Thus the masculine drive to conquer is led by an image of beauty that is his own mother, and the epic quest and the oedipal story are fused. H.D. metamorphically repositions Paris (the lover who took Helen to Troy and who slew Achilles) as the child of Achilles and Helen (222). The final three stanzas of this canto introduce an image by which H.D. symbolizes palimpsestic human experience: the shell, or its more dynamic parallel, the spiral, which represents the repetition of the same structures of human experience through differing times and places (see 107, 128, 193). Metamorphosis and mystical doubling are the methods by which characters disappear and reappear in each new circuit of the spiral. H.D. also makes structural use of opposed poles, binaries that are temporarily resolved in each cycle of the spiral or shell. Important among these oppositions are Egypt and Greece, mystery and intellect, the timeless and time, vision and memory, female and male, Achilles and Paris, Greece and Troy, fate and choice, peace and war, Eros and

Eris, and—fundamental to the entire narrative—Eros and Thanatos, love and death. Essential to understanding the structure and meaning of the narrative is the recognition that these contesting pairs require each other and are both destabilized and resolved in the recurring, eternal cycle. As the narrator's prose acknowledges in "Pallinode," "*there is this yet, unresolved—without war, there would have been no Achilles, no 'Star in the Night*'" (76). The resolution sought throughout the epic is anticipated in "Eidolon," when the narrator asserts, "La Mort, L'Amour *will merge in the final illumination*" (271).

Central Symbols

Many of the central symbols are implicit in the discussion of myth and structure. In addition to the shell and spiral, or winding stair, and the eidolon, or "doll," H.D. frequently uses the veil or scarf to refer to the feminine principle (55, 85) and the iron-ring to refer to the masculine (55, 87). Both accrue multiple nuances in their frequent repetition, and, in keeping with the associations the masculine and feminine principles have, the veil often points more broadly to the realm of dream or vision and the iron-ring to the realm of action and to the production of domination or violence. The caravel is both the ship of death of Osiris (26, 66) and the craft that bears Achilles from Troy to Egypt (57). In the Osiris myth it is a basic symbol of the fragmentation of the body and the harrowing of hell, or the underworld, before restoration to life by Isis. In *Helen* it serves to equilibrate Achilles and Osiris and symbolizes the vehicle or medium of transportation through the mythic cycles of experience, from action, time, and memory to dream and vision.

Perhaps the symbols most basic to the unfolding of the epic narrative are the Star in the Night, the Amen-temple, the hieroglyph, and Helen herself. The Star in the Night is the name Helen first gives her orgasmic or visionary experience of violence transformed into ecstasy with Achilles on the desolate beach (17). That experience is redefined as the "*eternal moment*" in "Eidolon" (269), and the reference is steadily repeated throughout (see 77, 84, 86, 92). In this repetition there is slow accretion of meaning until the image takes on the sense of encounter with the timeless in time. Each of the other of these basic symbols encodes something of the same meaning, in different ways. We encounter the Amen-temple on the first page as Helen's residence in Egypt, a place of "peace" to which she was brought by Amen/Zeus. It is defined in "Eidolon" as "*the same Amen-temple, at all times, in all places, on all planes of existence, whether they are symbolized by Athens, the intellect, or by Eleusis, the mysteries*," and it is "dedicated to Isis, / or if you will, Thetis" (212). It is thus suggestive of the infinite creative principle at work in all phases of existence. The hieroglyph symbolizes constant wisdom preserved from time, just as the inscriptions in stone in the temples and sarcophagi of Thebes can still be read six millennia later, but it is also a sign of something else, as a letter or word may be. Achilles demands of Helen on the beach, "are you a witch? // a vulture, a hieroglyph, / the sign or the name of a goddess? / . . . // who are you?" (16). Almost immediately we are told that Helen has a knowledge of the temple writing beyond that of the instructed scribe, for "She herself is the writing" (22). In "Pallinode" Helen must contend with the patriarchal myth of woman as the source of the fall, of Helen as the cause of the fall of Troy, and she is described as *"the admitted first-cause 'of all-time, of all-history'"* (47). Over the course of the narrative, her association with Thetis and Isis builds, and she comes to terms with her guilt in abandoning her daughter Hermione in Sparta (a rhyme with her twin sister Clytemnestra's failure to forbid the intended sacrifice of her daughter Iphigenia). She is lover of Achilles and mother of Euphorion/Paris and a kind of mother-goddess, the principle of creativity incarnate, and thus an expression of the union of the timeless with time.

Interpretive Questions for Student Response and Discussion

Once armed with this information about myth and symbol, students should attempt to construct a meaning for the uses of those myths and the evolving significance of the symbols. To facilitate that effort, I hand out a list of questions. In graduate classes, each student will be responsible for a question. In undergraduate classes, this exercise is a splendid opportunity for group work, and different teams of students may be assigned each of the questions, ideally for work outside the class and presentation within it. The following questions are suggested for "Pallinode":

> What are the oppositions in *Helen in Egypt*, and how are they negotiated?
> What is the role of epic convention in the poem? How is it realized, and how and to what purpose is it altered or transformed?
> What is the relationship of choice, chance, and fate? (See 59, 99.)
> What is the relation of myth (narrative or story) to reality?
> What happens on the beach? What is the meaning of Achilles's attack?
> "Helena? who is she?" (37).
> "[W]hat was the question / to which she gave the answer" (54)?
> "Helen—come home" (108). What is home?

If time permits equally sustained attention to "Leuké" and "Eidolon," additional questions applying to all three sections are useful:

1. What are the esoteric, kabbalistic, and related mystical materials of *Helen in Egypt*, and what role do they play in an understanding of the poem?
2. What is the meaning of history in the poem? How is memory related to it?
3. What is the role of the lyre, the story?
4. What is the meaning of "the mother"?
5. "[W]hat can a woman know / of man's passion and birthright" (294; cf. 304)?

Theoretical Frameworks from Poststructuralist Critics

If students are already theoretically sophisticated, I call attention to the ways in which H.D. anticipates poststructuralist concepts or practice as we read the text. If not, near the middle of the discussion—too late to displace students' interpretive efforts by the theories of others—I introduce several key concepts in poststructuralist criticism that seem applicable. One is the performativity of the text. I ask students to locate places in which H.D. signals that an experience or perception is incommensurable with language by using such devices as ellipsis or by breaking off the grammatical or narrative line and interposing absence. I also ask them to identify points of contradiction in the text, locating places where the prose alters the poetic canto that follows or differs from it and places where a character contradicts his or her previous assertions. In both cases the text performs the instability of reality, and the reader must replicate Helen's uncertainty about what is real and what is dream, what is fact and what is fiction.

A particularly useful essay is Luce Irigaray's "The Power of Discourse and the Subordination of the Feminine." Irigaray points out Freud's a priori valuation of "Sameness," saying that Freud uses "analogy, comparison, symmetry [and] dichotomous opposition" from ordinary discourse to reflect *"the sexual indifference"* of the scene of representation and to ensure its coherence and closure (72). Asserting the power of the Western philosophic system "to *reduce all others to the economy of the Same*" (74), Irigaray advocates interrogating *"the conditions under which systematicity itself is possible"* (74):

> the *scenography* that makes representation feasible . . . that is the architectonics of its theatre, its framing in space-time, . . . its actors, their respective positions, their dialogues, indeed their tragic relations, without overlooking the *mirror* . . . that allow the logos, the subject, to reduplicate itself. (75)

She then calls for women writers *"to work at 'destroying' the discursive mechanism"* (76). Though written some two decades before Irigaray's essay, *Helen* could almost be a textbook demonstration of the ways in which Irigaray called for women's writing to jam the machinery of discourse—and students take delight in finding and describing these strategies. Among those strategies is *"mimicry,"* which is, "for a woman, to try to recover the place of her exploitation by discourse, without allowing herself to be simply reduced to it" (76). Here we see Helen assuming the feminine role deliberately—functioning as the ur-female, the seductress with the power to enchant men with her beauty; as the victim, the object of violent possession; and as the mother. The instability of these positions challenges the stereotypes of the female.

The framing of the epic in time and space destabilizes the coherence of both. The characters in Egypt demand to know "how are Helen in Egypt / and Helen upon the ramparts / together yet separate?" (63). The multiplicity of personality and fluidity of subject position for Helen is dizzying—Isis is Cypris/Aphrodite and she is Thetis; she speaks for Helen and merges identity with her (178)—but there is similar mutation of subject position for some other characters, as when the lover Paris becomes the son. In fact, the entire text offers itself as a rupture in the economy of the same, and at every turn Helen escapes from the efforts of Achilles and Paris to discover in her the Helen that reflects them as they would be. There is a similar undoing of stable binaries, such as the opposition of youth and maturity, spring and winter, Eros and Eris, darkness (Typhon) and light (Osiris), and even love and death. The text rejects the primacy of knowledge, and Helen is the apogee of the writing of the body, for she is the script. Woman is revealed to be the other of the patriarchal order, the scapegoat or object of blame, and Irigaray could almost be describing Helen when she writes, "[C]ertain properties attributed to the unconscious may . . . in part, be ascribed to the female sex, which is censured by the logic of consciousness" (73), or asserts, "[W]oman, in order to correspond to man's desire, has to identify herself with his mother" (70). Lastly, just as Irigaray envisioned the "interpretive rereading" of ordinary discourse to be "a *psychoanalytic undertaking* as well" (75), H.D. stages "Leuké" as a kind of regression into the unconscious, first into memory of the recent past with Paris at Troy, then under the guidance of Theseus/Freud into deeper recesses of memory, including childhood. In this process she "lost the Lover, Paris, / but to find the Son" (155) and actually takes up a position on a couch before Theseus, so that "my Psyche, [may] disappear into the web, / the shell, re-integrate, / nor fear to recall" (170).

These suggestions support a considerable amount of elaboration, and instructors may well find equally compelling theoretical texts in work by Julia Kristeva or Judith Butler. In any event, this kind of treatment of *Helen in Egypt* gives rise to the important understanding that H.D. in particular and modernism in general shatters the coherence of the world in ways that anticipate and provide models for poststructuralist theorizing.

NOTES

[1] See H.D.'s comparison of "my own *cantos*" to Pound's in *End to Torment* (32, 41).

[2] For the biographical significance of this pattern, instructors may wish to read H.D.'s *The Sword Went Out to Sea*.

SEXUALITY, FEMINISM, RACE

Teaching Sex and Sexuality in H.D.: "I Had Two Loves Separate"

Susan McCabe

A colleague of mine once remarked, Ovid shows that one can metamorphose the body without changing the mind. But can this be possible? In the world and thinking of Ovid, the soul or mind may indeed successfully separate from physical form. Then is desire only of the mind? H.D. was in dialogue and "psychic collaboration" with the ancients, among them Sappho, Homer, Stesichorus. She drew on the volatile characters of Demeter, Circe, Cassandra; she became one of Sappho's gymnasium, garlanding Artemis. She retold the story of Eros and Psyche; she adapted Euripides in *Hippolytus Temporizes* to emphasize the desire for the mother figure. With this sketch, I claim that H.D.'s particular attractions to literary tradition were also bodily, even erotic. Her poetry, novels, and film work all suggest that mind and body intermingle, that sex belonged to both realms. In her *Notes on Thought and Vision*, drafted in 1919, during a time of personal sexual and romantic upheaval, H.D. was trying to set forth a gendered ontology, identifying the brain as "jelly-fish consciousness," with feelers and streamers reaching from the womb to the head (18–20).

H.D.'s project ensued well before *"l'écriture feminine,"* but it helps establish the link to H.D.'s wider readership beginning in the mid-1980s, when her novels started to appear. Susan Stanford Friedman, in her groundbreaking study, *Penelope's Web*, identified the novels—lyric works—as revealing glosses on H.D.'s poetry. For H.D., their contents constituted incendiary material; she had marked them "DESTROY" or relegated them to a drawer, since they were explicit in sketching forth the complex permutations of her sexual desires. But in my experience, a first principle in teaching H.D. is to teach her poems beside one or two of her novels, which enhances the shimmering of her sculpted poems and reflect back on her distinctive prose, expressive of an eroticism both transcendent and intensely personal. H.D.'s novels are also useful as transcriptions of the period and of H.D.'s specific artistic and sexual development. The short unfinished *Paint It Today* (composed in 1921) charts H.D.'s attraction to her first love, Frances Gregg, which overtook her romantic involvement with the "erstwhile fiancé," Ezra Pound (9). The novel offers a template for many of H.D.'s later triangular relationships. In fact, H.D.'s autobiographical novels, also highly lyrical, mesh with a flood of bodily and sensory consciousness, linked to the work of other modernist female novelists such as Virginia Woolf, Dorothy Richardson, Djuna Barnes, or Bryher. *Paint it Today* features a key moment to many motifs I touch on here—Midget's epiphany in the Diocletian gallery when she spots the small figure of Hermaphroditus, with its honey color and double sexuality (64–65). The moment is based on H.D.'s experience but connects the poet to a whole tradition of statue love as well as decadent Hellenists (Oscar Wilde, J. A. Symonds, Algernon Swinburne) who steadily illuminated divergent sexuality. Modernism pivots on unresolved definitions of sexuality; thus there is great pedagogical value in immersing students in the specifically literary and cultural speculations about modernist erotic life.

During the period extending from H.D.'s famed entry into imagism in 1912, her unpublished novels meditating on multiple kinds of relationships, her steady infusion of Greek mythology, up through her film work in the late 1920s, analysis with Sigmund Freud in the 1930s, and finally in the work of her last decades during and after World War II—including the postwar *Trilogy* and the epic poem *Helen in Egypt*—her entire career was enmeshed in a debate over cultural representations of embodiment and sexuality. Moreover, she transformed how sexuality and desire were lived and to what extent experience could safely speak in art. But why so much fuss about eroticism and sex? Sappho's fragments, for instance, are hermeneutical for delineating the poet's apparitional place outside "modern" constraints. In her "Fragment 36," H.D. writes, "[M]y mind is reft" (*Collected Poems* 165), and plays off the David A. Campbell translation "I am in two minds" (qtd. in Collecott, *H.D. and Sapphic Modernism* 51), reverberating with being divided by "bitter-sweet" love (*Collected Poems* 173), a recurring motif in H.D.'s bisexual poems. To invoke Sappho, rejecting "old desire—old passion" in H.D.'s "Fragment 113" (131), was not then to take on a mask but rather to enact a sexualized identity and to identify with a tradition valorizing aesthetic and erotic vision. Modernism was a period of major changes in how one could express and embody one's desires; it was a period when language highlighted its erotic significations, its place in poetic vision.

Biography: Triangles and Occlusions

H.D.'s sexual politics emerge out of the male modernism (the hard and dry verse claimed by T. E. Hulme as the banner of modernist lyric) and the Victorian milieu she both militated against and drew on. Teaching H.D. has always involved the teaching of her biography. Most important, teaching her writing gives the lie to clearly defined categories of masculine and feminine and also those of sexuality: homosexual, lesbian, bisexual, and the more contemporary parlance of gay, queer, or transgender.

I offer a synopsis of what might read more like melodrama than life: H.D. was briefly engaged to Ezra Pound who gave her the moniker of imagist; then she had an affair with Frances Gregg in 1910 (the "unwholesome" femme fatale of *Paint It Today* [9]). After her love affair with Gregg, H.D. married the imagist poet Richard Aldington in 1913. Aldington went to the front in 1916 and on leave began an adulterous affair with a mutual friend, Dorothea Yorke. H.D. went to Cornwall, had an affair with the musician Cecil Gray, and became pregnant with Perdita. Enter Bryher, daughter of a wealthy shipping magnate, who, after memorizing *Sea Garden*, sought H.D. out in Cornwall in 1918 and rescued her, nursing her back to health from pneumonia and a difficult pregnancy. She took both H.D. and Perdita under her wing and whisked H.D. to Greece, where they believed H.D. would heal from her recent traumas, which included the death of her brother serving at the front and her father's subsequent death. These circumstances are only the tip of the biographical iceberg. On the trip to Greece, Bryher and H.D. took along Havelock Ellis. He had diagnosed Bryher (to her relief) as really only a girl by chance, as a boy trapped in a female body. Bryher might well be best considered as transgender in today's terms; nevertheless, it is essential to recover the historical context of inversion to understand H.D. and her romance with Bryher and others—as well as her poetics of sexual indeterminacy. In *Hedylus*, H.D. depicts Bryher, who was written as the character Irene, as "not wholly gracious" (117) and as a "tiny Aphrodite" (129), with "tiny, improbably fine hands" (117), picking among the seaweed and fishnets in Cornwall.

Although H.D. spent the rest of her life with Bryher (corresponding extensively with her when they spent time apart) as her main supporter, lover, and admirer, H.D. persisted in calling Bryher a cousin in public, though in private she was busy sorting out her various love lines, disappointments, or failed attachments. Further, H.D.'s public persona occluded her complex relationship with Bryher as well as with others, and thus Barbara Guest's groundbreaking biography *Herself Defined* still constricted Bryher to the roles of patron or friend, underestimating the emotional and erotic spectrum of a relationship that colored and facilitated all of H.D.'s creative efforts after *Sea Garden*. H.D.'s most important book of poems to follow *Sea Garden* was *Hymen*, dedicated to Bryher and Perdita and in a sense acknowledging the significance of H.D.'s redesigned ménage. To teach H.D. and her modernist culture, the instructor needs to shadow forth H.D.'s conflicted but creatively energizing sexual explorations. After all, in a marvelous reinvention of the Edwardian family, Bryher—who entered into two marriages of convenience over the course of her relationship with H.D.—legally adopted Perdita in 1926, during her second marriage to bisexual Kenneth Macpherson. Bryher remained Perdita's central and most consistent guardian, directing and shaping her education. Amplifying the triangular dynamic, H.D. was for a short period involved in an affair with Macpherson.

Flash back to a hotel room in Corfu with Bryher in 1919, where H.D. experienced a series of hallucinations, helped along, as she later told Freud, by Bryher, who even completed some visionary sequences. These visions prefigured the pair's involvement with film (for they saw among other things a tripod and a light show etched on a screen). This visionary experience was also a mediating of H.D.'s lesbian choice—to live with Bryher and separate from her husband. The visions constituted a kind of folie à deux and attest to the "apparitional lesbian" that Terry Castle has identified as prominent in attempts to express (while repressing or etherealizing) deviant desire.

H.D. never openly called herself either bisexual or lesbian. By the time she died in 1961, she was still trapped in the modernist closet. Teaching H.D.'s biography as preface to her poetry allows students entry to the volatile cultural dynamics going on at large, and writ small, if in maelstrom, of H.D.'s life and her search for connection. Biography does not substitute for reading her poems or novels but supplements the sweep of H.D.'s erotic vision.

Freudian/Modernist Sexuality

When H.D. saw Freud in 1933, he diagnosed the Corfu visions as symptoms of grave mental disturbance—namely, the desire to connect with the preoedipal mother through her island travel and association with Bryher, who arranged and financed the analysis. H.D. writes in "The Master," her poem homage to Freud, "I had two loves separate," echoing Shakespeare with his "master-mistress" love (*Collected Poems* 453). Before she met Freud, H.D. was reading Freud with Gregg in German. During her analysis with Freud, H.D wrote Bryher, "It appears that I am that all-but extinct phenomenon, the perfect bi[sexual]" (Friedman, *Analyzing* 497).

While Freud supported her creativity and to some extent her "deviant" sexuality, he still situated her in an oedipal economy, one that shaped modernism as a whole, so that the apparitional lesbian still had to roam without full recognition. I recommend that students read Freud's *Three Essays on the Theory of Sexuality* and "Femininity" (both from *The Standard Edition* [7: 125–48; 22: 112–35]) alongside H.D.'s memoir of her therapy, *Tribute to Freud*, constructed almost a decade after it took place and written in a style suggestive of the flashing images of both her film work just before analysis and her earlier "writing on the wall" in Corfu (*Tribute* 76). Yet Freud offers more than just content; he is a modernist and provides a methodology of dream interpretation indebted to literature but also conducive to the kind of poetic excavations and dream work H.D. produced throughout her life. Thus it is optimal if students read at least some of Freud's *Interpretation of Dreams*, given how influential its mode of repeating, retelling, and linking dream fragments was to H.D. as well as to modernist literary texts and films at large.

One of H.D.'s major motifs (perhaps more than for any other modernist) is psychosexual development. H.D.'s sexual biography—seen through Freud's lenses—almost becomes another text she was writing but never published. In *Orlando*, Woolf sought to understand her androgyny or transsexuality in her mock biography of a character changing sex and literary style across the centuries, entering a taxi as one sex and leaving it another. The throbbing taxi cab drove other writers, male and female. T. S. Eliot's Tiresias in *The Waste Land*, "old man with wrinkled dugs," takes the transcendent time view, prophetic and double-sexed (*Collected Poems* 61). The mystery of sexuality obsessed most modernists, yet H.D. brought her life experiences into closer contact with her writing, demonstrating, by juxtaposition, how much the exploration of sexuality informed all the modernists. If modernist aesthetics aimed for an impersonal vantage, then it injected this impersonality with a migrating sexual identity.

Some Poems: The Modernist Speaker

Most H.D. critics agree that H.D. was never the imagist Pound imagined her. Instead of submerging her self and sexuality, her initials liberated her: the classical, cut, sharp lines distinctive of *Sea Garden* were also strangely romantic, excessive, repetitive. Her poems defy singular voice or a unilateral heterosexual scoring of addressees. The first poem in the debut collection, "Sea Rose," never uses the word "I," yet emotion and sensuality enter nonetheless. The culturally feminized rose is here something "harsh," a figure "marred and with stint of petals, / meagre flower" (*Collected Poems* 5), while in "Pursuit," the speaker becomes Daphne seeing the footprint of her pursuer:

> But here
> a wild-hyacinth stalk is snapped
> . . . .
> where your heel pressed. (11)

Without delimiting the speaker's sexuality, H.D. creates a world riddled with desire and embodied images in flux. As Cassandra Laity clarifies, H.D. uses male/male desire to evoke her sexual longings as well as to discover a vocabulary that describes multiple sexual trajectories. H.D. thus transfers between sexes; she is one of the followers of Artemis, bearing "deep-purple / bird-foot violets" in "Sea Gods" (30), inhabiting the landscape of the dryads (Pound called her his "Dryad" [qtd. in Kenner 174]), and "haunting the groves" along with "nereids / who dwell in wet caves" in "Acon" (32); she is the messenger Hermes "of the triple pathways" in "Hermes of the Ways" (*Collected Poems* 37). Her triangular erotic and aesthetic collaborations meant that she often considered more than one beloved.

Sea Garden creates a Sapphic geography of desire:

> no flower ever opened
> so staunch a white leaf,
> no flower ever parted silver
> from such rare silver.
> ("Pear Tree" 39)

The poem is a kind of Georgia O'Keeffe reverse ekphrasis, creating a painting that does not exist except in words. With its interrelated motifs of encroachment, sensuous pleasure, and painful differentiation—in its choreographing of a bodily imprint "where sea-grass tangles with / shore-grass" ("Hermes of the Ways" 39)—the volume expresses anguished losses of World War I along with split desire.

The conventional manner of reading voice and speaker cannot be sustained in any of H.D.'s modernist lyrics. Consider, for instance, the poem heralded as paradigmatically imagist, "Oread." The poem is a snapshot like Pound's "In a Station of the Metro" (*Selected Poems* 35), but one that has an anamorphic lens, taking its voice from a mythic Greek figure; several mountain nymphs are a chorus commandeering verbs. The boundary between subject and object, lover and beloved violently and erotically dissolve in "pools of fir" (*Collected Poems* 55). H.D. revised mythic characters from within, as it were. As with Pound, the gods and goddesses had a reality that coexisted with the so-called reality of modern life; to invoke this panoply was not mere exercise.

Borderline *to* Close Up

H.D.'s sexually inflected writing demands a contextualizing within cinematic discourse. A film enthusiast, H.D. collaborated with Macpherson and Bryher in their joint publication, the first film journal in English, *Close Up* (1927–33). In teaching H.D., I generally complement the reading of her poetry and prose with several pivotal articles in *Close Up* that link film and sexuality.[1] The convergence of poetics, psychoanalysis, border sexualities, and racial identities culminates in the jointly created film *Borderline*, with Macpherson as montage artist and director, H.D. and Bryher as actors, and both women finally as film editors. The collaborative *Borderline* purposely pushed the limit of imagist aesthetic along with the representation of race and sexuality. With unglamorous, penetrating stares back at the camera, H.D. starred as inverse femme fatale, the hysteric (the dominant figure of bodily dissociation in the nineteenth century that continued to shape modernism). Combining avant-garde techniques and psychoanalytic insights into the unconscious, *Borderline* literalized the way the gaze cuts and splices the other's body in dominant culture. Pete and his wife (played by Paul and Eslanda Robeson) find themselves scapegoats for the unrealized or taboo desires of the white characters; homoerotic and frustrated desire circulates between the actors performing in the film as well as off-stage. *Borderline* used a specialized "clatter montage," editing that required very small shots to be knit together, later transposed as more meditative method in H.D.'s *Helen in Egypt*. On an aesthetic level, a cinematic vocabulary also seems necessary in teaching H.D., given that the cutting, influenced by Sergei Eisenstein, underlines the methods H.D. was already using in her poetry to reveal how bodies are cut out, fragmented in their desires, and expressive of a variety of embodied figures of femme fatale, bisexual, or hermaphrodite. She revamped these cultural bodies, with her "camera," to explore deviant desire as an aesthetic principle.

Thus it is essential in teaching H.D.'s sexuality to screen *Borderline*. Beforehand, I suggest setting up the erotic vocabulary H.D. was drawing on in her immersion in German Weimar film, especially the work of G. W. Pabst, who evoked the expressive possibilities for sexuality as well as the repressive mechanics of patriarchal culture. Pabst's *Joyless Street* (1925) let H.D. fixate on Greta Garbo as a remodeled Helen of Troy, whose every gesture connected to a larger, more layered historical reality. The screen turned palimpsest. H.D. believed that film could overcome the split of emotion, body, and mind by allowing for a merging between self and image that felt like the discovery of a "sub-strata of warmth," a version of Freud's notion of the preoedipal state ("Cinema" 116).

"Helen"

Charlotte Mandel was among the first critics to see how H.D. manipulated close-ups to destabilize gender identity ("Garbo/Helen" 130). "Helen" (*Collected Poems* 154–55) is for me a prototypic cinematic poem that presents the cultural body of the femme fatale and bisexual desire while offering a template for transferential identification. Helen's face signals not only a receptive blank but also a palimpsest, layered with at least three superimposed bodies: the mythic Helen as femme fatale; H.D.'s mother, Helen; and an idealized Garbo. "Helen" presents a dead woman in bits and pieces. Like a camera, the poem pans the living/unliving body of Helen, composing her through syntax dependent on delayed appositions and dissecting takes. By disrupting expected syntax, the body part is constituted as a fragmentary afterimage ("and the white hands"); the part persists as phantom limb. Rather than think of it as a voice or speaker, H.D. adopts the male heroic gaze that traces the physiognomy of the femme fatale, desired only when mortified and broken. In the process, she simulates a statuesque vamp, caught as if in several freeze frames. Yet the "still eyes" are the poet's own, a shade away from the gaze of the female hysteric.

For H.D., male desire can project fatality on an apparently passive object of beauty, living out Edgar Allan Poe's poetic principle that the most beautiful subject is a dead woman's body; in fact, in H.D.'s poem, love of Helen's body appears to depend on her being "laid" and dead. By inhabiting Greece's "hating" and lusting or indifferent gaze, H.D. superimposes another possibility for the female spectator or for the gaze "unmoved" by "the beauty of cool feet," enacting a looking that is not climax oriented, that deflects compulsory heterosexuality. The erotic charge in H.D.'s poem lies in its lingering over Helen (and the Sapphic fragment) as tableau, suspended between animation and death, who returns a look from eyes with "lustre as of olives." Hysteric in fractured gestures and femme fatale in alluring but desecrated beauty, Helen is the apparitional object of female desire. In *Helen in Egypt*, H.D. proposes (through Stesichorus) that Helen never went to Greece but was always a specular phantom, a hallucination of male desire.

Modernism, Sexuality, and Repression

H.D. can provoke a student's or reader's desire for essentialism: Can we name her desire as lesbian or bisexual? Should we rename her transgender or queer? Or is she really a heterosexual woman, given her significant relationships with men? In the end, what becomes most pedagogically useful is this difficulty in definition in a phenomenological sense: her writing returns the reader to a gendered and embodied perspective, which undermines normative models of identity. It is thus impossible to read or teach any of her works without thinking about how modernism dates back at least to the 1890s, when sexual status was on the stand, when ways of being sexual and showing sexual desire were being debated in cultural spheres. After the scare of the Wilde trial, there was "the cult of the clitoris" libel trial in 1918 (see Doan), in 1921 the parliamentary debates over criminalizing female homosexuality, and in 1928 the obscenity trial over Radclyffe Hall's publication of the lesbian classic *The Well of Loneliness*. These historical frames are necessary for teaching H.D. and her circle. Given that H.D. spent a significant portion of her adult years in Britain, these trials must have shaped her impulse to cloak and refashion her sexual desires. In teaching H.D. and sexuality, instructors of modernism courses might confront a pervasive cultural homophobia and then begin to identify how sex (both its repression and queer expressions) shaped H.D.'s creativity.

NOTE

[1] For a selection of H.D.'s articles in *Close Up* that illuminate her sexual poetics, see all three installments of "The Cinema and the Classics"; "*Expiation*"; "*Joan of Arc*."

Teaching H.D.'s *Trilogy* from Transnational Perspectives

Mary K. DeShazer

Over the past twenty-five years, I have frequently taught H.D.'s World War II epic *Trilogy* to graduate students, in a course entitled U.S. Women Poets of the Twentieth Century and in a seminar entitled Women, Modernism, and Border Crossings. Although my primary theoretical and pedagogical frame in both classes has been feminist, my focus has shifted from gynocritical and gynetic modes to transnational ways of reading the poem.

In approaching H.D. as a transgressive woman writer and *Trilogy* as a project of feminist mythological reclamation, I relied heavily on Susan Stanford Friedman's *Psyche Reborn* and Rachel Blau DuPlessis's *H.D.: The Career of That Struggle*, as well as Susan Gubar's essay on H.D.'s gendered imagery and my study of her female muses. Although I continue to find this approach fruitful, since 2001 I have reevaluated H.D. as a geopolitical writer and *Trilogy* as a project that interrogates the experience of war from a civilian perspective and reenvisions postwar culture. In so doing, I have turned for theoretical insight to books on transnational feminisms by Friedman (*Mappings*) and by Caren Kaplan (*Questions*), to Georgina Taylor's study of H.D. and the public sphere, and to the September 2006 issue of *Modernism/Modernity*, *Modernism and Transnationalisms* (Gikandi). In my seminar I ask students to examine, in *The Walls Do Not Fall*, the poet's representation of the expatriate writer in London as a documentary "border-crosser" during wartime and to reflect, in *Tribute to the Angels* and *The Flowering of the Rod*, on H.D.'s ecumenical approach in synthesizing ancient spiritual belief systems as an antidote to cultural violence. In addition, I encourage students to consider H.D.'s writing of *Trilogy* during the Blitz as a type of political activism. "Resurrection is a sense of direction," the poet claims, and in *Trilogy* her direction is feminist, modernist, and transnational (123).

Since the 1990s feminist theory has intersected productively with postcolonial theory, border/diaspora studies, and modernist studies. In my course Women, Modernism, and Border Crossings, I assign students exemplary critical texts that explore these intersections and offer ideas and terminology useful to understanding feminist and modernist transnationalisms. When students read chapters from Friedman's *Mappings*, they grapple with "the geopolitical as a distinct axis" of analysis and the "migratory meanings" of "*home* and *elsewhere*" (108–10). As Friedman notes, "[T]ransnational geopolitical thinking acknowledges . . . that *any* 'domestic' setting serves as a site for absorption, appropriation, and transformation of cultural formations from elsewhere" (112). When students engage with Taylor's *H.D. and the Public Sphere of Modernist Women Writers*, they analyze *Trilogy* as H.D.'s public reflection on her cultural milieu, part of an ongoing dialogue with other women artists about their historical moment, and reflect on the wartime involvement that H.D. and Bryher (H.D.'s longtime companion) had with European Jewish refugee work and with Mass Observation, the political, literary, and psychoanalytic project of documenting ordinary people's response to daily life (Taylor 137). And when students encounter Jahan Ramazani's "Modernist Bricolage, Postcolonial Hybridity," they explore his key words and probe his assertion that "the space of a [modernist] poem is neither local . . . nor global" but manifests itself instead as "a translocation, verbally enabling and enacting, between specific times and places, cross-cultural, transhistorical exchange" (446).

In assigning *Trilogy* I apply to H.D. three questions that originated in Friedman's chapter in *Mappings* on reading Virginia Woolf geopolitically: What might it mean to read H.D. transnationally? How are the spatial and the geopolitical imprinted in her work? Just who might the geopolitical H.D. be, and how does she relate to the H.D. read through lenses of gender, sexuality, class, race, and religion? (115). In addition, I generate a series of theoretical and textual questions that facilitate both a transnational feminist perspective and a close reading of the poem's themes, images, and linguistic or rhetorical strategies. Below I present six of these questions and offer analytical frameworks and insights that my students and I have used in interpreting *Trilogy*.

> *Question 1*. In *The Walls Do Not Fall*, where do you find and how might you assess H.D.'s representation of the American poet as a "border-crosser" writing from London's "doodle-bug alley" during World War II? Consider spatial juxtapositions from the poem such as "here/there," "over us / under us," "tombs/temples," and "haven/heaven"; other images of borders and crossings; and comparative cross-cultural references (e.g, to Pompeii during the eruption of Mount Vesuvius in AD 79, Karnak during the excavation of the pharaohs' tombs in the 1920s, and London during the Blitz of the early 1940s).

To address the first question, students and I consider possible "migratory meanings of *home* and *elsewhere*" (Friedman, *Mapping* 108) in section 1 of *Walls*, especially the shifting yet reciprocal positioning of "here/there" in such passages as "[a]n incident here and there / and rails gone (for guns) / from your (and my) old town square"; "there, as here, ruin opens / the tomb, the temple; enter, / there, as here, there are no doors"; and "here, there / sand drifts" (3). We also probe the significance of the dedication of the poem to Bryher "*for Karnak* 1923 / *from London* 1942" and view online the Karnak excavations, the Pompeii ruins, and bombed-out scenes from postwar London as tools for comprehending H.D.'s visual imagery.

We discuss how the themes of withstanding conflagration, the struggle to endure, and the hope of survival and recovery are enhanced by imagery of liminal spaces and border crossings: "gods always face two-ways" (5), "unlock[ing] the portals" (8), "a half-open hut-door" (10), "eat[ing] my way out of it" (12), a "cross-roads" (26), "still half-at-home in the world" (39), a "schism in consciousness" to be "bridged over" (49), and movement "*cross-wise*" (58; see *Walls*, secs. 5, 8, 10, 12, 26, 39, 49, 58). Also significant are depictions of inspiration as a "go-between, interpreter" (29) and of poets/survivors as "*voyagers, discoverers / of the not-known, // the unrecorded*" (59).

> *Question 2*. How might you analyze and evaluate H.D.'s spiritual and poetic quest in *Trilogy*? Consider ways in which H.D. draws creative inspiration from such cross-cultural sources as ancient Greek, Roman, and Egyptian deities, including Hermes, Venus, Amen, Isis, Osiris, Thoth; the Roman cult of the Bona Dea; the Christian Book of Revelation; the various angels; and "Our Lady" in *Tribute to the Angels*.

In her introduction to *Trilogy*, Aliki Barnstone indicates that she assigns students Web-based presentations on H.D.'s allusions to Greek, Roman, Egyptian, and Christian deities, angels, and myths. I do the same, but my students emphasize the transnational affiliations that H.D. makes among these religious systems. The Lady in *Tribute* is especially intriguing to examine through a transnational lens because, while H.D. claims that the Lady has long been recognized worldwide (from cathedral to museum to cloister to palace stair), "none of these / suggest her as I saw her" (96). We consider why this originality of perception is important to H.D. and whether her representation can be read as appropriative and hierarchical or communal and geopolitical.

Students also analyze the Lady's association with border crossings: before approaching the Lady, the speaker and her compatriots "crossed the charred portico, / passed through a frame—doorless— / . . . entered a house through a wall" (83); the Lady "carries over the cult / of the *Bona Dea*" (103) in a way that evokes "the same—different—the same" spiritual understandings (105). Through Isis and the Lady, H.D. transnationalizes female creative power.

> *Question 3*. How does Mary Magdalene in *The Flowering of the Rod* extend H.D.'s use of biblical allusions, her goal of feminist mythic revision, and her emphasis on border crossing? How might her attribution of "mage" status in *Flowering* to Kaspar, an Arab man, transnationalize the poem's spiritual vision?

In reflecting on the third question, students and I discuss H.D.'s references in *Flowering* to "Marys a-plenty" and to Mary Magdalene as both "of a tower-town" and herself a tower (135). We consider the significance of verbs that begin with the prefix *trans-* (*transcribe, translate, transmute*) and of the noun *transfiguration* (151, 156, 160, 165). In addition, we explore references to Mary's location in liminal spaces: blocking a "half-open door," leaving various houses, crossing thresholds, unfastening and sliding out of doors (134; see *Flowering*, secs. 10, 13, 15, 20, 35, 39). We also probe connections between the Mary Magdalene of *Flowering* and the Lady of *Tribute*: their mysterious power to cross borders at will, their function as muses bringing transhistorical insights, and their mythic connection to "a tale of a Fisherman, / a tale of a jar or jars" (105; see *Tribute*, sec. 39 and *Flowering*, secs. 12, 20, 35, 39, 43).

Despite the sexism Kaspar must unlearn and all he does not understand about his mission, H.D. repeatedly associates this enigmatic figure with diasporic movement and cross-cultural knowledge: he is a merchant, a "stranger in the market-place," or possibly he is "a Chaldean, not an Arab at all" (130, 139). Yet Kaspar is also an "ambassador" (132), a "great wanderer, // a renowned traveller" (156), "master of caravans" (137), and a wise man who receives "the title Magian" (151). Kaspar possesses the "innate capacity / for transcribing and translating / the difficult secret symbols" that link humans across cultures and belief systems (165); he can interpret a "hieroglyph, a parchment of incredible worth / or a mariner's map" (164); and he is someone who "saw further, saw deeper, apprehended more // than anyone before or after him" (165).

> *Question 4.* How might H.D.'s use of the following poetic techniques contribute to a transnational interpretation of *Trilogy*: compound words, aggregations, neologisms, rhetorical questions, multiple personae, and imagined dialogue with interlocutors?

In assigning this question, I draw on Patrizia Lendinara's essay "Binding Words and Feelings" to explain to students how the three hundred compounds, aggregations, and neologisms that H.D. employs might have geopolitical implications, for example, "old-self," "new-world reconstruction," "not-known" (compounds); "pearl-of-great-price," "self-out-of-self" (aggregations); "Christos-image," "death-symbol," "not-war" (neologisms). As Lendinara notes, many of H.D.'s compounds highlight the theme of liminality, such as "grave-edge," "field-edge," "lake-edge" (117, 134, 134). Certain aggregations—"before-and-after," "the-healing-of-the-nations," "fire-to-endure"—urge consideration of how H.D.'s coinages reconfigure what Friedman describes as modernism's "space/time borders" by "moving from singularities to pluralities of space and time . . . and from nominal modes of definition to relational ones" ("Periodizing" 425–26).

To help students evaluate the poet's personae and rhetorical strategies, I offer them insights from Marina Sbisa's essay on *Trilogy*, which assesses the poem's "linguistically indicated enunciating subjects," the poet's choice of pronouns, and textual moments of self-exhortation and "intersubjective confrontation" (94, 97). The last of these occur especially in *The Walls Do Not Fall*, whose dominant persona asserts her authority to speak about war and cross-cultural transformation.

> *Question 5.* How might H.D.'s writing of *Trilogy* in London during the Blitz be interpreted as a type of geopolitical activism? Explain your point of view with reference to Taylor's study of H.D. and the public sphere; to images in *Trilogy* of bombs, flames, and incendiary rain; and to H.D.'s elucidation of "protection for the scribe" as a literary and perhaps a political goal (15).

To answer the fifth question, students and I discuss how H.D.'s engagement with other politically oriented modernist women writers affects our understanding of her aims in *Trilogy*. We evaluate Taylor's claim that in its emphasis on resurrection and reconstruction, *Trilogy* "attempt[s] the fullest examination of the forces that lead to war, and, ultimately, the forces that can lead to peace, of any work by any woman writer of the period" (174–75). In addition, we examine H.D.'s comments on writing *Trilogy* during the Blitz as recorded in her letters to Norman Holmes Pearson, probe examples in *The Walls Do Not Fall* of her vivid descriptions of the chaos the bombings generated in London, and assess her designation of *Tribute to the Angels* as "a sort of premature peace poem" (Pearson ix). We then discuss Taylor's assertion that in *Trilogy* H.D. moved away from formal experimentation and intense introspection for their own sake to recontextualize both within the needs of contemporary sociopolitical reality, "including the need to abandon neutral or pacifist orientations in the face of the Nazi and Fascist threats" (144).

Students also read Kaplan's essay "The Politics of Location as Transnational Feminist Critical Practice" and apply to H.D.'s writing the concept of a "politics of location," a phrase originated by Adrienne Rich that, Kaplan notes, "both functions as a marker of Western interest in other cultures and signals the formation of diasporic identities" (138). We examine how H.D.'s ambivalent politics of location as a resident alien rather than a British citizen affects her perspective in writing *Trilogy* and how her position as someone privileged by race, class, and nationality yet marginalized as a woman and vulnerable as a poet in a civilian war zone informs her representation of military bombardment and cultural transformation.

> *Question 6.* How might Ramazani's concept of "modernist bricolage" be applied to *Trilogy*, and how might H.D. adapt the "hybridizing literary strategies" that Ramazani associates with both modernist experimental poetics and postcolonial poetics (449), namely translocalism, mythical syncretism, heteroglossia, and apocalypticism?

In approaching this question, we define Ramazani's key words and find examples of how each strategy is manifested in *Trilogy*. Ramazani defines *modernist bricolage* as "the synthetic use in early twentieth-century poetry of diverse cultural materials ready to hand" (448); *translocalism* as a "mode of intercultural syncretism" characterized by Western and non-Western spatial allusions layered through montage and dissolve effects (449); *mythical syncretism* as the use of "intercultural amalgamations" including ecumenical religious imagery and rites (451); *heteroglossia* as "rapid [linguistic] turns from high to low" cultural registers, the effect of which is "crisscrossing voices" (453); and *apocalypticism* as a strategy that "uncovers" a poet's response to the crisis in modernity as one in which language and meaning threaten to implode—"a compressed, visionary evocation of modernity as cataclysmic violence, a modern history trembling on the verge of dramatic and perhaps ultimate transformation" (454). *Trilogy* illustrates each of these concepts beautifully, and students can apply Ramazani's insights and terminology to selected passages from the text.

Since a transnational reading of *Trilogy* is not the only viable approach, I acknowledge to students that the poem might instead be interpreted as participating reductively in the Eurocentric internationalism that Ramazani posits as endemic to "high" Euromodernism. To explore this perspective, students apply to H.D. this quote from Ramazani:

> Writing in the metropole at a time of imperial and ethnographic adventure, massive immigration, world war, interlingual mixture, and accelerated communication and travel, the Euromodernists—many of them exiles and émigrés themselves—were the first English-language poets to create a formal vocabulary for the intercultural collisions and juxtapositions, the epistemic instabilities and decenterings, of globalization. (448)

Students analyze *Trilogy*'s metropolitan setting, World War II context, formal strategies and recurring vocabulary, cultural juxtapositions, and epistemic decenterings. In addition, they read the first chapter of Kaplan's *Questions of Travel* and discuss the contradictions that existed for modernist expatriates who considered themselves exiles but often behaved like tourists, "escap[ing] from the nation-state into the cosmopolitan and polyglot city" in search of "imperialist nostalgia and aesthetic gain" (30, 33).

Finally, I invite students to assess the extent to which *Trilogy* employs the narrative strategies that Simon Gikandi argues are centrally "involved in the transnational reach of modernism": a "reconfiguration of the time and space of modernity," the "re-routing of modernity through a set of texts that might initially appear to be marginal to its economy," and the "reopen[ing] of the old question of the political agency of modernism" ("Preface" 422–23). Usually we reach consensus that H.D. engages the first two strategies by weighting her language with spatiotemporal liminality and by rerouting modernity through esoteric spiritual texts from around the world. We debate, however, whether the centrality of Old and New Testament scripture and of Bethlehem as the site of cultural redemption reifies orthodox Christianity in ways that undermine the poem's claim to transnationalism or whether, in Susan Schweik's words, *Trilogy* offers "an altered Jerusalem narrative" that contains "a powerful, sanctioned lode of anti-militarist sentiment," thus affirming H.D.'s place as a war poet with a geopolitical focus (247, 245). After dissecting these diverse theoretical texts and questions, students are well positioned to evaluate whether H.D. presents a Eurocentric grab bag of cross-cultural allusions or forges a feminist transnational worldview that moves beyond Eurocentrism.

Teaching Race in H.D.'s Work

Rebecca Walsh

In the wake of literature's turn to cultural studies, H.D. scholarship has gained new vigor from the scholarly study of race and national identity. Our classrooms can do justice to the shared genealogies of Anglo-American, African American, and orientalist modernisms that punctuate H.D.'s work, helping students grapple with the ways that American exceptionalist, expansionist ideologies and other empires, specifically Britain in H.D.'s case, have historically comingled (Stoler 24). While critical race theory and postcolonial ideas about orientalism can provide students with analytics for talking about the politics of these formations, materials from the various cultural fields relevant to H.D.'s artistic production can equip them to notice and to historicize how race and nation function in her work.

Students can begin to gain purchase on these issues through elements of H.D.'s biography. I begin classroom discussions with a brief introduction of her Moravian ancestry. Pacifist, religious exiles from Eastern Europe who eventually settled in Bethlehem, Pennsylvania, Moravians valued tolerance and sought ethical ways of relating to Native Americans. H.D.'s exposure to these values and her recognition of the realities of the Moravians' international dispersal and exile helped shape her "modernism of the margins," to use Susan Stanford Friedman's phrase, which empathizes with and gives voice to populations disenfranchised through race and other forms of difference ("Modernism" 104). Early enculturation about social marginalization and contemporary awareness are not necessarily one and the same, however. H.D. had limited direct contact with African American modernist movements early in her career, although several figures in her circle actively supporting the Harlem Renaissance movement—Nancy Cunard, Carl Van Vechten, Robert Herring, Kenneth Macpherson—kept her apprised of its challenges and successes (Friedman, "Modernism" 96–98). Van Vechten's and Macpherson's erotic interest in young, black male artists tinged their involvement with an opportunism that Aldon Nielsen claims affected H.D.'s perceptions (85). And yet H.D.'s private writing of the 1920s and 1930s records evidence of her holding antiracist positions, as Annette Debo has shown ("Whiteness" 157–58).

H.D.'s novel *HERmione* and her involvement in the production of Macpherson's 1930 film *Borderline* give students the opportunity to explore the degrees to which H.D.'s constructions of African American identity might constitute a productive "modernism of the margins" or operate, as Nielsen warns, not as a project of empathy but as an instrumentalist, self-interested fabrication of sympathetic black subjectivity created to be empathized with (85). At stake in this discussion is modernism's fascination with the primitive, which associated African American subjectivity with savagery, naturalness, and the exotic, as critics like Marianna Torgovnik have discussed. These primitivist gestures surface in *HERmione* in moments when H.D.'s eponymous heroine Hermione ("Her") Gart objectifies and aestheticizes Mandy, her family's African American domestic servant. During a storm, Hermione imagines that Mandy "was a brazier burning in that bleak room . . . was bronze like a brazier," turning Mandy into an elemental, mechanistic heat source (88).

Such dehumanizing constructions generated for white modernists a perception of distance from African American embodiment and served to naturalize and normalize whiteness. Other moments in *HERmione*, however, refuse both of these operations by intermingling African American and white identities and by insisting on whiteness as a racial category. I ask students to read closely the often discussed scene in the Gart family kitchen in which "Her" helps Mandy prepare a bowl of cherries: "Her slipped a white hand into the deep bowl, black arm lifted from the deep bowl" (27). The syntax creates a unified, coordinated performance out of Hermione's and Mandy's movements and even suggests that their appendages figuratively belong for a moment to a single body. The symbolic cross-racial hybridity strikes students as especially arresting in an era anxious about miscegenation and in which narrative instances of racial mixing often circulated around the "tragic mulatta" figure. In this gesture, H.D. strains against the "symbolic gesture of expulsion" of modernist primitivism that, as Sieglinde Lemke explains, was meant to manage and drive underground an active copresence of blackness that exerted a shaping force on white literary texts (10). H.D. also exposes students to the operations of whiteness as a racial category, as Hermione's race is marked by her "white hand" rather than remaining a privileged, and hence invisible, norm against which otherness is measured (Debo, "Whiteness").

Since some students are not used to perceiving the racial operations of whiteness, I distribute handouts containing excerpts from David Roediger's historical analysis of the shifting, contested nature of whiteness in nineteenth-century America and from Peggy McIntosh's autoethnographic recounting of her experiences of whiteness as an "invisible knapsack" filled with unearned, unasked-for advantages. Though not without limitations, McIntosh's list of forty-six "ordinary and daily ways" in which she enjoys white privilege in the world illustrates the luxury of existing in an unmarked, invisible racial category that is typically constructed as "morally neutral, normative, and average, and also ideal" (96). Although white privilege is never fully surrendered in H.D.'s work, as Debo reminds us, Hermione's racial positionality is at least kept in view even when Mandy is not present ("Whiteness" 155, 160).

An even more overt critique of Anglo-American white social dominance appears in the film *Borderline*, to which H.D. made multiple contributions. It was produced by the small film company POOL Productions, founded in 1926 by Bryher (H.D.'s longtime companion), H.D., and Macpherson (Friedberg 369), who at the time was H.D.'s lover and Bryher's husband. H.D. starred in the film; wrote "The *Borderline* Pamphlet," the explication and theoretical manifesto that accompanied the screenings and was published by London's Mercury Press in 1930 (376); and, along with Bryher, created the film's montage structure while Macpherson sat out ill (380). In this unusually nonhierarchical arrangement, H.D. and her cohorts also solicited feedback in the preproduction stage from the film's African American stars Paul and Eslanda Robeson (Debo, "Interracial Modernism" 377). Depravity defines *Borderline*'s central white couple, the racist and neurotic Astrid (portrayed by H.D. under her stage name, Helga Doorn) and her husband, the dissolute and violent Thorne. The film opens with his violent temper on display, as a point-of-view shot suggests he has just shoved Adah (Eslanda Robeson), the mixed-race wife of an African American man named Pete (Paul Robeson) who presumably has just broken off her relationship with Thorne. Astrid's jealousy at Thorne's affair is unleashed in a racist diatribe, and Thorne's evasion of his responsibility in Astrid's murder enables the racist town to scapegoat Pete. The film thus solidifies the connection between these characters' impulsive and compulsive behavior and material violence directed toward African Americans (see McCabe, "Borderline Modernism"), which Debo argues culminates in the final café scene; images of raised fists and fire intercut with an image of a dark male body refer to ongoing instances of lynching in the United States ("Interracial Modernism" 373).

Against this background of interrogated whiteness, students can explore the complex impact of the film's portrayal of Pete, the aspect of the film that has attracted the most scholarly commentary. The film's dominant use of the close-up to linger on Pete's face and, like Mandy of *HERmione*, his hands participates in the broader primitivist logic that reduces blackness to physicality while attributing spiritual and psychological interiority to whites, as Hazel Carby has suggested about the film (*Race Men*). And yet Pete's characteristics as dignified, hardworking, and mature stand in stark contrast to both Thorne's alcoholic excesses and the animalistic and physically frenetic appearance of "black" characters like Gus in D. W. Griffith's *Birth of a Nation* (1915), whose attempted rape of Flora takes place in an outdoor chase scene that suggests unbounded and dangerous black male sexuality. Showing students a brief clip of this chase scene makes Pete's stillness, his loyalty to Adah, and his disinterest in Astrid all the more powerful.

To extend student conversation beyond tidy binaries of black and white, I invite students to focus on Adah's role in *Borderline* as a light-skinned, mixed-race expatriate black woman. Adah has been viewed as symbolizing liminality and border crossing (see McCabe, "Borderline Modernism"; Walton, "'Nightmare'"), but when put in dialogue with modernist novels featuring mixed-race heroines, her structural position becomes even more complex. Adah's affair with Thorne opens up several interpretive possibilities for students; her actions could play into the "loose black woman" stereotype that lingered from nineteenth-century discourse (Christian 15), but, given her dignified comportment in the film, Adah more likely contributes to the empowering "re-sexualization of black womanhood" by African American women's novels of the 1920s that Ann duCille has charted (10).

Indeed, examining Adah in relation to the larger set of fictional representations of black and mixed-race black women gives students traction for considering these questions as well as the broader potential for the film to resignify heterosexual romance and courtship dynamics. Students familiar with second-wave feminist critiques of gender might dismiss Adah's role in the film as flat or her purpose limited to the traditionally feminine script of heterosexual partner. But given that black women suffered a long history of legal disenfranchisement cutting them off from sanctioned and recognized marriage under the law, a successful heterosexual relationship between an African American man and an African American mixed-race woman in the modernist period is politically multivalent if not subversive of white domination (see duCille).

If color and skin tone was an "overriding preoccupation" for African American women during the early twentieth century (Hull 17), the implied racial politics of Adah's romantic choice again become visible when students consider a character like Angela Murray, the light-skinned, mixed-race heroine who "passes" for white in Jessie Redmon Fauset's *Plum Bun*. While it is unclear whether Adah, too, could pass, and the film certainly does not suggest she attempts it, Angela Murray's calculations can help students fill out ways that gender and race shape Adah's possibilities and limitations. Angela's relationship with a Thorne-like caddish white man, Roger Fielding, provides her with economic, social, and geographic mobility that her black suitors lack. Indeed, racism interrupts romance when her date Matthew Henson, a dark-skinned black man, is refused admission to the movie theater. As the end of *Borderline* reveals all too well, Adah's happiness with Pete is similarly vulnerable to the operations of racist policing, visible in the town's decision to make Pete the scapegoat.

If Fauset rewrites a familiar "tragic mulatta" plot (Christian 15–16), *Borderline* moves beyond this narrative plot entirely with Adah. While stories about mixed-raced heroines often ended tragically, with a heterosexual match undone by a "black" past that catches up with a "white" heroine, *Plum Bun* closes with at least the promise of happiness; in the final scene, Angela is about to restart her life in Paris with Anthony Cross, a man of black and Spanish descent whom she truly loves. *Borderline*, on the other hand, ends with Adah apart from Pete, although it is clearly white persecution of blackness targeted at Pete, not the awkwardness of her navigations of biracial identity, that created the situation. The European setting of the film facilitates only temporary romantic freedom from the incursions of white racism ostensibly more virulent in the United States.

While I want my students to grasp the fullness of racial politics regarding African American identity and to allow room for modernism to counter mainstream America's investment in (white) racial homogeneity, emphasizing only this dimension can run the risk of reawakening models of first-world feminism that, in focusing on race within the West, treated forms of racial and national otherness as separate areas of knowledge. Examining the politics of H.D.'s turn to Egypt as source material and as the setting for several works chips away at the implicit "nationalist-exceptionalist lens" that undergirds subtle ideologies of United States uniqueness (Shohat 7), not to mention traditional assumptions that imperialism only affects texts produced by "official" colonizer-colonized relationships.

When I teach "Secret Name: Excavator's Egypt," the third story in *Palimpsest,* or *Trilogy,* H.D.'s World War II long poem, I assign brief passages from Edward Said's landmark *Orientalism,* which makes the now familiar argument that British and French scholarship and literature about Egypt and the Levant fashioned the Orient as "irrational, depraved (fallen), childlike, 'different,'" while constructing Europe as rational, morally upright, mature, and normative (40). I also offer students Said's suggestion that orientalist discourse is not "what [orientalists'] eyes and minds showed them immediately" (177) but rather is shaped by a "textual attitude" (93), by what has been said already by academic orientalists, explorers, and travel writers of the past.

H.D.'s "textual attitude" can be located in the Egyptological texts by Margaret Murray and James Henry Breasted and nineteenth-century British travel narratives about Egypt that H.D. and Bryher had amassed and read in preparation for their trip to Egypt in 1923. These Egyptological materials rejected reigning classicist models that had elevated Hellenic Greece as the seedbed of Western European civilization and claimed Egypt as a new "monumental past" for the West, as Marsha Bryant and Mary Ann Eaverly have demonstrated (435). Students can explore the Egyptian turn in *Trilogy*'s first section, *The Walls Do Not Fall,* in which London's bombed-out landscape shifts imperceptibly into an Egyptian temple complex where, reassuringly, "still the Luxor bee, chick and hare / pursue unalterable purpose" (3). H.D.'s appeal to ancient Egypt throughout this section thus challenges "traditional narratives of Western culture by making Egypt its source and spiritual center" (Bryant and Eaverly 450). But much of *Trilogy*'s Egyptian imagery is of a vast, silent past, denying contemporary Egyptian context, as orientalist discourse tends to do, and relegating it in an analeptic leap to the achievements of the past. The only Arab to appear in *Trilogy* is the biblical figure of Kaspar, a character who reinscribes Arabness within a familiar Judeo-Christian narrative.

"Secret Name: Excavator's Egypt" offers a similar take on Egypto-modernism's obsession with Egypt as the new past, although here H.D. foregrounds American identity and forges transnational alliances. Set in British-controlled Luxor/Karnak of the 1920s, the story conveys the thoughts of its American heroine, Helen Fairwood, an Egyptologist of sorts on holiday. Helen experiences terror just as she is about to descend into the tomb of King Amenophis II, where she also encounters a "crouching Arab" at the top of the steps (182). Though her companions take no notice of him, Helen seeks "frantically for baksheesh," a combination of tip and alms, which would allow all to "be right." Dehumanizing him and fragmenting his body, she observes that "[t]he warm monkey-like palm reached upward." The Arabic that he speaks to her is a "sort of serpent sibilance" that calms her "like the hypnotic siss-siss of some beatific serpent." Meredith Miller's analysis lays bare Helen's transformation of the Arab into something "more and less than human" who functions as a "symbol of her own right of entry" (90). Certainly by conscripting him as her "psychic guarantee" Helen makes him into a conduit to a spiritually rejuvenating ancient Egypt (89), one of many examples in the text of an orientalizing, evolutionary logic that pits the modern West against a premodern Orient.

But scenes like this can also prompt students to scrutinize how femininity and Americanness might inflect the nature of authority over an ostensibly British colonial other. British women travelers who wrote about Egypt enjoyed relative privilege from education, class, and national belonging, though their gender meant that they were in an uneasy, unstable relationship with the British imperial project and with the masculine forms of authority that underwrote it (see Monica Anderson). Amelia Edwards, whose 1891 travelogue *A Thousand Miles up the Nile* H.D. owned, proclaims in her preface that she will remain mum on recent changes in Egypt "because I in no sense offer myself as a guide to others." What does it mean for an American writer like H.D. to inhabit this already ambivalent narrative space? These questions give students the chance to join in the recent critiques offered by Lisa Lowe and others that take Said to task for failing to consider the impact of cultures or nations outside a European-orientalist dyad (7–8). Helen, students point out, recognizes that her toll is "unrequired" (*Trilogy* 182), suggesting that as an American woman she at least lacks the assumed colonial authority of the British traveler that the British Captain Rafton seems to exude. Moreover, Helen constantly questions her assumptions in this scene, leading students to see critical distance between H.D. and her protagonist.

If anything, Helen gradually reinhabits an American identity she had lost sight of through her relationship with Mary Thorpe-Wharton, another American tourist. The two settle into a "racially attuned companionship" (227). But exactly what kind of Americanness is being deployed in the text? One option is to assume H.D. imposes a form of rugged individualism onto Egypt, given that Helen and Mary form "this type, this American, beaten and weathered machine type, thin as rails, steel-bone and sinew" (231). Bryant and Eaverly see this gesture as of a piece with Breasted's desire to claim Egypt to establish a legitimate and distinctively American branch of Egyptology (448). Another option is to recognize the links that Helen draws between African American modernity and Egypt. As Helen heads with Rafton to Karnak on the last night of the moon, she recalls an image of the chariot that had been carried out of King Tut's tomb, captured in one of Rafton's photographs. She quickly associates it with the famous African American spiritual, "Swing Low, Sweet Chariot": "This was a chariot, set low—swing low, sweet chariot—rolling with a soundless smooth ease over the road. This was the low swung chariot, but of some intermediate world, not the gold flamboyant harnessed chariot of the soul" (200). For students in an American modernism survey who are familiar with the images of Egypt in Langston Hughes's "The Negro Speaks of Rivers" (*Collected Poems*), this detail resonates as part of a larger project of black diasporic consciousness. Even the cadence of H.D.'s language, "rolling with a soundless smooth ease over the road," loosely echoes some of the spiritual's second line, "coming for to carry me home." Whatever personal associations this reference may express for Helen, it linguistically reenacts modes of African-diasporic belonging central to the Harlem Renaissance. If this comparison is not a "modernism of the margins," it is at least a modernist meeting of the margins.

How to best involve students in considering these discourses of race and coloniality depends on their backgrounds and previous exposure to modernism, especially experimental aesthetics. Instructors of upper-division seminars and graduate classes on modernism or on American literature and race can ask students to read multiple works by H.D. as well as primary historical literature and theoretical lens texts. In a twentieth-century literature survey course, some of this historical and scholarly context can be made available through handouts with selected passages or excerpts, while other material can be covered by students divided into groups, tasked to bring various parallel readings to life in class.

H.D. and the British Modernist Tradition: *Kora and Ka*, Mythopoesis, and England's Great War

Bret L. Keeling

I never hesitate to incorporate H.D. into my reading lists for courses in British modernism. As an undergraduate, I read both Ezra Pound and T. S. Eliot in British survey courses, just as I read Joseph Conrad, William Butler Yeats, and James Joyce. For me, "British literature" comprises writers of any nationality who write in Britain. In my section on World War I literature, I integrate H.D.'s *Kora and Ka* with Rebecca West's *The Return of the Soldier* and Virginia Woolf's *Mrs. Dalloway*. Before reading the fiction, however, students read some of the most frequently anthologized poets of the Great War: Rupert Brooke, Siegfried Sassoon, Wilfred Owen, and Isaac Rosenberg. Frequently, I also ask students to read excerpts from chapter 2 of Paul Fussell's *The Great War and Modern Memory*. Fussell introduces students to the concept of the Great War and to the British concern for the western front and the troops literally dug into the trenches of France and Belgium. Students learn from Fussell that it is not the air and naval wars and not the wars fought in the Middle East and Africa but rather this Great War of the trenches that is uniquely British. And it is H.D.'s concern for and experiences in this war that tie the American-born author to her adopted home in England and to her British contemporaries.

Most of my students come to the course having never heard of H.D. I share with them a passage Robert Duncan wrote in regard to H.D.'s *Palimpsest*:

> Language becomes throughout a ground of suggestion and association, a magic ground, weaving of phrases echoing in other phrases, a maze of

> sentences to bind us in its spell, so that we begin to be infected with the sense of other meanings and realms within those presented. We must come back and back to the same place and find it subtly altered each time. (*H.D. Book* 109)

Significant here is Duncan's emphasis on connection and relationship, his insistence that one will return again and again to the text and yet still not know the text in the conventional ways students may expect to know what they read. I encourage students to be comfortable with their uncertainty about the reading and suggest that if they allow themselves to be "altered" each time they read and reread a passage, then they may become inquisitive about the concept of uncertainty itself and avoid feeling frustrated at not finding or achieving a sense of knowing what H.D. means.

Duncan's passage alerts students to the difficulty most of them will experience when they encounter H.D.'s use of ancient religious concepts, stories, and icons in *Kora and Ka*. I draw their attention back to our reading of Yeats's poetry earlier in the term and remind them that a revisioning of mythology, or mythopoesis, is one tool a modernist artist uses to tap the reader's knowledge of an ostensibly shared past to secure the reader's emotional response to the artist's new text. Her mythopoesis is complicated because H.D. not only relies on more than one myth for resonance in her texts but also uses myths from numerous cultures. I return to Duncan's passage and stress his use of the words "echoing" and "weaving," telling students that in *Kora and Ka* they will find H.D. weaving together stories and icons from Egyptian, Greek, Christian, and Celtic religious traditions. I urge them to think of this convergence of mythologies as evidence not of H.D.'s attempt to create a parallel between hers and a specific existing text but of her desire to create connections—or echoes—among many texts.

To familiarize students with these numerous religious traditions, I have them read Robert Spoo's brief introduction to *Kora and Ka* before they read the novella. Spoo explains that "Ka" refers to the Egyptian belief in "a 'double' or 'dweller' born with every person" that is like a "soul that survived the death of its host" (x). Spoo also tells us that this Ka is the soul of the main male character, John Helforth, and that Ka and John alternate as the story's first-person speakers. This information helps most students understand the narrative's point of view. Finally, as a supplement to Spoo, I ask students to conduct online or library research to learn as much as they can about Ka and several additional icons and stories: Kore/Persephone, Dionysus, the Last Supper, and the Holy Grail.

Despite all this preparation, we do not begin our next class meeting with a discussion of these mythological allusions. Instead, because we have already read and discussed both *The Return of the Soldier* and *Mrs. Dalloway*, students begin by focusing on the ways West and Woolf inform their readings of H.D. Students concentrate on the story's "soldier," John Helforth, and discuss his emotional collapse in relation to Chris Baldry's amnesia (*The Return of the Soldier*) and Septimus Warren Smith's shell shock (*Mrs. Dalloway*). But they are also quick to note the differences among the three men. First, students recall that Chris is "cured" of his amnesia and is sent back to the front; Septimus is never "cured" and, after the war, he commits suicide. John Helforth's condition troubles them. Completing their reading of *Kora and Ka*, students insist they do not know whether John is recovering from his breakdown or spiraling ever deeper into suicidal madness. Students also point out that while Chris and Septimus both experience the Great War in battle, John Helforth experiences it by way of his two brothers—Bob and Larry—who have both died in combat.

Here, if they do not do so themselves, I direct students to explore these differences of experience, reminding them that we have already encountered the noncombatant or home-front experience of World War I in our discussions of the three women characters who care for Chris in *The Return of the Soldier*: Jenny (his cousin), Kitty (his wife), and Margaret (his first love). What makes John Helforth's noncombatant home-front experience of war different from theirs? Or, why does John, who has never experienced battle, seem as shell-shocked as Septimus? Students struggle a bit with these kinds of questions. Most of them are reluctant to dismiss Helforth's predicament. Some point out that John's experience of the war in *Kora and Ka* is similar to Jenny's experience in *The Return of the Soldier*: both characters imagine the mutilation, dismemberment, and death of loved ones in trench warfare based on trench representations in newspapers (*Kora* 36) and "war-films" (West 5). Other students focus on the unique pressures John feels as a man who, because of the deaths of both brothers, cannot legally be conscripted but who nonetheless cannot ignore his mother's seeming eagerness to sacrifice another son to the war effort. Such class discussion often leads us back to the war poems we read to open our World War I section and to our discussion of the "white feather" phenomenon, in which women gave white feathers signifying cowardice to civilian men. Inevitably some students recall that the three women in *The Return of the Soldier* all determine that Chris is better off "well" and back in trench warfare than he is "sick" and at home with them. And students recognize with some surprise that in *Kora and Ka*, Kora Morrell—John's lover (perhaps) and a soldier's wife—expresses no acceptance of war propaganda and no dismissal of war experience.

As we explore these ideas regarding war experience, we also explore the literary elements that help illuminate them. Even if Spoo's introduction had not prepared students for the dual voices of Ka and John Helforth, they are ready to focus on the relevance of a narrative's perspective to make meaning of modernist fiction. After all, we have previously talked about the first-person point of view in *The Return of the Soldier* and explored the significance of questioning that single point of view rather than simply accepting it as real or true. In addition, students have already discussed the myriad third-person points of view in *Mrs. Dalloway* and considered the many levels of human awareness those points of view imply. Here I pause to point out the recursiveness of these kinds of class discussions. While I would argue that H.D. attains a useful accessibility when read in the contexts of West and Woolf, I would also contend that the complexity of *Kora and Ka* facilitates and enhances our understanding of the richness of *The Return of the Soldier* and of *Mrs. Dalloway*.

Now that students are engaged with the formal aspects of their readings, they are more likely—or, at least, more willing—to pursue the issue of modernist mythopoesis. I ask students to gather general information about myth and to relate that information to specific details in the text. When we turn to H.D.'s mythopoeic engagement with the figure of Persephone, I begin by asking students to list details about this Greek figure. Because they have read Spoo's introduction, students know that "Kore or Kora is another name for Persephone" (xiii). And because they have completed their online and library research, students are aware of additional information: Persephone is the daughter of two gods, Zeus and Demeter; while she was picking flowers, she was abducted by the god Hades and made his queen of the underworld; in response Demeter refused to fertilize the world's crops unless her daughter was returned to her; and Zeus agreed to Demeter's demands, but because Persephone had eaten some pomegranate seeds, he required her to spend half of each year in the underworld, among the dead. Depending on their sources, students may also be aware that Persephone's annual ascent from the underworld signals the beginning of spring, that her annual descent into the underworld signals the inevitability of death, and that Persephone is sometimes said to be the mother of Dionysus—which Spoo also mentions (xiii).

Once they have shared and compiled this kind of information, students consider how their knowledge of the myth of Persephone informs their reading of *Kora and Ka*. I make a distinction here between what I am asking and what they might expect me to ask. Often students expect professors to require that they explain the allusion (or the symbol or the metaphor). But I do not want them to decide immediately what this allusion—or the text, for that matter—means. To do so would be to suggest to them that the meaning is stable, knowable, and closed off from further exploration. Instead, when I ask students to consider how their knowledge of Persephone informs their reading of *Kora and Ka*, I am asking them to redirect their attention back to the details in the novella and to allow those details to proliferate in meaning.

I remind students that it is significant for them to realize that they cannot possibly know *Kora and Ka*—or any modernist text—in terms of information alone. Instead, they can explore the novella in terms of what E. M. Forster in his 1925 essay "Anonymity: An Inquiry" calls atmosphere, which he distinguishes from "common knowledge" that is the stuff of "information" (82). For Forster, the text that foregrounds "atmosphere" ("uncommon knowledge") does not attempt to convey informational "truth"; instead, it aims to create a "universe that only answers to its own laws" and that offers "a new standard of truth" (82). Students can create a kind of "truth" of the relationship between the figure of Persephone and the character of Kora using the "laws" H.D. provides in her details. Approaching mythopoesis in this way encourages students (and their professors) to become infected with and altered by H.D.'s text, to refer back to Duncan, and to take an exploratory stance toward meaning and meaning making.

This stance allows students to look at details in *Kora and Ka* in new ways. Some students make a connection between Kora and Persephone based solely on the last section of the novella, in which John Helforth says explicitly, "I saw Kora then just as the Kore-Persephone and I realised that I too have proper affinity with her" (52). Because this last section is the one place in the novella where all the stories and icons I have asked students to research come together, it makes sense that students begin here. But they rarely stay here. Why? Because they now know that Dionysus is the son of Persephone, which leads them to return to and rethink certain details in the novella: John belittles what he calls Kora's "mother complex" (30) and tells Kora not to treat him the way she treats her children (40); John's Ka says he follows Kora "as a child follows its mother" (9); Kora, in Freudian fashion, insists that John is secretly "in love with" his mother (35). In addition, knowing that Persephone was abducted while gathering flowers and subsequently is fated forever to annually ascend from and descend back into the underworld has implications for thinking about the relevance of Kora's questions to John: "Can't you just *love* your mother?" and "Can't you see the flowers growing and ignore the grave-yard?" (41).

Details about flowers and graveyards return students to their research focusing on Persephone's death and rebirth. They revisit the passages when John compares Kora to a "caterpillar" (21, 31, 53). In *Kora and Ka*, H.D. never explains that the caterpillar "dies" and is reborn in the form of the butterfly. But students realize this parallel themselves and attempt to make meaning of it in connection to Persephone, focusing on exploring how the information from their mythology research echoes as atmosphere in the details of the text. And this focus on death and rebirth leads students to reconsider John's last lines in the novella: "We were Kora of the Underworld and Dionysus, not yet risen. I was then Larry and those others, had no place then in any living landscape. Now we are Kore and the slain God . . . risen" (54). Armed with their research and class discussions, students make several insightful observations. They remark that the Greek and the Christian sacrifices echo each other: John makes no distinction between the Greek Dionysus and the Christian God. Students note, too, the shifts in tense and person: "We were," "I was," "We are." The shift from past to present tense seems to mirror the shift from death to rebirth. Moreover, the shift from plural to singular and back to a plural suggests that, although communities are destroyed and individuals suffer in isolation, there is hope for reconciliation and for new communities.

The concept of atmosphere might not lead students to discover the "new standard of truth" that Forster suggests awaits them. Yet using this concept when reading and writing about World War I and mythopoeic texts such as *Kora and Ka* can help students enjoy being inquisitive about meaning making without feeling the pressure—and the frustration—of being wrong or right. What matters for me when I teach British modernism and the literature of World

War I—and what matters whenever I teach H.D.—is the rich humanity inherent in the reading that we can impart in discussion and in written response. If, in the aftermath and in the midst of war, H.D. can devote herself to constructing worlds of atmosphere and "uncommon knowledge"—and if we can devote ourselves to accepting the uncertainty of what we can ultimately know of these worlds and to appreciating the limitations of that knowledge—then perhaps we, as students and as teachers, can become more skilled at preventing the wars of the future and more likely to foster the hopes that symbolize rebirth and that keep us human in the plural sense of community.

Teaching H.D.'s Work in a War Literature Course

Raffaella Baccolini

I intend to show here how I have situated and analyzed H.D.'s *Trilogy* in a course on the literature of war, trauma, and conflict that I have developed for third-year students in a program for interpreters and translators at the University of Bologna. This course allows me to stress the necessity of becoming a good listener—an essential skill of the translator/interpreter who is going to render in other words someone else's words, a most appropriate challenge in these years that many see as characterized by a "clash of civilizations" (see, e.g., Huntington). I use *Trilogy* and (anti)war literature in general because they offer excellent opportunities to reflect on a timely subject, both for what these texts say and how they say it and because it seems relevant to ask what the role of the artist is, or that of the "worker in ideas who uses words as the primary means of production" (Ngũgĩ 33). By looking at H.D. in relation to other writers—such as her contemporaries Ezra Pound, Richard Aldington, Katherine Mansfield, and Ernest Hemingway, as well as later writers such as Denise Levertov, Bruce Weigl, Tim O'Brien, and Marina Warner—I show how war and trauma pervade her work and influence her ideas about the function of art and the artist in wartime. These writers are arguably engaged in antiwar literature, since their works attest to the complex and contradictory situation in wartime: they record feelings of guilt and resentment, enthusiasm and despair, as well as the need to remember and forget. But while some accounts reflect and maintain the binary soldiers/civilians, thus revealing an involuntary complicity with the discourse of war, those of H.D. and others attempt to go beyond by critiquing this opposition and exposing its destructiveness.

The course is structured chronologically—dealing primarily with World War I, World War II, and Vietnam—and ends with more current events such as the wars in the former Yugoslavia and in Iraq and the 9/11 attacks. For each historical event, I select literary and visual works by soldiers and civilians. A series of introductory lectures focuses on the theoretical debates surrounding such literature, including the conventions of the war literature genre, the difficulty of representing trauma and war, the contradictions and fears linked to such an attempt (guilt, need to remember, inadequacy of language, fear of exploitation), our access to the past, and the use and abuse of memory.

We examine H.D.'s *Trilogy* in the cluster on World War II literature, and I focus students' attention on four main points: the role of the intellectual and the responsibility of the artist in times of conflict; the transcendence of binary logic in general and that of men/women and soldiers/civilians in particular in the discourse of war literature; the idea that religious differences, often divisive and the source of conflicts, can also draw people and cultures together; and the healing power of literature. Two class periods of two hours each are devoted to discussing the first part of *Trilogy*, *The Walls Do Not Fall*, the part that most explicitly deals with the description and the effects of World War II. This discussion is preceded by an introduction to H.D.'s work (the characteristics of her poetry) and the assignment that students look up the word *palimpsest* and all the references and allusions they find in the first ten sections of the poem.

In the preceding classes, we have discussed some of the features of war writing, in particular as they were developed in World War I literature. One feature I focus on is how the canon of English war literature unequivocally rests on an exclusionary discourse, since war has traditionally been considered a male experience. It includes only the authentic stories of frontline soldiers, which are meant to correct the distortions perpetrated by those who have not been there. Studies on war literature (see Bergonzi; Cobley; Fussell) present the genre as motivated by the fear of exclusion: these stories need to be told to set the record straight, because the official story has distorted and excluded what "really" happened. Such an approach automatically excludes women and their production, since they are thought incapable of offering authentic, eyewitness accounts; it also undermines women's experience because it is not firsthand and, hence, cannot be legitimate.

Recent historical research about changes in warfare, however, has shown how war affects soldiers and civilians alike and yet differently, bringing to the fore new topics of analysis, such as the issue of violence against women during conflicts. Work of feminist critics has revealed how a polarized gender system—where men are the fighters and women the peacekeepers at home—overlooks female complicity in and resistance to the war discourse (see Condell and Liddiard; Cooper, Munich, and Squier; Gilbert and Gubar, *No Man's Land*, vol. 3; Hanley; and Higonnet et al.). But while this criticism has mostly recovered women's memoirs and novels, not enough has been done to challenge the idea of a canon of war literature that rests on the exclusion of those who the canon assumes do not participate in the war experience. H.D. is among those writers who question this politics of exclusion.

One function of war novels is both to recall and to commemorate the many dead. The novels serve as a memorial to the dead and a reminder for the living; they usually record contrasting feelings such as pity for the dead and anger for the senseless death, alienation, and displacement of the soldiers, but also survivors' guilt and resentment for those—mostly women—on the home front. War literature thus defined omits writings by women and civilians and allows us to keep fostering the ideology of war with its myth of heroism. Such a vision, suggests Lynne Hanley,

> inhibits thinking about war as a continuous and ongoing condition of twentieth-century life. The memoir consolingly frames war, limiting it to a particular place and time and insisting that, outside this particular place and time, there is no war to remember. . . . [It] depicts war as an aberration rather than the habit of a culture. (33)

All the works examined in the course present the complex and contradictory characteristics that are typical of the genre. By stressing the disillusion and resentment of the soldiers, Pound's "Hugh Selwyn Mauberley" (*Selected Poems*), Aldington's "The Case of Lieutenant Hall," and Hemingway's *In Our Time* maintain two kinds of divisions between soldiers and civilians: between generations (the young men who were sent to die by the old men telling them lies) and between men and women. The exclusionary discourse prevents these writers from viewing both men and women as victims of war. The resentment against women is often displaced onto the women themselves and expressed as fear or hatred of and disgust for women and their sexuality. See, for instance, the image of the "old bitch gone in the teeth" for which the multitude of soldiers died in Pound's poem, the hatred for women's bodies in Aldington's story, or the fear of sexuality in Hemingway's "Soldier's Home."

It is interesting, then, for students to see what happens when we examine a text written by a woman. A similar division is found in Mansfield's story "The Fly," where a description of the Boss torturing an insect is an indictment of war and of the lack of responsibility on the part of the old generation that has sent its youth to die. Her story, however, does not display the misogyny expressed in the accounts of her male counterparts. Though her male characters resent women, the light in which she casts the men clearly undermines their statements. H.D. presents yet another position in *Bid Me to Live* when she insists that war differently affects all, "[v]ictims, victimised and victimising" ([1960] 7).

With this background, we start working on H.D.'s *Trilogy*. Since I use this poem to begin the unit on World War II literature, I make sure that the differences between the two wars are clear to the class. World War I exacerbated the division between soldiers and civilians but gave women a new sense of freedom as they gained power and visibility in society. World War II, by contrast, presented a changed and perhaps more complex setting. With the changes in warfare, the home front was not safe any longer, so the divide between soldiers and civilian was slightly diminished. Yet the resurgence of patriarchal politics, the cult of masculinity, and notions of a pure race staged a reaction against the emasculation associated with World War I. In her memoir on World War II, Bryher (H.D.'s longtime companion) captures this contradictory feeling:

> [I]n spite of the bombing I found the Second War so much easier to bear than the First. We were all "in it" and there was not the dreadful gap between soldiers and civilians that had caused so much stress in 1914.
>
> (*Days* 7–8)

She also writes that if, for women, "the First War had opened a few doors . . . the Second slammed many of them shut again" (120). "[T]he bombs in both wars," she adds wryly, "made no distinction as to sex" (35). At this point in the course, we also look at the propaganda posters of the time, in which women are criticized for their "careless talk" that costs soldiers' lives (*World War II Poster*

Collection). Some of the posters, however, also serve to make clear that differing war conditions in the 1940s in Europe and in the United States resulted in different gender patterns.

In the two class periods devoted to *Trilogy*, I concentrate on close readings and discussions of the first ten sections of the poem. Like other modernist epic poems, *Trilogy* is characterized by a quest: the poet-prophet-mythmaker needs to find new values with which to counter the destruction of twentieth-century society. H.D.'s answer lies in a new syncretist religion that combines Judeo-Christian with Greek and Egyptian traditions. As with many modernist writings, there is a parallelism between content and form—in H.D. it can be explored through the notion and technique of the palimpsest. The work with students consists, for the first class period, in finding the different ways in which this notion is present in the poem. The presence of layers—literally of writings, but metaphorically the layered juxtaposition of traditions, cultures, religions, and historical periods—is identified as the essence of the palimpsest. The students are then able to point out that the many references and allusions represent different temporal, cultural, and religious layers. By superimposing past and present, places, religions, and the personal with the historical, H.D. foreshadows the shattering impact of war and violence throughout time.

We also discuss section 1 of *Trilogy* in relation to previous works studied in the class, how it records the poet's disorientation at the sight of total destruction and how its detached tone is in contrast with the horror of what is being observed. H.D.'s matter-of-factness, however, is not pervaded by the bitterness of Hemingway's vignettes. Rather, the tension between language/tone and subject matter suggests a numbness of feeling, a reference to the routine of the threat of death. By recognizing the effect of war on civilians and their desensitization to violence, students point out that H.D. represents the extraordinary as the quotidian. When urged to consider how this tone can be linked to the notion of the palimpsest, the students begin to see that H.D. is saying that there is no escape in the past: the images of destruction in London juxtaposed to the ruins in Egypt and the devastation of Pompeii are a vivid representation of how history repeats itself. But the long line of destruction in different time periods may also be suggesting that violence and war are conditions of our civilization, rather than aberrations.

As we approach section 2, our attention is still concentrated on H.D.'s language. Students usually note two things: H.D.'s play on words and the use of a binary "us/them" discourse, both of which contribute to creating a section that oscillates between opposites. The initial impression students usually have is that H.D. re-creates polarities that are specific to the discourse of war and its literature. By drawing their attention to other sections of the poem (e.g., *Walls*, sec. 39, and *Tribute*, sec. 8), I help students recognize that H.D's creative etymologies and free associations represent her alchemical use of language—the notion that words have the power to reconstitute and create an alternative and oppositional vision to that maintained by tradition, a vision that transcends its destructive binaries. In section 8 of *Tribute to the Angels*, for example, H.D., by playing on Hebrew, Latin, French, and English words, melts bitterness and fluidity with maternity to form the image of the female divinity (25–35). These are words that transform and are made flesh.

I also want students to understand that the second section presents yet another difference from the other accounts examined: the division among groups is not along lines of gender or age or between enemies and allies but between orthodox and heterodox believers. The poet speaks from within a sect of followers of beauty and art. This section asks, What is the function of poetry and beauty in war? What is the role of poets and intellectuals? I help students notice how the poet is already pointing to one of the important attributes of art: the power to heal and to regenerate, as made clear by her linking art with versions of the goddess of fertility in different religious traditions. Students can then see in the reference to Isis that just as Isis sewed together the scattered parts of Osiris's body, so can art and beauty re-create a vision of peace and life. As Isis, H.D. is sewing together the fragments of civilization with which to counter destruction. Subsequent references to the caduceus—the rod carried by Hermes that in the various transformations has become a symbol of medicine, fertility, and healing—and the serpent constitute other images of healing and resurrection (see *Tribute*, secs. 7, 11–12). The technique of the palimpsest is then perceived in its revolutionary potential: images of gods and goddesses from different religious traditions have "the same—different—the same attributes, / different yet the same as before" (105). Religion, which can divide people unnecessarily and ignite wars, is here linked with beauty, art, and rebirth.

For the second class period, when we concentrate on sections 6, 9, and 10 of *Walls Do Not Fall*, we analyze H.D.'s immediate answer to the question of the role of the artist in war. Analyses of section 6 usually point out a similarity with section 4: they each present a personification of the poet—a seashell and a silkworm, respectively, that share the condition of being humble and suggest that even despised creatures are capable of beauty within. Art that is despised and deemed futile is reevaluated in this section with a defiant tone that celebrates its persistence. The poet's task parallels that of the silkworm, which consumes detritus to spin silk, something precious and beautiful. For H.D., then, the task of the writer, his or her ethical responsibility, is to find inspiration in devastation. At this point, students are invited to compare H.D.'s position with Mansfield's ethical imperative not to leave the war out of the novel (Murry 380–81). And later in the course, H.D.'s position will be recollected when examining other texts, such as Levertov's "Advent 1966" (*To Stay*) and "Statement for a Television Program" (*Poet*). Returning to section 6, students are invited to reflect on palimpsest. If the opening lines of the section recall Psalm 22, where the worm is despised by the people, section 7 explicitly links the transformation of the worm to the "king-cobra," the serpent of the Ophite tradition, sacred in Egypt (13). Similarly, the worm/caterpillar that turns into a butterfly means different things in different traditions: butterflies are symbols of the soul in Greek culture, while in Christian symbolism they represent rebirth and immortality. Through H.D.'s reevaluation the students recognize the value of art and the role of the artists who can not only record destruction but also offer a vision with which to oppose that violence.

Finally, we analyze sections 9 and 10 of *Walls Do Not Fall*, where the poet turns her attention to male divinities while continuing her defense of art and writing. The students notice how these divinities (Thoth, Hermes, Mercury) share the attributes of writing, art, and creating and ordering the universe and are patrons of the arts. Against the conjuring of these gods, however, the society of H.D.'s time continues to show a widespread disregard if not hatred of books, as H.D. juxtaposes Nazi book burning with wartime use of "folio, manuscript, old parchment . . . for cartridge cases" (16). Against these images of destructions, the names of the male divinities and the figure of the powerful—and peaceful—female pharaoh Hatshepsut are conjured as symbols of the endurance of art against the continuous yet ephemeral violence. Section 10 reestablishes the two voices of *Trilogy* and addresses H.D.'s underlying theme: the struggle between violence and literature; the supremacy of art over war; the possibility to counter destruction with writing—in short, the healing and regenerative power of literature. Students notice how H.D. plays with the terms "sword" and "word"; content and language fuse to say that the "sword" derives—in yet another creative etymology—from the "word," it is "the latter-born" (17). The final lines of the section, "*in the beginning / was the Word*," quote the first words of the Gospel of John, a paraphrase of the opening of Genesis. Again, H.D. is superimposing different religious traditions and adds the God of Christianity to the images of Egyptian, Greek, and Roman gods. Eternal, healing literature is associated with both male and female divinities, in a vision that goes beyond the destructive binary divisions between men and women or soldiers and civilians that are so ingrained in war literature.

In teaching this course, I have also noticed the possible risks involved. War literature asks for a response from the reader, one that often comes through identification. But no one wants or tends to identify with the oppressors, ultimately showing that identification may not be the most effective way of understanding a complex event. Since the emphasis is primarily on events that are far away in time, the temporal and geographic distance may also serve as an excuse not to feel burdened with any sense of responsibility. But H.D.'s work, more than all the others', shows the students just the opposite: the superimposition of past and present, of the personal and the historical, invites them to think critically about our memory of the past and its link with present times. H.D., like other writers (Levertov, Warner), invites us—students, readers, and teachers—to go beyond the initial shock or wound, to "work toward the more subtle work of articulating the haunting presence of trauma [and violence] in everyday life" (Harad), and to think about war as the habit of a culture rather than an exceptional aberration. And yet, despite and because of the times we live in, this literature also makes clear that the role of the intellectual must be articulated again and with it our roles as teachers and students. Edward Said's intellectual is one who bears witness to "horror otherwise unrecorded" (qtd. in Stanton 9) and thus can become an agent of social change "that is both local and has broader, more global material and ethical consequences" (9). Against the "destroyers of the world," the intellectual can bring "the word that breathes life" and that connects and offers hope in defense of human life (Ngũgĩ 36, 39).

Burnt Offerings or Incendiary Devices? Ambivalence, Trauma, and Cultural Work in *The Gift* and *Trilogy*

Madelyn Detloff

Teaching H.D. is an exercise in ambivalence, in the technical sense of the word—an oscillation between intense extremes. On the one hand, H.D.'s writing provides moments of rewarding pedagogical pleasure; on the other hand, teaching her more intricate work to unsuspecting undergraduates can be arduous and sometimes exasperating. Taught in isolation, the *Sea Garden* poems or *HERmione* or parts of *Trilogy* fit nicely into a syllabus as examples of important forms—the imagist poem, *Künstlerroman*, modernist long poem, or feminist myth revision. It is more difficult to give students a sense of the approximately fifty-year span of H.D.'s writing career (from 1909 to 1961), a half century that coincides with some of the most turbulent and troubling decades of European history. The breadth of H.D.'s life and work presents challenges for those of us who teach from a cultural studies perspective that examines a work's articulation of ideologies, social contexts, and aesthetic expectations. Considered from the multifaceted perspective necessary to understand articulation, H.D.'s career is difficult to categorize. Was she a late modernist or an early imagist? American or British? poet or novelist? romantic heterosexual or bohemian queer? serious critic or dilettante? Was she worthy of our emulation for her forward thinking or deserving of our disapproval for her conservative lapses? Clearly such questions cannot do justice to the complexity of H.D.'s life and work, but their insufficiency can provide the motivation for what might be called a pedagogy of ambivalence—a pedagogy that draws its energy from the productive discomfort of inhabiting the awkward territory of the "both/and."

This ambivalent self-locating is an implicit necessity of cultural studies. As Rita Felski notes:

> Cultural Studies bears the unmistakable marks of its dual parentage, literary criticism and sociology. It is as much about form as about content, as much about pleasure as about politics. It does not abandon close reading but requires it. (507)

H.D. scholars have advocated a similar attention to the both/and relation between the formal elements of H.D.'s work and its cultural contexts. In her book on H.D.'s "cultural poetics," Adalaide Morris suggests:

> As forms of cultural meditation and mediation, [H.D.'s poems] instantiate, exercise, and advocate a kind of attention that is crucial to the ongoing life of a culture. In this sense, they think *about* thinking and they think

> *toward* action: they are, that is, philosophical and ethical. They do cultural work. (*How to Live* 2)

In what follows, I outline some pedagogical tools for understanding the cultural work done in H.D.'s World War II writings, *The Gift* and *Trilogy*. I discuss how H.D. might be taught in the context of trauma studies, a field of cultural studies that analyzes how loss, suffering, and catastrophe are articulated (or effaced) in formal and informal discourse. Trauma studies is less of a discrete discipline than it is a cluster of often overlapping scholarly and cultural endeavors in disciplines such as history, the fine arts, architecture, literature, sociology, psychology, and gender studies.[1] This cluster is connected by some common epistemological and ethical questions: How do we know trauma when we see it, hear it, remember it, represent it? What are its effects on those who witness, experience, remember, perpetrate, efface, ignore, repress, or express it? What are its cultural effects and legacies? What are the ethical responsibilities of those who come into contact with trauma through experience (as perpetrators, survivors, witnesses, or bystanders) or representation (in memory, symptom, scar, artifact, testimony, legacy, or history)? Can traumatic experience be represented, and if so, what are the effects of different modes of representation? Reading *The Gift* and *Trilogy* together as cultural artifacts produced during a time of trauma and providing representations of it gives students the opportunity to ponder these questions—and to hone their understanding of the ethical and epistemological dilemmas presented by trauma and trauma-producing practices.

My aim in presenting H.D.'s work through the lens of trauma studies is not to provide a reading of her texts as narratives of personal healing, although they certainly lend themselves to such a reading, especially her semiautobiographical prose. Suzette Henke's chapter on H.D. in *Shattered Subjects* provides an extensive reading of H.D.'s "scriptotherapy" (43), and I recommend making this essay available to students or assigning it in an upper-division course. Since a great deal of criticism focuses on H.D.'s personal struggles, I attempt to balance that perspective with a cultural studies focus on how *Trilogy* and *The Gift* might articulate the civilian-survivor experience. H.D. lived in London during the air raids of World War II, and thus both texts (written, as Susan Stanford Friedman notes, from 1942 to 1944) function as artifacts of the Blitz—a series of almost nightly air raid attacks on London, Coventry, and other British cities from 7 September 1940 through May 1941 (Friedman, *Penelope's Web* 364; Richards).

Because most North American students today (and perhaps British students as well) are not familiar with the devastation of the Blitz, I have designed a short background exercise to facilitate better understanding of the material circumstances informing the texts and subtexts of *Trilogy* and *The Gift*. The background exercise can be done as homework or in digitally enabled classrooms that have access to the Internet. The digital resources I list below can be linked to a Web page or be posted to one's course links page on course management software. The activity can be performed in small groups in class or individually at home or in the library.

The first resource I introduce is Louis Silverstein's *H.D. Chronology*, a Web version of his excellent chronology of H.D.'s life. Formatted for the Web by Heather Hernandez, Silverstein's chronology contains information on H.D.'s ancestors in Europe and Bethlehem, Pennsylvania, and can be used as a quick cross-reference for events noted in *The Gift*. The chronology contains entries on the death of Frances Gregg in an air raid on Plymouth in 1941; Sylvia Beach's internment in the south of France in 1943; H.D.'s comments on writing the manuscript of *The Gift* during the "bad raids" on London in 1943; and brief information on the war work of Perdita Macpherson Schaffner, H.D.'s daughter. Students can skim the chronology to get a sense of the personal and historical experiences that inform H.D.'s writing and then return to the chronology for particular details as they read *The Gift* or *Trilogy*, connecting the material circumstances of the war to the aesthetic achievement of the long poem or the fable-like quality of the memoir.

After delving briefly into biographical information about H.D., students turn to a few digital archives containing photos, news reports, and audio clips from survivors of the Blitz. The first site, *The Imperial War Museum*, contains photo

Fig. 1. An Anderson shelter standing intact amid a scene of debris in Norwich (Imperial War Museum, HU036196)

Fig. 2. Bomb damage in the center of Coventry, England, two days after the German Luftwaffe air raid on the night of 14 November 1940 (Imperial War Museum, H5600)

archives, timelines, and special exhibits about the "homefront" during World War II. I have reproduced a few of the photos available in figures 1–4. These photos offer a glimpse of the extensive damage that civilians encountered during the Blitz. Browsing through the archival images enables students to visualize the destruction of the Blitz when they read the first lines of *The Walls Do Not Fall*: "an incident here and there / and rails gone (for guns) / from your (and my) old town square" (3). The "ruin everywhere," the "shrine" that "lies open to the sky," the "fallen roof" that "leaves the sealed room / open to the air," and the "desolation" that H.D. refers to in the first strophe of the poem are more than just metaphors, although H.D.'s poem is highly figurative and polysemic. Similar photographic images are available on the BBC site *Coventry and Warwickshire*, under "History," as is audio footage of survivors describing the bombing aftermath. Finally, the London *Times* provides an online archive of newspaper coverage of the Blitz that allows students to read contemporaneous news accounts of the air raids and their aftermath ("Blitz").

There is an ethical as well as a historical dimension to a civilian-survivor approach to reading H.D.'s World War II writings. If we follow Elaine Scarry's sadly still-urgent analysis of war in *The Body in Pain*, we recognize that one of war's rhetorical and political ruses is to redescribe pain and devastation so that the direct effects of war ("dead bodies and ruined houses" as Virginia Woolf

Fig. 3. The western bell towers of Saint Paul's Cathedral in London seen through an archway after the heavy incendiary raid of 29 December 1940. Photo by Cecil Beaton (Imperial War Museum, MH2718)

would say [*Three Guineas* 11]) are deanimated: translated into the language of strategy, valorized as heroic sacrifice, or dismissed as collateral damage. Given this context, it is important to pay attention to the particular and recognize our tendency to make the devastation of war into a symbol without fully attending to its grim reality, to fast-forward to the end in a compensatory gesture that often forgets or neglects the suffering required to reach the end. This urge to transcend the particular is not exclusive to the rhetoric of war but also central to the rhetoric of memorialization. As James Young notes, however, a new generation of artists and critics attempting to memorialize the loss of millions in the Shoah have developed an "antiredemptory aesthetic" (10). These memory

Fig. 4. Firemen directing hoses on burning buildings in the city of Manchester (Imperial War Museum, HU49833)

workers, Young argues, "resist the temptation for redemptory closure in their work, but they can make visible why such history [of trauma] is worth recalling in the first place" (10–11). Contrasting *Trilogy* with these antiredemptory efforts heightens the ambivalence of reading H.D.'s poem. Without keeping the "ruin everywhere" (*Trilogy* 3) at the forefront of one's mind as a material reality, H.D.'s message of healing and resilience, apocalyptic rebirth and redemption, risks effacing what Victoria Harrison calls "the world-erasing realities of bombed-out neighborhoods, incinerated Jews, and the terror of daily life under attack, by creating its alternative vision—its 'spiritual realism'" (73). Additional online resources from more recent conflicts can be used to provide students an opening for thinking about how our discussion of H.D.'s representation of the devastation of World War II might give us tools for thinking critically about the violence of war in the present.

After completing the background exercise to situate *Trilogy* and *The Gift* as World War II writings—and more specifically as writings composed during the Blitz—we attend closely to the words on the page, reading long sections of the poem aloud (taking turns every few lines). We might read the last ten sections of *The Walls Do Not Fall*, which contain allusions to rationing ("let us measure defeat / in terms of bread and meat" [46]), the responsibility of the scribe (49), and pillars of fire (49). When we read the often quoted passage about cryptic words ("they are anagrams, cryptograms, / little boxes, conditioned // to hatch butterflies . . ." [53]), does it matter to us to know that H.D.'s daughter at this time was using her language skills to work for the Office of Strategic Services? When we read about the decomposition of Osiris (the dismembered brother/god) and enunciate the "zrr-hiss" of bombs (58), perhaps the picture we have seen of the bomb shelter covered in rubble will come back to mind.

Alternatively, students can be asked to trace the many images of fire, purifying destruction, and sacrificial wounds in *Trilogy*, attending to the literal meaning of the words and images. We are so good at reading symbolic meanings that we may forget that fire burns, hurts, kills. If I have time to assign *The Gift*—not generally practical in a survey course, but possible in an upper-division seminar—I may ask students to trace similar images of fire in the text. Perhaps because of its status as memoir or its less controlled formal structure or its closer association with childhood, *The Gift* is less redemptive than *Trilogy*. The spectacle of a little girl going up in flames is less easy to make into a meaningful symbol and is therefore perhaps a precursor to antiredemptory aesthetics.

When I teach *The Gift*, I find it helpful to give a brief overview of Judith Butler's theory of the role of "passionate attachments" in subject making from *The Psychic Life of Power*. Butler gives us language to begin analyzing the ambivalence of subject formation that is described so well in the story of Hilda's coming to consciousness. Butler argues that we come to our sense of subjectivity recursively, through submitting to our dependence on others and then disavowing our memory of that submission. As she explains:

> The desire to survive, "to be," is a pervasively exploitable desire. The one who holds out the promise of continued existence plays to the desire to survive. "I would rather exist in subordination than not exist" is one formulation of this predicament (where the risk of "death" is also possible). (7)

This theory may help explain why *The Gift* is littered with the corpses of dead girls and women. Among other things, Hilda is articulating her subjectivity as the story of her survival, which is contrasted to the litany of deaths that begins with the first line of the memoir: "There was a girl who was burnt to death at the Seminary, as they called the old school where our grandfather was Principal" (Gift 35). There is a clear parallel to be drawn between Hilda's childhood survival and H.D.'s survival in London during the Blitz, where one was constantly reminded that "the risk of 'death' is also possible."

Eventually, it is worth discussing at length H.D.'s allusion to the Bluebeard tale and its eerie references to lethal masculinity. The uncanny elements of the tale can be linked materially to wartime trauma as well: a house filled with corpses seems an anomaly exclusive to fairy tales and horror stories, until we think of the everyday realities of the Blitz, where one might indeed come upon a house filled with corpses and body parts. Such gruesome images are part of the landscape of *Trilogy* as well, where, among the ruins, "the flesh? it was melted away, / the heart burnt out, dead ember / tendons, muscles shattered, outer husk dismembered" (4). Because we tend to read poetry as much more metaphorical than prose, we might be tempted to look beyond the gruesomeness of this image, a vehicle for a metaphor whose tenor is the triumphant spirit, the undaunted city and nation, the "frame" that still holds (4). Pointing out the potential ambivalence of our responses to the poem is helpful here, for the poem is not simply gruesome; it is important to register its resilient, even defiant message—the expression of a Londoner's will to survive despite the "zrr-hiss" of the incendiary devices making the risk of death a very real possibility. For those of us reading the text decades later, without a memory of the Blitz, the challenge is to hear the story of loss as well as the story of resilience. Reading *Trilogy* and *The Gift* from the perspective of trauma studies allows us to notice what the texts communicate and cover, the "meaning that words hide" in our plain sight (*Trilogy* 53).

Ultimately, it is not my desire for students to read only trauma in what are also beautiful testaments to survival. My desire, as I mentioned above, is to tap the productive potential of the both/and of H.D.'s texts—survival implies loss, resilience implies suffering, mending implies brokenness, sacrifice implies death. My hope is that we can learn to see both one and the other in H.D.'s texts and, perhaps more urgent, in the texts of our troubled times.

NOTE

[1] For examples of work in trauma studies, see Dominick LaCapra, *History and Memory after Auschwitz* and *Writing History, Writing Trauma*; Judith Lewis Herman, *Trauma and Recovery*; and Cathy Caruth, *Unclaimed Experience*.

Teaching *Trilogy*: H.D.'s War and Peace

Susan Stanford Friedman

"It was the best of times. It was the worst of times." So begins *Bid Me to Live (A Madrigal)*, H.D.'s novel about love, war, and writing in World War I, a deliberate echo of Charles Dickens echoing Cicero. The post-9/11 world is both the worst and the best of times to be teaching *Trilogy*: the worst, because the world is full of wars, the violence of the times is frightening and critical for our students to think about; the best, because the questions H.D.'s poem explores about war and peace resonate richly with issues students care about, whether they are undergraduates, graduate students, or advanced high school students.

I recall vividly how intensely my undergraduate students responded to the poem's core quests and visions when I taught the poem during the Gulf War of 1991, once I figured out how to connect the poem's central engagement with war to the students' questions about current conflicts. No longer were the poem's allusions so daunting, its loose structure of lyric sequences so challenging to make cohere. Unlike teaching *Trilogy* in the late 1970s and 1980s, this teaching fed a spiritual hunger in the students to make sense of a violent and chaotic world, or at least to keep alive the dream of peace. "[W]*e are voyagers, discoverers / of the not-known, // the unrecorded*," H.D. writes at the end of *Trilogy*'s first volume, *The Walls Do Not Fall*: *"we have no map; // possibly we will reach haven, / heaven"* (59). Students of a country at war can connect with these lines, no matter how dense the poem's patterns, how wide-ranging its fragmentary invocations of past religious, hermetic, mythological, and literary traditions.

Trilogy can be taught in many different kinds of courses—courses on modernism or modernist poetry; the epic tradition and the twentieth-century long poem; women's writing; war poetry; thematically shaped courses around issues of gender, religion, spirituality, mythmaking revisionism, time and space, language, experimentalism, war, pacifism, and so forth. Each curricular context creates a framework within which students become accomplished readers for specific sets of issues and forms. *Trilogy* shines as a different poem within each of these curricular galaxies. Consequently, there is no one strategy for teaching the poem, any more than there is one definitive reading of it. I attempt here a doubly directed strategy that is adaptable to the many kinds of courses in which the poem can be successfully taught.

What I have found to be the most successful is a "both/and" strategy of looking at the big picture and the little: the overarching narrative structures and the discrete lyric sequences; the poem's cosmic mythmaking and its imagistic craft for rendering states of mind; the philosophical or spiritual meditations and the conversational engagement with the reader. I recommend using Aliki Barnstone's ably edited edition, with its brief but useful introduction reviewing H.D.'s composition of the poem in London during World War II (1942–44) and its equally useful and unobtrusive "Reader's Notes" at the end. But I urge students to relax about all the poem's allusions and to recognize how many of them H.D. actually identifies within the poem (in marked contrast to the allusions in Ezra Pound's *Cantos* or T. S. Eliot's *The Waste Land*). Constantly shifting to the volume's endnotes and trying to memorize the attributes of various deities, angels, and other allusions can be very distracting for students, especially on their first reading of the poem. Identification of specific allusions is best left to instances of close reading of particular passages. I urge students to get a sense of the whole, first by letting the poem's exceptionally lucid couplets flow over and through them and then by engaging with the poem's larger quest and prophetic structures. Invariably, students understand more than they think they do. Then, much as a cinematographer first pans over a landscape before zooming in for a close-up, I turn their attention to specific lyric sequences for highly detailed, close readings of selected passages.

Central to *Trilogy*'s cosmic scope is the questing spirit of the poet. She—the poem's "I"—tells the story of her and other civilians' experiencing the bombing of London, surviving the ruin everywhere, and seeking its deeper spiritual meanings. How to explain, she asks, the violence of war and what she metonymically calls the "pyramid of skulls" (122)? "[W]hat saved us? what for?" she wonders (4), the questions of all survivors of holocaust. Her answer lies in the search for "spiritual realism" (48), a forceful yoking together of the transcendent out-of-time with the materiality of the in-time in what appears to be an oxymoron. This quest for the sacred is not an escape from war but rather a plunge into the heart of darkness to find at least the hope of rebirth and regeneration. "[R]esurrection," the poet says, "is a sense of direction" (123).

The poet affirms the efficacy of search in the face of the doubters, those who would question the power of poetry to address the might of bombs. Poets are not "useless," "non-utilitarian," or "pathetic," as skeptics have charged (14). Instead, they are the poet-prophets of the modern world, with poetry as their medium of vision. The poet says:

> [R]emember, O Sword,
> you are the younger brother, the latter-born,
> . . . .
> *in the beginning*
> *was the Word.* (17)

I have found it effective with students to evoke the tradition of prophetic poetry and prior apologias of poetry such as Philip Sidney's *A Defence of Poetry* (1579–80) and Percy Shelley's *A Defence of Poetry* (1821). As a modernist, however, H.D.'s poet-prophet faces the uncertainty of quest and takes a Kierkegaardian leap of faith, not certain in the end if "*we will reach haven, / heaven.*" *Trilogy*'s defense lies in poetry as a medium of search, not of answers.

Trilogy's three volumes narrate the poem's overarching quest plot in different ways. *The Walls Do Not Fall* seeks the divine in its paternal form, while *Tribute*

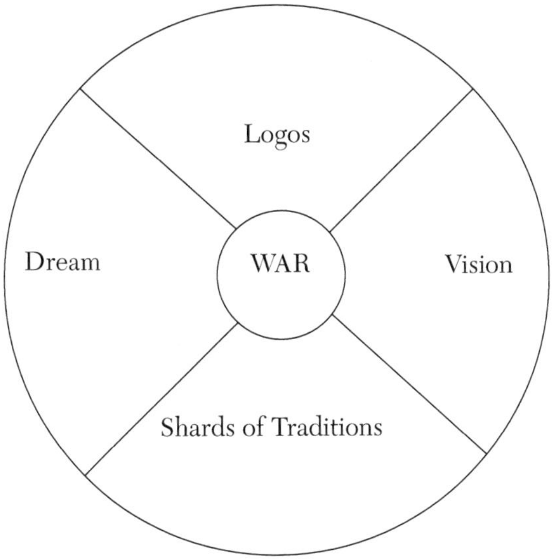

Fig. 1

to the Angels finds the divine in the heart of the maternal. *The Flowering of the Rod* finds paradise in a fleck of shining light in the poet's embedded "tale of jars," the encounter between Mary Magdalene and the Arab merchant Kaspar (see secs. 12–42). "[I]t was unseemly that a woman / appear disordered, disheveled," he thinks: "it was unseemly that a woman / appear at all" (137). But the light "as of moon-light on a lost river" that emanates from her hair, revealed as her scarf falls to the floor, was like the dream of water for a "parched, dying man, lost in the desert" (136). Before having students work through the narrative complexities of the three volumes, however, I return to the quest story to characterize how the poet engages in search rather than focusing initially on what she finds. A circular chart divided into quadrants provides an effective visual mnemonic device to characterize the poet's pathways and processes of search (see fig. 1).

"War" stands sharply in the middle of the chart to signal violence as the material condition of the poem's production. "Dream" and "Vision" represent the poet's directly experienced access to spiritual realism. "Logos" and "Shards of Traditions" represent the poet's meditations on words ("I know, I feel / the meaning that words hide; // they are anagrams, cryptograms, / little boxes, conditioned // to hatch butterflies . . ." [53]) and on the fragments from many cultural, religions, and esoteric traditions (such as those in ancient Egypt, Mesopotamia, Canaan, Israel, Ionia, Greece, and Rome; Judaism, Christianity, and Islam; the Kabbalah, Gnosticism, astrology, alchemy, numerology). Contextualizing these four areas in relation to modernism is helpful to students—dream and vision are akin to the epiphanic moments of being in James Joyce and Virginia Woolf; logos and paratactic fragments of many cultures resonate with Eliot and Pound.

Once students understand these distinctive pathways—two forms of direct experience and received traditions—they can more easily see how the poem moves fluidly, free associationally, and often imperceptibly among them. In *The Walls Do Not Fall*, for example, the poet speaks of "the dream parallel // whose relative sigil has not changed / since Nineveh and Babel" (24). What follows is the poet's dream of "the world-father," who appears in her dream as "Ra, Osiris, *Amen*" in "a spacious, bare meeting-house" built in that "eighteenth-century / simplicity and grace" reminiscent of the Moravian church in Bethlehem, Pennsylvania, H.D.'s birthplace (25). This dream initiates a sequence of meditations: it begins with the Christos image in painting ("He might even be the authentic Jew / stepped out from Velasquez" [28]); moves through the sensation of being "mothered again" in the wool, the "cocoon" of the Lamb, who is simultaneously Christ, Amen-Ra, and Aries the Ram (see *Walls*, sec. 21); experiences the dark night of the soul ("oneness lost, madness" [41]); and concludes with secret meanings hatched in the name of Osiris, the resurrection god of the Egyptians, O-Sire-Is (see *Walls*, sec. 40).

In *Tribute to the Angels*, the flow between dream and vision, logos and tradition, takes a decidedly woman-centered turn, as the world-father takes on the form of the divine as mother. The poem becomes an alchemical crucible of words where "a word most bitter, *marah*" and "a word bitterer still, *mar*" are melted, fused, and joined to become "mer, mere, mère, mater, Maia, Mary, // Star of the Sea, / Mother" (71). The alchemical recovery of the divine mother occurs in a sequence of invocations to guardian angels from Jewish, Christian, and Islamic traditions. These movements from logos to cultural tradition set in motion an epiphany of the divine maternal presence for the poet as she walks into a bombed-out garden square where she sees a "half-burnt-out apple-tree / blossoming" amid the ruins (87). "[A] new sensation // strikes paralysing, / strikes dumb" as the poet hears the music of the spheres even while she realizes "there is no escape from the spear / that pierces the heart" (85, 86).

This vision of "the flowering of the rood" (the wood as contemporary cross [87]) folds into the poet's dream of the Lady, who comes knocking in tune with the clock's ticking at her bedside (see *Tribute*, sec. 25). Arguably *Trilogy*'s central trope, the Lady in her dream reminds the poet of all the painters who have represented her. But the poet insists that the Lady of her dream, of her direct experience, is different. She holds not the child, as the mother of God, but instead a book whose "pages, I imagine, are the blank pages / of the unwritten volume of the new" (103). The poet's dream releases the Lady from the prison of former representations:

> she is not shut up in a cave
> like a Sibyl; she is not

> imprisoned in leaden bars
> in a coloured window,
>
> she is Psyche, the butterfly,
> out of the cocoon. (103)

The Lady is both the poet and the poet's muse. Like the maternal deities recovered through alchemical distillations earlier in *Tribute to the Angels*, the Lady is also the divine principle of sacred regeneration in female form.

To return to my cinematic metaphor for teaching *Trilogy*, once students have panned across the big quest structures of the poem, they can zoom in more narrowly onto resonant passages, densely packed images, and lyric sequences. Students and teachers can select their favorite passages for reading out loud (*Trilogy*'s rhythms are especially musical, reflecting H.D.'s Moravian background) and for close reading. As if viewing cinematic close-ups, readers can examine in minute detail the avatars and personae of the poet; the complex and fluid modes of address (the poet's "I" and "we"; the "you" and "they" who are addressed or invoked); the conversational tone and dialogic engagements created by the procession of pronouns; the poem's imagist craft and the palimpsestic layers of material, political, philosophical, and spiritual meaning that are embedded in words; the rhythms of rhyme, internal rhyme, off rhyme, and vers libre; the open space on the page created by the use of relatively short lines in couplets; the use of narrative insets that fold into the lyric and meditative sequences; and so forth. *Trilogy*'s formal aspects are endlessly rich and suggestive. Part of the poem's enchantment lies in the simplicity of its syntactic flow and lyric lucidity and the complexity of its poetics and cosmic scope—a contradictory quality reminiscent of the Japanese and Chinese poetry H.D. read in translation.

Section 4 of *The Walls Do Not Fall*—"There is a spell, for instance, / in every sea-shell" (8)—is one of the best sequences for close reading, useful on many levels, from prosody, through image, to religious allusion (see esp. in the Bible Matt. 7.6, 13.45–46) and cosmic vision. The poet takes on the persona of a sea-shell, a flabby hermit that opens to the tide flow and experiences the "invasion of the limitless" and the "shark-jaws / of outer circumstance" (9)—images that link back to the poet's opening walk through the bombed-out streets of London. "[I]ndigestible, hard, ungiving," the poet refuses to be overwhelmed by the whale of history that would swallow her:

> living within,
> you beget, self-out-of-self,
>
> selfless,
> that pearl-of-great-price. (9)

Echoing Marianne Moore's animal personae, the poet takes on as well the lowly avatar of the "worm" clinging to a

> grass-blade,
> the back of a leaf
>
> when storm-wind
> tore it from its stem. (11)

This image is a striking use of nature as objective correlatives for the poet's attempt to cling to life in the face of war. Echoing Romantic and American transcendental uses of nature and anticipating late-twentieth-century ecological literature, the poet as worm on a leaf sparks cosmic meditations, for the worm conflates allusions to the worm of death, the serpent of Eden, the sacred serpent of the mother deities, and the caterpillar who spins a cocoon. In the face of war, the poet is "the industrious worm" who must "spin my own shroud" (12), the cocoon that produces the butterfly, symbol of the soul and of Psyche reborn.

Trilogy is a poem that confronts war with an insistence on peace, finds in death the vision of rebirth. It is a poem that seeks revelation in the face of apocalypse. The poet's most defiant avatar is John, the prophet of Revelation, the final book of the Christian Bible. "*I make all things new. / I John saw. I testify*," the poet says, quoting directly from Revelation and calling him "He of the seventy-times-seven / bitter, unending wars" (65). The poet knows that John threatened any who would dare to change a word of his revelations—"*if any man shall add // God shall add unto him the plagues*" (65)—but she alters his text profoundly nonetheless. Weaving lines from Revelation and the Gospels describing Jesus throughout *Tribute to the Angels*, the poet heretically puts herself, a woman, in the place of John and Jesus. Instead of seeing the whore of Babylon who must be slain in the Apocalypse of the Second Coming, she finds the Lady carrying the book of the new. She locates in the poem's alchemical wordshop the "[b]itter, bitter jewel / in the heart of the bowl" and ultimately finds "Venus, Aphrodite, Astarte, // star of the east / star of the west" (72, 73). She finds the "heart-beat, pulse-beat" of the living jewel brought to life by her invocation of the deities of love (77). She finds Annael, the female archangel associated with Aphrodite and the planet Venus, whose name, she says, means "peace of God" (79). In her apocalypse, the fires of war morph into the purifying flames of alchemical transfiguration.

The syncretism of the poet's quest through dream and vision, word and tradition is important to stress. Unlike Eliot in his later work, H.D. turns away from orthodoxies of all kinds. Instead of seeking a single religious authority, she builds a hybridic blend of many religious traditions, including centrally heterodox and hermetic ones. This cosmopolitanism, I believe, is the secret to the poem's appeal to students today. In its engagement with war and peace, *Tril-*

ogy is profoundly antiauthoritarian and antifundamentalist, building a hope for peace out of the mystic's sense that there are multiple pathways to the divine. No one culture, no one religion, no one vision has an exclusive pipeline to truth or redemption.

Trilogy emerges out of the crucible of World War II, specifically out of London, the center of the once all-powerful British Empire, as it faced the onslaught of the Nazi invasion. For twenty-first-century students, World War II often seems like ancient history, distant not only in temporal terms but also in ethical and political terms, given the ambiguities of the post-9/11 world and worldwide conflict of a different sort. I have found that H.D.'s exploration of war and peace resonates powerfully with these students. But exploring the implications of the poem's geopolitics can also be worthwhile. On the one hand, *Trilogy* anticipates Martin Bernal's *The Black Athena*, with his thesis that ancient Egypt and the regions of the Middle East were essential to classical Greek, Roman, and Western civilizations. *Trilogy*'s religious and cultural syncretism refuses notions of Western exceptionalism or exclusive focus on the Judeo-Christian tradition. Not only is *Trilogy* in tune with the new interest in the three Abrahamic religions, but the poem broadly insists on an embrace of the divine in female as well as male forms and resists fundamentalisms of all kinds. On the other hand, the Egyptian, Middle Eastern, and Mediterranean worlds of the poem remain steadfastly ancient, not contemporary. Does the poem turn a blind eye to the colonialisms of the region before and during World War II, asymmetries of power that continue to affect conflict in the region today? Does the poem's religious syncretism largely bypass Islam as it blends Judaism and Christianity with Greek, Roman, Canaanite, Assyrian, Ionian, and Egyptian religions? Can we read the encounter between Mary and Kaspar in *Trilogy*'s final volume against the grain of the poem's vision and in the context of the meanings of "Arab" and the significance of the veil in Western orientalism?

Reading H.D.'s work through the lens of today's world conflicts is both inevitable and anachronistic. As teachers, we face a double task: to read a poem like *Trilogy* in the context of its own times and in our own and our students' times. We need to ask today's questions of poems of the past as well as the questions of past times. *Trilogy*'s war and peace invites us to do both.

INTERTEXTUAL AND INTERDISCIPLINARY APPROACHES

"She Showed a Way to Penetrate Mystery": Teaching H.D. and Denise Levertov

Donna Krolik Hollenberg

When I teach H.D. and Denise Levertov, I often begin with Levertov's "H.D.: An Appreciation," an essay written in 1969 that emphasizes the late poems in a time when H.D. was known chiefly as an imagist (*Poet*). Levertov's appreciation for H.D.'s long poems lauds the ways they represent the past and present, their musicality, and, most central, their ability to project darkness and mystery (Hollenberg, "'Within the World'" 247). As Levertov puts it, "She showed a way to penetrate mystery; which means, not to flood darkness with light so that darkness is destroyed, but to *enter into* darkness, mystery, so that it is experienced" (*Poet* 246).

This sense of the mysterious is a quality of Levertov's poetry, too. Students can fruitfully delve into the biographical connections between these poets of subsequent generations, H.D.'s influence on modern poetry in general, H.D.'s and Levertov's use of the erotic, their writing in the epic genre, their interest—or lack thereof—in narrative, their use of visual art, and even their fascination with dance. In addition to focusing on what these poets share, students can be prompted to recognize the ways in which Levertov's poetry developed in a direction H.D.'s did not. The title of H.D.'s last book, *Hermetic Definition*, reflects her immersion in magic and the occult as well as a desire to be cloistered. Unlike H.D., Levertov reconciled poetry with political action, becoming "the poet in the world." In her later years, however, even as she remained a political activist, her poetry became more visionary as she moved from agnosticism to Christian faith.

H.D. and Levertov first met in the company of Robert Duncan, when H.D. returned briefly to the United States in 1960 to accept an award in poetry from the American Academy of Arts and Letters—its first to a woman—and Levertov was delighted when H.D. invited her to meet again for tea at H.D.'s hotel. Levertov wrote an effusive letter in response to H.D.'s gift of her roman à clef, *Bid Me to Live (A Madrigal)*, which H.D. inscribed with a line from Levertov's poem "A Ring of Changes." As I have noted elsewhere, both H.D.'s novel and Levertov's poem are about the intertwining of life and work in the marriages of writers, particularly regarding conflict and pain. H.D.'s gesture conveyed to Levertov that "I am a woman writer, like you, and I understand the tensions and complexities of your life" (Hollenberg, "'Within the World'" 248). The ensuing correspondence indicates that the younger Levertov was grateful for attention from such a distinguished reader and role model. She sent H.D. manuscripts of new poems she thought would interest the older poet, including "The Depths," ". . . Else a Great Prince in Prison Lies," "Luxury," "The Thread," "The Presence," "The Grace-Note," and "Matins," all published in *The Jacob's Ladder*. Students may make useful comparisons in reading many of the poems in this volume, which are about the origins, in memory and repressed experience, of dream and vision—themes reminiscent of H.D.

Besides Levertov, many other twentieth-century poets have acknowledged H.D.'s influence in books, essays, reviews, epigraphs, and poems. In North America alone, in addition to Duncan, whose *H.D. Book* is a central contribution to the conceptualization of late modernism, and to the twenty poets and critics included in *H.D. and Poets After* (Hollenberg xi), a list of writers directly influenced by H.D. would include Robin Blaser, George Bowering, Hayden Carruth, Jane Cooper, Robert Creeley, Beverly Dahlen, Diane di Prima, Sandra Gilbert, Judy Grahn, Barbara Guest, Thom Gunn, Donald Hall, Lindy Hough, Susan Howe, Dale Kushner, Dorothy Livesay, Charlotte Mandel, Hilda Morley, John Peck, Robert Pinsky, Joan Rettallack, Adrienne Rich, May Swenson, Lola Lemire Tostevin, Edith Walden, and Anne Waldman. Still others, such as Rita Dove, Louise Glück, and Phillis Levin, have been compared with H.D. by critics (Curry). Topics addressed by these poets—but by no means exhausted by them—include the (female) imagination's responses to extremity and war; the handling of the erotic and the sacred; the role of dream in their work; issues of racial inheritance and gender; poetry's relation to the sister arts of painting, music, and film; and the connections with the Romantic tradition. As Robert Kelly put it, "If ever an American writer unselfconsciously connected our national striving to language, our word-dance, with the whole Western literary tradition—lightly, lightly!—it was H.D." (33).

To use Levertov as an example of H.D.'s legacy, at either the undergraduate or graduate level, an instructor might introduce the poem "September 1961," in which Levertov mourns the absence of Ezra Pound, William Carlos Williams, and H.D. at the end of their lives and contemplates the impact of that absence on the next generation of poets, to which she belonged (*Poet*; Hollenberg, "'Obscure Directions'" 737). This poem was inspired by the news of

H.D.'s muteness before her death, even though, of these modernist precursors, Levertov felt closest to Williams. She had "ambivalent feelings" about Pound, as I have written elsewhere (Hollenberg, "'Obscure Directions'" 737), and her feelings about H.D. were not entirely positive either. As Levertov wrote in a 1997 letter to me, not long before she died, she had had "a reaction" against some of H.D.'s work, particularly her fiction. In this letter, Levertov objected to H.D.'s mythologizing of Hugh Dowding, chief air marshal during the Battle of Britain, which she found "adolescent & silly" (qtd. in Hollenberg, "'Within the World'" 268). This criticism is curious in the light of Levertov's infatuations with younger men, recorded in many poems. Students might consider the title sequence of her book *Life in the Forest*, which is dedicated to "Jon,"

> Brother in dream
> Sometime lover
> Friend
> Imaginer. (113)

What was there about H.D.'s mythologizing of her romantic attachment to the air marshal that unsettled Levertov? And what does her critique of H.D. say about the lingering effects of old assumptions about the sexual and the erotic? about the figure of the muse in literary tradition?

Eros is present in both H.D.'s and Levertov's works, not only as sexuality, but as a multifaceted life force, a primary affirmation that enables spiritual growth. Through an innovative use of the childbirth metaphor, in *Hermetic Definition* H.D. transforms her initially debilitating infatuation with Lionel Durand, a young journalist, into an expression of spiritual ascendancy and poetic power. In fact, as Jane Augustine has pointed out, the title poem enacts one of her profoundest themes, "her desire for a pure and redeemed physical sexuality, sexual union inseparable from divine love" (45). At its close, wrapped in "nun-grey," H.D. achieves the peaceful homecoming of the imagination for which she has prayed (*Hermetic Definition* 55). Indeed, the attitude of prayer pervades the poem, as H.D. recognized, writing to her friend and mentor, Norman Holmes Pearson, that "nothing I ever wrote became such *incantation* such *prière*" (qtd. in Hollenberg, *Between History* 291). Similarly, facing what would prove to be a terminal illness, in *Sands of the Well* Levertov separates the erotic from the sexual. Reading "The Trace," a poem in which Levertov revisits tempestuous friendships with three men, along with one of her several poems about the mystery of divine love, provides a useful basis for students to compare Levertov's relationship to the divine with H.D.'s (70).

Another fruitful area of inquiry is each poet's handling of the long poem, or lyric epic. H.D.'s *Trilogy* is suitable for undergraduate courses, especially since it is available in an annotated edition, and I have included it in survey courses of twentieth-century literature, both British and American. Written during the Blitz in London, it harkens back (in feeling) to World War I as well. I have paired it with Levertov's "Staying Alive," the long documentary poem written during the protests against the Vietnam War (*Poems, 1968–1972*). These poems allow students to consider important questions about the relation between poetry and politics: What is the role of the artist in periods of crisis? What is the impact of ideology (and propaganda) on language? H.D.'s poem also critiques the male-dominated Judeo-Christian religious tradition and invokes a female godhead. While Levertov does not take that direction, there are important references to the Bible in her poem, whose meanings students can explore. They can also productively consider the relative merits of documents compared with symbols as poetic devices. Both poems are highly allusive and resonant, but in different ways.

Levertov certainly had read H.D.'s *Helen in Egypt*, and graduate students respond well to this late, long poem. (Undergraduates often appreciate the recording of H.D. reading the first part [available at *PennSound*]; they immediately understand the feelings she conveys.) Graduate students can compare a part of *Helen in Egypt*—say, part 3, "Eidolon," containing myths about Thetis—with one of Levertov's poetic sequences on biblical legends or events, such as "The Showings: Lady Julian of Norwich, 1342–1416" (*Breathing* 75–82). Just as H.D. entered deeply into classical mythology and transformed it, Levertov reimagines important Christian personages and events in the New Testament. As Levertov put it in the foreword to *The Stream and the Sapphire*, a collection of her poems on religious subjects, she thinks of this practice as "do-it-yourself theology" not unlike "what Ignatius of Loyola recommended in the 'Exercises'" (vii). "Sagesse," part of H.D.'s *Hermetic Definition*, was published in the *Evergreen Review* in 1958, along with Levertov's "Scenes from the Life of the Peppertrees" and poems by Robert Creeley, Edward Dorn, and Kenneth Koch. Graduate students can follow that lead in longer papers on these poets.

Unlike H.D., whose experimental fiction led to a stylistic breakthrough in her long poems, Levertov wrote no novels. Yet there is a strong narrative tendency in Levertov's late poetry that was influenced by thinking seriously about short story form. The sequence "Modulations for Solo Voice" has an epigraph from Carson McCullers's *The Ballad of a Sad Café* (*Life* 66), and Levertov's *Breathing the Water* has an epigraph from Eudora Welty's *The Golden Apples*. The former was written while Levertov was in love with the Australian poet Ian Reid, author of a book on the short story. We must acknowledge, also, that Levertov grew up hearing the great nineteenth-century novelists read aloud by her mother, and she loved, in particular, the works of Anton Chekhov. Students could read her essay on Chekhov, whose "vision of life" Levertov cherished (*Light* 279), and then compare her debt to him with H.D.'s affinity with James Joyce or Dorothy Richardson. Levertov also admired the stories of Katherine Mansfield, another writer of H.D.'s generation, whose work one can think of as imagist prose. Students might also compare the effects on readers of short stories and narrative lyric poems. What impact does silence have, particularly in poetry, and when is less not more?

H.D. and Levertov shared several other interests, including a love of visual art. Works of art, particularly classical sculpture, appear often in the poetry and prose of H.D., who frequented museums in London, Paris, Athens, and New York. Through such films as *Borderline*, she also participated in an exciting phase of art cinema, which was then informed by psychoanalytic theory. Levertov, too, was an art and film lover throughout her life. Until young adulthood, she considered being a painter as well as a poet, and she wrote many poems about paintings, too many to list here. She was also influenced by photography; the group of poems titled "Spinoffs, One," in *Breathing the Water*, is inspired by the photographs of Robert McAfee Brown (9–15). A comparison of the ekphrastic poems of both poets allows students to explore the added dimensions these bring to their poetry.

The two poets' mutual interest in dance is perhaps less well known. H.D.'s poem "The Dancer," with its plea to be "wild and free" (*Collected Poems* 446), seems to anticipate the "open" forms of Levertov and her compatriots in the Black Mountain school of poetry. Levertov studied ballet in her youth and modern dance as an adult; in its free-flowing, "organic form," her poetry lends itself to choreography. Her poem "A Tree Telling of Orpheus" abounds with dance imagery, and, as with H.D.'s "The Dancer," the poem was transitional in her artistic development, written before the sequence "Relearning the Alphabet" (*Relearning* 81–85). Students could develop this topic with special attention to the interplay of sound and syntax in these poems. In "The Dancer," a hymn to Rhodocleia, future goddess of the feminine, H.D.'s speaker is carried out of herself into a new relationship with nature and the divine. In her ecstasy, she becomes "more than human" and is moved to "build an altar" to the gods (*Collected Poems* 443, 450). We find this impulse, a speaker stretching out and up, in Levertov's poem, too. The tree tells of its transformation by the song of Orpheus. It is "wrenched from the earth root after root" and achieves a "new life" (*Relearning* 83, 85). Even when Orpheus leaves, all those trees who have witnessed his presence are changed forever: "But what we have lived / comes back to us. / We see more" (85).

Among the most beautiful and inspiring lines in H.D.'s *Trilogy* is the famous opening of *The Walls Do Not Fall*, written during the bombing of London:

> ruin everywhere, yet as the fallen roof
> leaves the sealed room
> open to the air,
>
> so, through our desolation,
> thoughts stir, inspiration stalks us
> through gloom:
>
> unaware, Spirit announces the Presence;
> shivering overtakes us,
> as of old, Samuel (3)

Like so much of H.D.'s poetry, the passage reconciles contradictory experiences we regularly confront in the world—darkness/light, despondency/inspiration, earth/heaven—in language that mediates between the sacred and the profane. This attempt to reconcile opposing entities is a hallmark of religious experience, writes Mircea Eliade in his book *The Sacred and the Profane: The Nature of Religion*. We find this desire for wholeness in many of Levertov's poems as well, particularly those that consecrate a particular space, be it a mountain or lake, or dramatize an opening that represents the possibility of communication with the sacred like "The Jacob's Ladder" (*Jacob's Ladder* 37). Students could apply Eliade's ideas fruitfully to the work of either poet, for both H.D. and Levertov help us experience mystery. In Levertov's words, it is "the Hiddenness before which man must shed his arrogance" (*Poet* 246).

Robert Duncan's *The H.D. Book*

James Maynard

Many critics and biographers of H.D. have long recognized the scholarly value of Robert Duncan's *The H.D. Book*, published for the first time as a single volume in January 2011 as part of the University of California Press series The Collected Writings of Robert Duncan. Commenting on the number of readers who over the years have credited his critical tribute and creative homage for introducing them to H.D.'s writings, Eileen Gregory has observed that what Duncan's project "has meant for the study of H.D. can hardly be estimated" (Preface). Rachel Blau DuPlessis describes *The H.D. Book* as "a major meditation on modernism, the impact of *Trilogy* and H.D." (*H.D.: The Career* 144). Reflecting on his experience of discovering the first published installment of *The H.D. Book*, the poet Robert Kelly identifies it as "one of the greatest repertories of critical insight and poetics [he'd] ever read" (44). Mary S. Mathis and Michael King go so far as to call it "the most extraordinary continuing critical and aesthetic attention to H.D.'s work" (393). Given the project's initial piecemeal publication in mostly little magazines, however, the full text of Duncan's study of H.D. has yet to find wide inclusion in the average classroom. In what follows, therefore, I would like to introduce *The H.D. Book*, focusing on its particular contributions as a form of writing and thinking about poetry and poetics while highlighting its potential pedagogical value for students and teachers of H.D.

The H.D. Book belongs to that mercurial genre of formally innovative, often highly personalized critical studies written by poets. Such a line in the American tradition—the basis for an exciting upper-level or graduate course—includes William Carlos Williams's *In the American Grain*, Charles Olson's *Call Me Ishmael*, Louis Zukofsky's *Bottom: On Shakespeare*, and Susan Howe's *My Emily Dickinson*. An encyclopedic reading of Duncan's life in poetry, *The H.D. Book* incorporates aspects of autobiography, biography, literary explication, accounts of transatlantic modernism, protogender studies, process-oriented philosophy and aesthetics, comparisons of poetry and psychoanalysis, a defense of pluralism and heterodoxy, studies of religion and the occult, a dream diary, responses to Cold War politics, and a history of the spirit of romance. As Susan Stanford Friedman rightly observes, the multidiscursive prose of *The H.D. Book* is in many ways "influenced or foreshadowed" by H.D.'s "generic hybrids" *Tribute to Freud* and *The Gift* (*Penelope's Web* 285). Occupying a central place in each of these threads is Duncan's reading of H.D., which, like his poetry, continually emphasizes its inexhaustibility. The central method of the book, if one can speak of it as having such, is establishing a network of potentially significant associations and contexts that keep the meanings of H.D.'s texts alive. For those who recognize this process as fundamentally related to the activity of teaching literature, *The H.D. Book* stands as a model for the work of the classroom.

Duncan began working on *The H.D. Book* in 1960, shortly after he and Denise Levertov visited with H.D. in May at the Stanhope Hotel in New York, where she was staying when she returned to the United States to receive the American Academy of Arts and Letters poetry award. In April of that year Duncan had visited Norman Holmes Pearson at Yale, where he gave a reading and taught a graduate class. Afterward, Pearson wrote H.D. to report that Duncan had "an uncanny understanding of what [she was] after" (Hollenberg, *Between History* 270). Pearson and H.D. had previously been impressed with Duncan's review of her *Selected Poems* in *Poetry* in 1958 ("In the Sight"), and, as Duncan writes later, the first idea of *The H.D. Book* "had been commissiond by Norman Holmes Pearson as a Book for H.D.'s Birthday" ("H.D. Book: Outline").[1] Most of the initial writing of *The H.D. Book* was done between 1960 and 1961, with revisions and additions to certain sections made in 1963 and 1964. Over the years, subsequent chapters appeared in some of the most important little magazines of the 1960s, 1970s, and 1980s, including *Coyote's Journal*, *Caterpillar*, *Sumac*, and *Credences*, as well as such established university publications as *Chicago Review* and the *Southern Review*. For courses focusing on the material history of twentieth-century literature, these magazines and literary journals provide an interesting counterpoint to such modernist publications as *Life and Letters To-day* and the *Egoist* (of which H.D. was an assistant editor) that published H.D.'s work a generation before Duncan.

As a pedagogical resource, *The H.D. Book* offers a series of readings of H.D.'s work and her development as a poet, a retelling of American modernism that places her at the center, an intervention into early New Critical dismissals of her writing, an alternative to Bloomian models of poetic influence as struggle, and an exploration of poetry and the feminine. Throughout the various chapters, Duncan continually develops a poetics of initiation—not in terms of indoctrination, since he rails against dogma and convention, but rather as a sense of beginnings, the title of part 1. Thus the writing shifts back and forth between different levels of initiation, into H.D.'s writing specifically, but also more generally into language as a communal consciousness and into poetry as a historic evolution of forms. Indeed, much of Duncan's thinking about historical being pertains to locating oneself in a nexus of traditions, and so he derives his poetics from the writing of H.D. The first chapter of *The H.D. Book* opens with a scene of instruction and personal discovery to which many students can relate: Duncan's introduction to H.D.'s poem "Heat" as a high school student in Bakersfield, California, in the mid-1930s, a text shared by a beloved teacher not as part of an institutionally regulated middle-class upbringing but rather as "a personal revelation" or cathexis (38). What unfolds is a long and complex reading of H.D.'s work that, regardless of its shifts and errancies, continues to proceed on the trail of a secret message at first only dimly intuited and to emphasize poetry's subversive marginality, which Duncan often associates with the cultural position of the feminine.

Starting from the iconic imagism of H.D.'s early poems, Duncan traces her career through the temporal, biographical, and cultural palimpsests found in stories like "Murex" (from *Palimpsest*) and "Narthex"; the political turmoil and social alienation of the war years in London; the value of poetic fictions in texts like *Helen in Egypt*; and H.D.'s relationships with Bryher and Sigmund Freud. Duncan focuses at length on the complexity and inclusiveness of the writings collected in *Trilogy*. It was "The War Trilogy," he wrote H.D. on 20 July 1959, that "made it possible, gave a link in a tradition, for me to follow lines of my inheritance within the main body of a given poetics" (Bertholf 9). Together with *The Cantos*, *Paterson*, *The Waste Land*, and *Finnegans Wake*, Duncan examines *Trilogy* as an example of what he calls "poems of a world-mind in process" (*H.D. Book* 196). Addressing *Trilogy* as the poetic response to a series of personal and historical crises, Duncan concludes part 2, chapter 6, of *The H.D. Book* with the following observation:

> The sense that "we are at the cross-roads" then has structural as well as historical and psychological meaning in The War Trilogy. Given the name *Imagiste*, H.D. was never satisfied that it meant what she seemed to think it meant, and even after her analysis with Freud, she did not rest with the Freudian image but went on to the *eidola* of *Helen in Egypt*. What was required was that there be the full power of a double meaning, that the real refuse to be defined. In word and image and then in story her sense was always that "the tide is turning." (426)

Such a reading restores a certain historical prominence to H.D. in opposition to the New Critical dismissals of her by Dudley Fitts and Randall Jarrell, both of whom Duncan explicitly refutes. From a more general perspective of H.D.'s historical reception, moreover, Friedman, writing in the mid-1970s, credits Duncan as one of the "few people [who even] read her poetry" ("Who" 47).

In keeping the terms of "the real" open against the increased commodification of daily life under the modern war state, H.D.—along with Ezra Pound, William Carlos Williams, D. H. Lawrence, and to some extent T. S. Eliot and James Joyce—stands as one of the central figures of what Duncan variously describes as a Romantic or visionary modernism. Crediting "that group of poets printing in the pages of *The Egoist* between 1914 and 1917" with "the beginning of a phase in poetry that has not ended," Duncan places not only himself but also his contemporaries in a direct line with H.D. and her extended company:

> For my own generation, our elders—for me, specifically Pound, H.D., Williams, and Lawrence—remain primary generative forces. Their threshold remains ours. The time of war and exploitation, the infamy and lies of the new capitalist war-state, continue. And the answering intensity of the imagination to hold its own values must continue. (*H.D. Book* 183)

Having traced the work of these modern "elders" to a historical context of spiritual and cultural impoverishment and having witnessed the imagination continuing to be under threat at mid-century from a host of repressive sources,

Duncan positions his "own generation" as direct inheritors of a political struggle to counteract alienation through a participation in the life of poetry capable of reimagining the real to include all that has been excluded. The result is not just a fascinating study of H.D. but also an open and exploratory enactment of a poetics.

The complete edition of *The H.D. Book*, published in 2011 by the University of California Press, gathers together for the first time all the chapters of parts 1 and 2 and a transcription from Duncan's notebook of a preliminary draft of part 3 (as an appendix). Duncan revised his works actively and often, and in this volume the editors Michael Boughn and Victor Coleman "interpolate *all* changes that were made . . . on all available manuscripts" to present a text "as close as possible to the state it was in when Duncan stopped working on it" (17). The result is a complete and accessible edition that includes the editors' useful introduction to the text and Duncan's working process, a composition and publication history for each chapter, a list of the many books cited, and select images of Duncan's manuscripts from his archive in the Poetry Collection at the University at Buffalo. Reproduced below, a list of this publication history draws the peculiar arc of *The H.D. Book*'s serialization while providing a glimpse into an overlapping community of little magazines associated generally with the New American and Black Mountain poetries of the 1960s and 1970s in which many readers first encountered Duncan's writing.

Part 1: Beginnings

Chapter 1. "Beginnings. Chapter 1 of the H.D. Book Part 1." *Coyote's Journal* 5-6 (1966): 8–31.
Chapter 2. "The H.D. Book, Part I: Chapter 2." *Coyote's Journal* 8 (1967): 27–35.
Chapter 3. "Two Chapters from *H.D.*" *TriQuarterly* 12.2 (1968): 67–82.
Chapter 4. "Two Chapters from *H.D.*" *TriQuarterly* 12.2 (1968): 82–98.
Chapter 5. "The H.D. Book: Chapter 5." *Aion: A Journal of Traditionary Science* 1 (1964): [7–29]; rpt. as "From the *H.D. Book*. Part 1: Beginnings. Chapter 5. Occult Matters." *Stony Brook* 1-2 (1968): 4–19.
Chapter 6. "Rites of Participation." *Caterpillar* 1 (1967): 6–29; 2 (1968): 125–54.

Part 2: Nights and Days

Excerpts from Part 2 selected by Cid Corman. "From the Day Book." *Origin* 2nd ser. 10 (1963): 1–47.
Chapter 1. "Nights and Days. Chapter One." *Sumac* 1.1 (1968): 101–46.

Chapter 2. "The H.D. Book. Part II *Nights and Days*: Chapter 2." *Caterpillar* 6 (1969): 16–38.

Chapter 3. "The H.D. Book, Part 2, Chapter 3." *Io* 6 (1969): 117–40.

Chapter 4. "The H.D. Book: Part II. Nights and Days. Chapter 4." *Caterpillar* 7 (1969): 27–60.

Chapter 5. "From the H.D. Book, Part II Chapter 5." *Stony Brook* 3-4 (1969): 336–47; *Credences* 1.2 (1975): 50–52; rpt. (with additional material) as "From the *H.D. Book*, Part II, Chapter 5." *Sagetrieb* 4.2-3 (1985): 39–85.

Chapter 6. "H.D. Book: Book II, Chapter 6." *Southern Review* 21.1 (1985): 26–48.

Chapter 7. "Chapter 7 Part Two." *Credences* 1.2 (1975): 53–67.

Chapter 8. "Chapter 8 Part Two." *Credences* 1.2 (1975): 68–94.

Chapter 9. "The H.D. Book. Part Two: Nights and Days Chapter 9." *Chicago Review* 30.3 (1979): 37–88.

Chapter 10. "The H.D. Book Part II Chapter 10." *Ironwood* 22 (1983): 47–64.

Chapter 11. "Glimpses of the Last Day [from Chapter 11 of the H.D. Book]." *Io* 10 (1971): 212–15; rpt. (with additional material) as "From The H.D. Book Part Two: Nights and Days Chapter 11." *Montemora* 8 (1981): 79–113.

NOTE

[1] These epistolary relationships between Duncan and H.D. and between H.D. and Pearson can be triangulated using Robert J. Bertholf's *A Great Admiration: H.D. / Robert Duncan Correspondence, 1950–1961* and Donna Krolik Hollenberg's *Between History and Poetry: The Letters of H.D. and Norman Holmes Pearson*.

Teaching H.D. in the Creative Writing Classroom

Heather H. Thomas

> The muse is one of the major emotional institutions of poet and poem-making.
>
> —Rachel Blau DuPlessis, *The Pink Guitar*

As a memoir of artistic awakening, H.D.'s *The Gift* represents her childhood discovery and mature understanding of her creative gifts. The narrator's double voice across time also positions *The Gift* as a spiritual autobiography. Speaking with inquisitive wonder as a child in the Moravian enclave of Bethlehem, Pennsylvania, and with the wisdom of a mature poet under siege during the Nazi bombardment of London, H.D. seeks to discover the mystical gift of her heritage. This quest uncovers long-buried family secrets, including the suppression of her mother's artistic gifts. *The Gift* dramatizes moments when the child Hilda discovers a new way of seeing herself, others, and the world. This changed perspective sparks the imaginative transformations eventually spelled out in her poetry and prose.

In re-creating H.D.'s Pennsylvania roots and the formation of the child Hilda, *The Gift* reinscribes the family as empowering rather than suffocating in Victorian constraints and Moravian religious tradition (Friedman, *Penelope's Web* 330). Writing this book as bombs fall around her, H.D. also demonstrates creativity as an act of survival amid the wartime threat of death. These transformative struggles achieve the "(re)creation of the poet who writes *Trilogy*," the epic poem of World War II written during the same period as *The Gift* (350). For creative writers, *The Gift* offers a rare model of how the creative process begins in acts of attention that charge the imagination, how sensory perception and memory provide vital raw materials transformed in the process of writing, and how this process generates creative work.

Given the difficulty of her modernist poetry, H.D.'s visionary writing project may seem unlikely to engage creative writing students. Yet students respond to the emotional intensity and complexity of her work, and when prompted to read more closely, they learn a fundamental writing lesson: it is not abstraction or big ideas that make a poem effective but the chiseled materials of precise, condensed, concrete language. Students notice how H.D.'s use of clear diction placed in surprising contexts avoids anything predictable. Her work provokes students to seek the fresh turn of phrase and, beyond this, to articulate the unsayable within themselves, the other side of utterance waiting to be voiced on the page.

Creativity Narrative

As material for reflection and writing, *The Gift* is a *Künstlerroman* demonstrating an artist's recognition of her childhood discovery of the creative process. It has relevance for students learning to connect with their own creativity and to trust the creative process. Chapter 1, "Dark Room," provides students with several approaches to discovering and inventing a creativity narrative, a story or prose unfolding of their awakening to the role and value of the creative process. H.D. describes the creative process as a physical, psychological, and spiritual struggle with all these forces "*pressed down and shaken together, and running over*" (50).[1] This convergence of urgencies occurs in "the dark-room of memory" where one's treasure trove of images and mental pictures, under the pressure of the senses and imagination, is constantly being transformed. But we must train ourselves to notice this mysterious process. It is made difficult by the burial of our creative gifts under years of social strictures. It is in

> all these bone boxes, these *coffres fort* [strong boxes, safe-deposit boxes] or the *camera obscura* where our living inheritance is stored . . . buried under the accumulated rubble of prescribed thinking, of inevitable social pruning and trimming of emotion and imagination. (50)

Camera obscura means "dark chamber"; this early version of the modern camera consisted of a small darkened room with light admitted through a single tiny hole. Given that the image projected on a wall was upside down, the way through this chamber, at least for writers, must involve the "spell" of words. As H.D. explains, "A word opens a door or just a few remembered facts doled out, apparently indifferently or received apparently with little or no interest, become later, a clue, a focus, a centre or node for the growing branches of ideas or imaginative speculations" (51).

When the child Hilda witnesses a dramatization of Harriet Beecher Stowe's novel *Uncle Tom's Cabin* performed on a local stage, the darkness of the theater is like "the dark-room of memory," showing "continuous images like a moving-picture," where we can "watch people enter a room, leave a room, to watch, not only those people enter and leave a room, but to watch the child watching them" (50). As the play unfolds on stage, "the film unrolls" in her head as Hilda sees her life transformed through the artist's eye into material for creative composition (53).

Hilda's creative awakening also taps into a deep well of conflicted feeling about the mysteries of her family life and her place in it. A special, secret agency, a sense of her difference in a newly empowering way, as her "gift," stirs in her. At the same time, her empathic understanding of others, including her parents, also blossoms. In the construction of her memoir and her myth, H.D. represents this awakening as a defining moment that gives birth to the poet. The following four prompts based on passages from this scene highlight phases for students in the process of this "dawn of art" (47).

Prompt 1: "[T]hat aisle *all at once, was the same as the aisle in Church" (46).* Hilda compares the theater with church, another place where routine habits of mind are interrupted and imagination, or spirit, is unleashed. Even as the amateur quality of the production at times ruptures her suspension of disbelief, the theater is a magical place where life is transformed into art. Being in this special, even sacred, unfamiliar place awakens an urgent alertness, and Hilda notices the scene around her as well as the scene on stage with sharpened powers of attention and observation. Comparing the theater with a church implies that the creative process is a valuable way of getting beyond the "rubble of prescribed thinking" to a way of seeing that can prompt a poem (50).

Recall a time when you were in a new or unfamiliar place. Describe this place. What happened there? What felt familiar amid the strangeness? Write about this place or experience as it might be associated with sparking a changed way of seeing yourself, another, or the world around you.

Prompt 2: "The theatre was dark and the lights . . . were like ours in Church, when we sit in rows . . . and the Sisters walk down the aisles to hand the candles to the children" (46). Hilda's recollection of a Moravian ritual of lighting the literal darkness implies the dilemma of darkness incumbent in a creative or spiritual struggle. "What do we fear when, in solitude, we fear absolute darkness?" Susan Stewart asks in her work exploring the origins of poetry. We fear, Stewart says, "that the darkness will not end" (1). To counter this oblivion, to light the darkness, is to do the "cultural, or form-giving work of poetry . . . the production of a form that enters into the transforming life of language" (2). Metaphorically we might think of the candle as an instrument for writing the light within, an illuminated pen for writing word pictures in the dark room of memory.

Describe what it feels like to be in the dark by comparing it with something else. How does the darkness look? sound? feel to the touch? What is it made of? Where is a light in that darkness? What is the source of the light? Think of yourself in relation to this light. Where is the light inside you?

Prompt 3: "[I]n the light of the play itself, the details of the parade came into different perspective, everything came true" (47). When the play ends and Hilda goes outside, the street looks different ("really everything would always be different" [47]). She recalls the cast's parade through the streets of Bethlehem the previous day. In a voice fusing childhood wonder with adult wisdom, she observes:

> I know it was only Little Eva in a jerry-built, gold chariot, and yet it was the very dawn of art, it was the sun, the drama, the theatre, it was poetry,

> why, it was music, it was folk-lore and folk-song, it was history. . . . [T]he three children . . . who stood watching, were all the children of all the world. (47)

The magnitude and power of aesthetic experience to change oneself through one's point of view are conveyed here. Art becomes a force for empathy and connection. As she writes this childhood memoir during the London Blitz, H.D. envisions a world of peace as an antidote to the reality of bombs falling around her.

Write out in detail a time when you awakened to the importance of a book, film, art work, or song. How did this aesthetic experience change you? What did it provide for you at the time? In retrospect, how is this insight significant?

Prompt 4: "There would be someone else who was myself" (48). When Uncle Tom has a vision of Little Eva after she has died, Hilda is reminded of a princess in her storybook. She mentally projects the image of herself as Little Eva or a princess with golden curls, although Hilda has "short hair with, at best, mousy duck-tails at the nape of the neck" (48). When the play ends and she goes home, her heightened awareness persists. She begins to see herself as a character and her home as a stage for the family drama. Besides imaginative identification and projection, this experience demonstrates artistic invention and a form of play. Hilda invents her own play, noticing how the faces of the family, under the lamps, appear different, as faces did in the glow of the theater's footlights.

Look at a picture. What part or element of the picture speaks to you? Imaginatively project yourself into the picture. What part do you play? What do you do or say? Imagine yourself as a character in your life. What scene comes to mind? Write down all the details. What do you see, hear, touch, feel, smell, and taste? Who else is there? What happens? What is your felt sense about why this scene is important?

Poetry Writing

H.D.'s early poems from *Sea Garden*—available in *Collected Poems, 1912–1944*—have long provided anthologized models for teaching early-twentieth-century imagism. An introduction to the three principles of imagism will give students an approach to poem making that remains relevant today: direct treatment of an object, spare language, and rhythm based on music. These principles enumerate fundamental lessons to "show, don't tell"; compress the language; and tune the ear to the rhythms and music of speech. Even as H.D.'s later poems stretch far beyond this prescription, her imagist poems also escaped its limits. Unpacking Ezra Pound's definition of the image in "A Retrospect"—"an intellectual and emotional complex in an instant of time" (*Literary Essays* 4)—can help students understand that imagism, while grounded in concrete diction and concision, was actually a "visionary enterprise" (Longenbach 108).

Approaching poetry writing in this context, teachers can "make it new" (to quote Pound) by challenging students' received ideas of metaphor and personification to avoid prefabricated retreads of "grim reaper" or "happy daffodil" verse. In a rigorous avoidance of cliché, students' "visions" will have to be fresh. A discussion of "Garden," for example, can show H.D.'s radical revision of the rose, a rupture of the predictable symbolism of delicate feminine beauty and love. Students can identify the surprising and unconventional figuration of the rose as ice, hail, rock, and a stone sculpture (*Collected Poems* 24–25).

"Garden" focuses on small natural objects—the rose, pears, grapes—or on large, uncontainable natural forces like heat and wind, figured in comparison with small things, such as tattered fabric. The images are often partial: petals of the rose, points of pears, the roundness of grapes. H.D. employs synesthesia, mixing the senses of sight and touch in the figure of heat as "thick air" that "presses up and blunts / the points of pears / and rounds the grapes" and that is cut into "tatters" by the wind (25). Through an implied metaphor, the wind is both small scissors and a large "plough." The poem's closure, an image of the wind-plough "turning" the heat-blanket over, suggests a reading apt for creative writers (25). Through inventive technique, H.D.'s stirring turns of language transform ordinary things before our eyes, prompting us to see anew the transformative possibilities of language.

But H.D.'s speaker in "Garden" struggles to stir herself. Static and lethargic, she appeals to the wind to open a way out of this oppressive garden and toward agency. The metaphors also illustrate the poem's intellectual and emotional complex. Here is the juxtaposition of a stifled, beleaguered, passive person with her vitally active and willful imagination. It is a complex audible in the shifts of voice from an apathetic tone to one that appeals or commands and in the sentence style that shifts from the conditional to the imperative.

Exercise 1: Image Invention

Have students bring a natural object to class or choose a small object that they have with them. Ask each one to show his or her chosen object and to tell both a predictable image or association and a contrasting fresh image or association. Then have them track the object through the senses of sight, sound, smell, taste, and touch, listing descriptive phrases, images, and verbal associations and making comparisons through metaphor or simile. Explain and illustrate synesthesia as a transfer or mix of the senses ("sharp barks," "heat's tatters") and have students write at least one example.

After they have contemplated the object, ask students to draft a short word-picture poem for a sightless person. They might approach this draft by circling four details or images that interest them and using one detail or image in each line or by finding a series of related details or images, then focusing the poem around these phrases. For revision, use the principles of imagism as a framework. Remind them of Pound's advice to "go in fear of abstractions" and to concentrate on concrete diction (*Literary Essays* 5).

H.D.'s poems brim with turns and crossings, feats of altered seeing, identification with an other, and projection into intersubjective relationships, sometimes through mask, metaphor, or personification. Her early Greek personas give way to transformative identifications with small creatures. Her voices range from personal to prophetic, intimate to bardic, and often employ shifting perspectives. In the 1930s poem "Sigil," contemplative analysis and close observation of parts foster intimacy and shift the reader's perspective. As the speaker directs you to "pull dry sea-weed from the sand" and examine it, "your eyes // look out as they did here" (*Collected Poems* 412). The perspective shifts from sky to beach and then underground, as the speaker "perceiv[es] the other-side of everything" (413).

In the well-known fourth section of *Trilogy*'s *The Walls Do Not Fall*, H.D. figures the mollusk as a "stone marvel" whose shell protects it from the mighty, battering "sea thrust" (8). Then the speaker projects herself into the creature, an oyster, and speaks from within the shell. The shift from third-person outside observer to first-person interior occupant of the thing observed initiates a voice of prophetic wisdom. This voice issues not from grandiosity but from a creature considered humble or insignificant, yet with transformative inner resources of great value. H.D.'s refiguration of the pearl as a self-constructed soul occurs through turns that take the speaker from the exterior of the small shell into its tiny interior, and then back out with a changed, enlarged vision. Singular and focused at first, the perspective of the speaker multiplies as she crosses boundaries (self, self-out-of-self, selfless), moving fluidly between inner and outer worlds. The poem inscribes a place between these boundaries, an intersubjective space that contains something of the speaker and the oyster, but is itself other, the third inscribed space of the poem.

Exercise 2: Borderlines

This exercise works well with a natural object. If possible, send students outside to find something—a twig, stone, leaf, petal, or shell, whatever they find or finds them. You might frame this as a search for their natural "gift," something with which they spontaneously connect or would consider giving to another as a metaphorical part of themselves.

Have students show the object and identify one aspect, quality, or element that intrigues or appeals to them, then write a word picture describing the object in detail and drawing images from each of their senses. Ask students to write a memory chain for a few minutes: for example, "The leaf reminds me of ______, which reminds me of ______, which reminds me of ______," and so forth.

In addition to undertaking observation and memory work, students should interact with the object to discover a metaphorical relation with it. They will want to notice what happens in the flow of perception and thought as it moves from outside to inside, from exteriority to interiority, or the other way around, inside-outside. Through this process, the borderlines of perception and thought open and converge. Students can explore the crosscurrents, intersections, and imaginative points where inner and outer worlds meet.

To illustrate the process of writing from shifting borderlines, refer students to section 4 of *The Walls Do Not Fall* and take as an example H.D.'s shifting speaker position in relation to the oyster shell and the pearl. Ask students to write in response to the following: Where are you in the object? Within its natural environment, where are you? In what part, aspect, or element of the object might you find yourself? What happens then? Finally, to prompt them to write from the inside out, ask them, Where is the object inside you? What part of your body connects with the object? What happens then?

As they compose their poems, encourage students to use imagery from at least two senses, details from two different memories, and shifting perspectives of outside and inside in the poem's interaction with the object. As they revise, urge students to use precise words and images, omit clichés and all unnecessary words, and chisel the lines and stanzas with shape, sound, and rhythm in mind.

Teaching H.D.'s work in the creative writing classroom provides students with an astonishing range of opportunity to learn and practice new reading and writing strategies. Inspiring, relevant, and useful in both undergraduate and graduate classes, H.D.'s work fosters a fruitful inquiry into voice, language, and form. Her work also catalyzes students' discoveries about themselves, others, and the world through instances of attention to the senses, memory, and empathy—powerful tools for creative writers. Exploring this major modernist's work in both memoir and poetry enables a breadth of understanding about H.D. as a writer, a sense of what Rachel Blau DuPlessis has called "the career of that struggle." H.D.'s signature engagement with the process of imaginative transformation—the "spell . . . in every sea-shell" (*Collected Poems* 512)—invites students to explore possibilities in language and to engage in the transformation of familiar forms wherever the "spell" of writing may lead them.

NOTE

[1] All quotations from *The Gift* are from Jane Augustine's edition.

Projecting H.D.: Film, Criticism, and Visual Culture

Rachel Connor

In 1929, H.D. responded to a questionnaire for the *Little Review*, "I spend literally hours alone in my apartment making the mountains and village streets and my own acquaintances reel past me in light and light and light" ("Confessions-Questionnaire" 364). Her commentary on watching what were essentially home movies locates H.D. as a fascinated spectator, and yet she was intimately acquainted with the technical apparatus of film. We know from her correspondence that she had learned how to operate her daughter's "magic lantern" and had "peeled and prepared" the reels herself (Connor 107).

This essay reveals the scope and some of the complexities of H.D.'s engagement with film and contextualizes it within debates and developments in visual culture during the 1920s and 1930s. Between 1927 and 1933, H.D. appeared in films and edited them. She collaborated in the production of *Close Up*, a quarterly journal promoting serious intellectual debate about cinema, and was a regular contributor: in the journal's six-year life span, H.D. wrote two poems about film, three theoretical essays, and eight reviews.

H.D.'s involvement in film unquestionably defined the aesthetics of her poetry and prose, as Charlotte Mandel has argued ("Garbo/Helen"). And although this introductory essay does not analyze these texts in any detail, it offers several suggestions for intertextual approaches to H.D.'s work, promoting a fruitful mediation between the fields of literature and film.[1]

Filmmaking: "A Meticulous Jigsaw Puzzle Technique"

In 1927, along with her lovers Bryher and Kenneth Macpherson, H.D. established the independent film company POOL Productions. With a small budget and simple apparatus, they made four films; the first two—*Wing Beat* (1927) and *Foothills* (1929)—were shot with a handheld Debrie model L camera. POOL's aesthetic was primarily influenced by Soviet cinema and German expressionism, the work of directors like Robert Wiene (*The Cabinet of Dr Caligari* [1920]), Fritz Lang (*Metropolis* [1927]), F. W. Murnau (*Nosferatu* [1922]), and G. W. Pabst (*Secrets of a Soul* [1926], *The Loves of Jeanne Ney* [1928], and *Pandora's Box* [1929]). These films employed dark sets, heavy framing, and techniques such as extreme close-up, intercutting, and montage to explore the characters' interiority. POOL drew self-consciously on these same techniques; indeed, *Foothills* (in which H.D. takes the part of a city woman visiting the countryside) explicitly borrows the plot of Murnau's *Sunrise* (1927).

After *Foothills* POOL went on to make the short *Monkey's Moon* (1929), a copy of which was found in 2009 and can now be viewed at the Beinecke

Library's Web site. In 1930, POOL completed *Borderline*, the only one of its full-length films still existing in its entirety. Set in a Swiss mountain village, *Borderline* explores the neurotic relationship between white lovers Thorne and Astrid (played by H.D.) and another couple, a mixed-race woman (Adah) and a black man (Pete), played by the celebrated singer and actor Paul Robeson. From our postmodern, multicultural perspective, it is difficult to imagine how *Borderline*'s subject matter would have been considered so contentious. Yet it would have been seen as shocking, if not explosive, in an early-twentieth-century context in which migrants of color had not yet begun to arrive en masse in Europe and in a culture of racial segregation in the United States.

Several critics have analyzed the film's problematic racial politics. It is not my task here to repeat that analysis, but it is worth commenting briefly on how the film's liberal treatment of black identity is potentially and ironically undermined by its experimentalism—in particular, by the eroticism of H.D.'s response to Robeson, whom she likens in the film's explanatory pamphlet to a bronze statue. In the close-up shots of Pete, H.D. states, "[A] head is sculptured, gouged out in planes and focus of light and shadow and inset with eyes like those Mena period Egyptian heads with amber glass" ("The *Borderline* Pamphlet" 227). H.D.'s intention is to draw analogies between film and sculpture—Macpherson, as director, she says, "sculpts literally with light" (227). Yet her description serves perhaps to romanticize—and therefore objectify—the black male body in a similar way to that of her poem written in 1931, "Red Roses for Bronze" (*Collected Poems* 211).

Borderline abounds with close-ups of hands and faces. H.D. frequently adopts this same technique of intense focus in her prose, particularly in her representation of the troubled female psyche in the novels of the *Asphodel* cycle (*HERmione*, *Paint It Today*, and *Asphodel*), on which she was working during the 1920s. The most striking cinematic device employed in *Borderline*, though, is montage. Sections of the film move swiftly and repeatedly between characters, inviting comparisons between their consciousness and experience. At the point at which Pete and Adah embrace, for example, the image of Pete is intercut with shots of a fast-moving waterfall. This effect is produced not by superimposition but by the painstaking method of "clatter montage," which H.D. describes as "the meticulous cutting of three and four and five inch lengths of film and pasting these tiny strips together" ("*Borderline* Pamphlet" 230).

In the accompanying pamphlet to *Borderline*, H.D. compares the film's cinematographic devices with Sergei Eisenstein's technical ingenuity achieved in *October* (1928). Specifically, she discusses a dramatic war sequence in which Eisenstein achieves "the lightning-like effect of repeated firing" through intensive editing: "the lift, fire pause, lift, fire etcetera, were repeated in metronomic precision," H.D. writes, "and the effect was produced by the cutting and fitting of minute strips of soldier, gun, gun-fire, soldier, gun" ("*Borderline* Pamphlet" 230). It is clear from H.D.'s "Autobiographical Notes" that she had firsthand knowledge of such techniques and that she and Bryher were responsible for much of the technical work on *Borderline*: "when finished [shooting the film] K[enneth Macpherson] develops a bad throat and Bryher and I work over the strips, doing the montage as K indicates . . . very hard work" (qtd. in Connor 24). One possible direction for study of H.D.'s work, then, might be to consider how her technical expertise in filmmaking—intercutting, splicing, focus on the close-up image—illuminates the reading of her literary texts.

Borderline was screened in thirty to forty art houses in England, France, Germany, Scotland, Belgium, Spain, Holland, and Denmark, but because of its technical innovation and radical subject matter, it was not a commercial success. It was never shown in the United States, despite plans to do so, because its interracial relationship could not pass United States Customs (Debo, "Interracial Modernism" 380). To the enormous advantage of students and teachers of H.D. today, *Borderline* has been digitally remastered. Previously only viewable in archives, the film is now readily available for purchase or hire both in the United States and the United Kingdom. As a result, *Borderline* can assume its place as a key text, not just in the H.D. canon but in the broader fields of cinema and modernism. *Borderline* provides an excellent case study for the discussion of early cinematography and, in cultural studies, for an analysis of discourses of sexuality and race. It has a place, too, in debates about the politics of modernist cinema—specifically in the (arguably artificial) construction of the polarity between high art and popular culture, to which this essay now turns.

Film Writing: Close Up, *Sound, and Internationalism*

H.D.'s involvement in cinema coincided with the rise of the Hollywood studio system and the growing commercialization of the American film industry. It is into this climate in 1927 that *Close Up* was born, a journal founded by POOL and distributed from Europe that sought both to counter the cultural dominance of American film and to celebrate film as a serious art form. As already discussed, POOL greatly valued the German expressionists, particularly Pabst, whose *Joyless Street* (1925) H.D. claimed as the film that was most influential on her thinking about cinema.

Set in Vienna during a time of acute poverty and hyperinflation, *Joyless Street*—as its name might imply—employs a dark urban setting, as well as close framing devices of its central female characters, one of whom is played by Greta Garbo. The plot pivots around the dilemma of one of these women over whether to prostitute herself to the local butcher in return for food. It is the character played by Garbo who remains morally upright, resisting temptation and so evoking the spectator's sympathy.

Pabst's film—and Garbo's appearance in it—was the subject of H.D.'s first essay for *Close Up*. In the first installment of "The Cinema and the Classics," on beauty, H.D. compares Garbo's appearance in *Joyless Street* with her role, after her move to Hollywood, in *The Torrent* (1926). H.D. delivers a blistering critique of the commercial values represented by American film. In *Joyless Street*, she argues, Garbo is a "Nordic flower," a "camellia" who demonstrates "icy mermaid-like integrity" (109); in *The Torrent* she has been made up to act the part of a black-eyed "vamp" with artificial eyelashes and a "black dyed wig" (107). Underpinning this examination of cultural politics is the issue of how femininity is constructed. Arguably, H.D.'s association of femininity with purity and whiteness is problematic, yet the trope appears to have haunted her throughout her career. Her late revisionist poem *Helen in Egypt* (1961) draws heavily on this central image of transformation from "purity" to dark-eyed vamp when the iconic Helen takes up a "blackened stick" to disguise her eyes and is "transformed" into Isis (16). In *Borderline*, H.D.'s portrayal of the neurotic, kohl-eyed Astrid perhaps owes something to her reading of Garbo's transformation, for, as Susan McCabe argues, H.D.'s performance of the "femme noire" locates Astrid as a "monstrous figure haunting the modernist male psyche" (*Cinematic Modernism* 181).

A key issue covered in *Close Up*'s pages was the resistance to sound technology in film, which grew steadily more sophisticated through the lifespan of the journal. *Close Up* objected not to sound, however, but to the introduction of speech. In the earliest talkies, reproduction quality was so low that the voice sounded unnatural, prompting resentment of the technology as well as the industry behind it. The fear was that film would become homogenized, that "the novelty of hearing people talk would put an end to visual experimentation," and that the integrity and coherence of the film would be disrupted (Forbes and Street 30). The "inner speech" invoked through montage in silent film would disappear.

The third installment of the "Cinema and the Classics" essay, "The Mask and the Movietone," is H.D.'s personal response to synchronized sound in film. Having the aural and the visual senses evoked simultaneously, she implies, serves only to reveal the mechanism by which the film is made:

> Voice follows face, face follows voice, face and voice with all their subtle blending are accurately and mechanically welded. They are *welded* that is the catch . . . [The actress's] voice and herself moving with so finished artistry were welded not (and this seemed some odd catastrophe) *wedded*. (115)

H.D. points out what she regards as the intrinsic paradox of the film sound track, that despite the heterogeneity of the sound film, commercial filmmakers are striving for a realistic, homogeneous effect. And this effect ultimately removes the spectator's capacity to collaborate in the text's meaning: "Here is art," H.D. writes, "but is it our own art? Isn't cinema just a matter (or hasn't it been) of inter-action?" (116). The loss of this "inter-action," of the collaboration between filmmaker and spectator, is what—for H.D. and for *Close Up*—ultimately detracts from the transformative power of art.

There were further reasons for *Close Up*'s resistance to the speech sound track. Until the advent of the talkies, silent cinema represented an "international language" that easily crossed national and cultural boundaries. This internationalist ethos colored the tone of the writing in *Close Up*; witness, for example, H.D.'s rhetorical stance in "Russian Films": "We are no longer nations. We are, or should be, *a* nation" (136). This broadly pacifist stance, a commitment to transnational communication, surfaces again in the work H.D. was to complete during World War II, in particular *Tribute to Freud* and *The Gift*.

Dubbing techniques in the film industry remained unsatisfactory until the 1930 arrival of the Moviola, a machine that allowed film editors to view the film as they edited, after which there was a more accurate mixing and synchronization of the sound track. For *Close Up*, however, such technology sounded a death knell for the film as an art form. When Bryher referred to cinema as the "the art that died," she spoke not just for herself, for POOL, or for *Close Up*; she was lamenting for an era of visual experimentation on an international scale that may never, perhaps, be repeated.

Suggested Topics and Questions for Classroom Use

Teachers intending to explore the wider connections between film and H.D.'s poetry and prose might consider how specific cinematic techniques are employed in the writing. A useful case study is the prose work *Nights*, which follows the period of H.D.'s involvement with film and uses effects (especially in relation to light) directly borrowed from the cinema. Teachers might also consider the extent to which the filmic nature of H.D.'s writing is evident even before her involvement in making and editing films. The narrative equivalent of techniques like intercutting, extreme close-up, and montage are apparent in the novels H.D. was writing (namely, *HERmione*, *Paint It Today*, and *Asphodel*) in the decade of her work with POOL. Since H.D. was an avid moviegoer, it is perhaps unsurprising that the vocabulary of film finds its way into her writing.

In discussions of *Borderline*, teachers might address the various representations of female identity in the film: through the marginal characters of the local residents, the café manager (played by Bryher), and the barmaid, as well as the more obvious hysteric figure of Astrid. Students might be asked to consider how female identity is rendered more complex by the representation of race—namely, through the film's treatment of Adah—as well as bisexuality. For those wanting to broaden discussion of female identity beyond the confines of a single text, reference might also be made to *Joyless Street* and *Pandora's Box*.

While H.D.'s film criticism can be challenging and, at times, somewhat oblique, the following essays provide a reasonably accessible starting point for a discussion of cinematic spectatorship: "Conrad Veidt: *The Student of Prague*," "*Expiation*," and "*Joan of Arc*." Questions to consider might relate to issues of social class and educational privilege and their implications for the study of modernism—both in literature and in film.

NOTE

[1] Teachers looking for additional helpful material addressing H.D. and film might also consult J. Brown; Carby, *Race Men*; Connor; Debo, "Interracial Modernism"; Donald, Friedberg, and Marcus; Friedman, *Penelope's Web*; McCabe, *Cinematic Modernism*; Morris, "Concept"; and Walton, "'Nightmare'" and "White Neurotics."

The Cinematics of H.D.'s Poetry

Charlotte Mandel

In a culture dominated by visual dynamics, where images and words continually appear and disappear on screens of varying sizes, students can access the poetry of H.D. through its cinematic energy and structure. Her early short lyrics defined as imagist in *Sea Garden* (1916) show intense focus on visual objects juxtaposed in dynamic association. Acquired technical and theoretical knowledge of cinema enriched the evolution of her poetry toward the lyric-narrative long poem *Helen in Egypt* (1961). Crucial to her progress is the period from 1927 to 1933, when H.D. gained direct hands-on experience with filmmaking; wrote reviews of films studied today as classics; and played a leading role in an experimental film, *Borderline* (1930), which starred Paul Robeson, already internationally known as a stage actor and concert singer. Examining the ways her cineaste years enter her poetry deepens understanding of H.D.'s prosodic practice and offers insight into her artistic aspirations. This essay follows chronologically four topics in H.D.'s poetic-cinematic advance: her grandfather's microscope and her father's telescope; cinematic analysis of some early poems; biographical and cultural events of her work with film; and cinematic elements of late long poems, particularly *Helen in Egypt*. The four parts interweave—nearly twenty years before H.D.'s conscious involvement with film art, her poems vibrated with cinematic tension. Teachers might consider using the film *Borderline*, now available in DVD in the set titled *Paul Robeson: Portraits of the Artist*, and the anthology *Close Up, 1927–1933* (Donald, Friedberg, and Marcus), which provides selected articles and photographs from issues of the film journal *Close Up*, including H.D.'s film reviews.

From birth, Hilda Doolittle was influenced by two remarkable paternal scientists—her astronomer father and her microscopist grandfather. Gazing through "magical" lenses, they discovered life and signs in the universe invisible to the naked eye. Francis Wolle, her maternal grandfather who lived next door, published three volumes of scrupulous drawings of microscopic freshwater algae, identifying and naming over five thousand species; her father, Charles Doolittle, spent long nights glued to a telescope and days entering written symbols of astronomical calculations. Their avid visual study of detail reappears in the poems of H.D.'s first book, *Sea Garden*. Her poem "Sea Gods" catalogs almost a naming of species: "wood-violets, stream-violets, . . . blue violets, moss, cliff, river-violets" (*Collected Poems* 30). Given the interests of her father and grandfather, it is clear that the making of "the perfect Imagist" began well before her meeting with Ezra Pound in her late teens (G. Hughes 104).

H.D.'s poetic vision, however, encompasses more than attention to surface detail. In her impressionistic memoir *The Gift*, H.D. tells of a moment of profound discovery when she was allowed to look through her grandfather's microscope: "we saw that where there is nothing, there is something" (Gift 42).

Her astronomer father traced, by mysterious symbols on paper, the progressions of stars invisible in daylight. Throughout her life, H.D.'s art would concentrate the focus of her psychic inner lens in a search for timeless meaning hidden beneath visible surface (see Mandel, "Magical Lenses").

In 1913, H.D. became an icon of the Anglo-American short-lived but pivotal literary movement called imagism. From the first, H.D.'s poetry demonstrated extraordinary ability to elicit motion within a single frame view of an observed object. It is important to distinguish the two-dimensional static effect of a photograph from that of the three-dimensional living sense the viewer experiences in front of a motion picture screen, even when the subject is motionless. The movie camera operates by means of the physical paradox of nonmotion: the viewer's impression of continuous action is illusory, a subjective response to a series of photographs, called frames. Film is composed of frames. A section of film resulting from a single camera operation (with no displacement of view or break in time) is a shot. Film editors vary the sequence and duration of shots to control the viewer's experience. The shot, therefore, becomes the filmmaker's work material in the same way the poet's medium is the word.

An essay by the pioneer Russian filmmaker Sergei Eisenstein compares the dynamics of an imagist poem to his theory of montage, where conflict between successively juxtaposed images on-screen makes meaning dynamic in the mind of the reader-viewer (45–63). The language of an effective imagist poem employs the visual image as a catalyst for idea and emotion. Eisenstein's writings on film theory, fundamental texts to this day, resonate with H.D.'s imagistic poetic process. To reveal a striking similarity of thought, teachers might set H.D.'s poem "Toward the Piraeus" beside Eisenstein's visualization of a "linguistically accurate" film portrait of a man:

> His raven-black hair
> The waves of his hair
> His eyes radiating azure beams
> His steely muscles. (59)

Compare H.D.'s verbal portrait:

> to watch you turn
> your great head, set on the throat,
> thick, dark with its sinews
> . . . .
> and the noble chin
> and the throat.
> (*Collected Poems* 178)

Her poem creates a filmic continuum—the lines focus attention on the man in close-up, detail by detail enlarged, adoration told by the verbal camera's long holding of the shot. Independently, Eisenstein and H.D.—the one as generative filmmaker, the other as transforming poet—were tuning their arts to a vibrating central dynamic. Technology was making it possible for H.D. to see her poetic aims articulated on-screen. She saw all of Eisenstein's films and read his essays in *Close Up*.

Students can analyze any of the poems in *Sea Garden* as though viewed on a screen. "Sea Violet" uncannily merges the microscope's concentrated magnifying power, the telescope's power to bring a star near at hand, and a cinematic held shot (in which the camera does not move while focused on a living subject) as the flower shimmers within the frame of the short poem:

> Violet
> your grasp is frail
> on the edge of the sand-hill,
> but you catch the light—
> frost, a star edges with its fire. (26)

In "Oread" we observe the superimposition of sensual green water over rock:

> Whirl up, sea—
> whirl your pointed pines,
> splash your great pines
> on our rocks,
> hurl your green over us,
> cover us with your pools of fir.
> (*Collected Poems* 55)

The dissolve is a film technique where one image appears over another, taking its place. In "Oread" images of pines have dissolved into pools, and the superimposition is aided by internal rhyming. The violent opening "whirl" settles into a quiet punning noun, the textural surprise of "fir."

The poem "Helen" functions in the manner of a cinematic held shot, which produces a very different effect from that of a photograph. Viewing the screen, one is aware of the action of light and the tension implied by the subject's imminence of movement. "Helen" focuses the reader's gaze on a beautiful shimmering woman of "the white face . . . and the white hands," recalling a full-length figure projected on a 1920s silver screen (154). The poem's opening lines, "All Greece hates / the still eyes in the white face," transform readers into an audience of spectators gazing at the woman (154; see Mandel, "Garbo/Helen" 130).

H.D.'s active involvement in cinema took place in Switzerland during the years 1927 to 1933 at a pension in Territet and later at a Bauhaus-design villa on the shores of Lake Geneva. There radiated from these locations a vortex of cinematic-literary-artistic creation sparked by H.D., her then lover Kenneth Macpherson, and her lifetime intimate friend Bryher, who married Macpherson as a social convenience. Their complex erotic and intellectual energies generated international exchanges on the possibilities of cinema as an art form. This period compares with the brief but stunning vitality of imagism, which influenced change in the direction of twentieth-century poetry. Here again, H.D. occupied a central space in a circle of intimate colleagues seeing themselves as seeing the world in new ways. They idealistically envisioned the silent cinema as a force for an international community that could transcend language barriers.

Bryher founded, financed, and coedited the pioneer—now classic—magazine *Close Up*, one of the first journals designed to foster the artistic and social significance of cinema as an art form. Macpherson edited the magazine and reigned as cameraman-auteur, eventually creating his ambitious full-length feature *Borderline*. H.D. learned to use a lightweight projector, acted in Macpherson's films, and contributed eleven review essays and two poems titled "Projector." These writings offer immediacy to her ardent response to cinema as visionary art. Editing strips of film inch by inch, at a time when "cut and paste" meant literal hands-on painstaking work, would be significant toward her later technique of assembling her nonlinear lyric-narrative long poems.

Close Up provides an invaluable view of the international discourse on cinema at a remarkable period of cultural ferment. The anthology *Close Up, 1927–1933: Cinema and Modernism*, edited by James Donald, Anne Friedberg, and Laura Marcus, features selections of the magazine's contents, with interpretive introductory essays by the editors. This anthology demonstrates the impact of cinematic awareness, fostered by the magazine's self-conscious avant-garde sensibility, as inseparably rooted in the development of modernist aesthetics. The pioneer journal published work from international contributors dealing with film theory, reviews, psychoanalysis, and film in education and featured an entire issue devoted to the "Negro" in film. Eight of H.D.'s eleven film reviews are reprinted in the anthology, as well as her incisive essay describing Macpherson's creative process, generally referred to as "The *Borderline* Pamphlet" because it was originally produced as a separate pamphlet. Not included is her enthusiastic review of the Russian film *Turksib* on the unlikely theme of building the Trans-Siberian Railroad. In this review, H.D. lauds the ability of film to actually picture "thought" on the screen ("*Turksib*" 490–91).

Friends among members of the Harlem Renaissance opened the way for Macpherson to invite Paul Robeson to act with his wife, Eslanda, in *Borderline*, Robeson's second film. The couple came to Switzerland en route from Paul Robeson's scheduled performances in London and Berlin. A showing of the movie enlarges the scope of any course on H.D. The DVD version has added a modern jazz musical sound track composed by Courtney Pine, a background that, while well played, is anachronistic. There are no records that reveal the music, if any, chosen by the film's creators. Students can fruitfully discuss the effects different musical choices have on the film's content.

If possible, students should read H.D.'s promotional essay on the making of *Borderline* before seeing the film ("*Borderline* Pamphlet"). Her description provides rare insight into the filmmaker Macpherson's camera technique, his highly ambitious style of European expressionist jagged juxtaposition, his use of images to elicit psychoanalytic association, and his intent to achieve a narrative exposing racial bigotry—while also oddly downplaying her and Bryher's substantial contributions. H.D. and Bryher took exact direction from Macpherson in the roles they played (H.D. as a rejected and racially bigoted wife, Bryher as a pragmatic pension manager) and painstakingly edited the film while Macpherson was ill. Any of these aspects offers topics for student discussion and research. The film was never exhibited in the United States, because of its daring—for the times—depiction of an interracial sexual relationship, although Bryher corresponded with the owner of an art film house in Baltimore about American distribution (Debo, "Interracial Modernism" 380). Macpherson's camera foregrounds the Robesons against mountain, sky, and waterfall, signifying purity and closeness to nature as opposed to the neurotic white characters cramped inside small pension rooms. While meant as admiration, this attitude, also expressed in *Close Up* reviews about the "Negro" in film, may be termed "romantic racism." Aldon Lynn Nielsen in *Reading Race* cites *Borderline* as an example of white modernists' stereotypical use of "blackness . . . as a part of nature," even though he also praises the film because it "offers one of the first compelling denunciations of racism in the history of American cinema" (26, 88).

In her film essays H.D. reveals her immediate attraction to cinema and excited discovery of an art form she speaks of in near-evangelistic language. The classic silent films she reviews, such as G. W. Pabst's *Joyless Street* ("Cinema" 105–09), Carl Dreyer's *Passion of Joan of Arc* ("*Joan of Arc*"), and *The Student of Prague* with Conrad Veidt ("Conrad Veidt"), are available on video or DVD. By reviewing these films before reading H.D.'s reviews, students can not only learn to write reviews but also compare their responses to H.D.'s.

H.D.'s cineaste period enabled passage from the fixed frames of imagist lyrics to the nonlinear narrative flow of *Helen in Egypt*, her long poem published in 1961, the year of her death. The poem's juxtapositions play with the influence of conscious and unconscious memory on present experience. Students can read the work in one sitting, passively allowing the changes of images, voices, and sounds to be encountered as in a cinema. Each lyric verse sequence is preceded by a prose voice that wonders and questions. The effect compares with the dual levels of consciousness experienced while watching a film: one part of consciousness absorbs the images on-screen, while another intellectually judges what is being viewed. Images of Helen appear in various locales, like camera shots, often repeated. Coincidental similarities appear in a film of the same period, the 1961 *Last Year in Marienbad*, by Alain Robbe-Grillet. This modernist film evokes a similar sense of searching within a woman's memory using nonlinear juxtapositions of striking images as found in dreams. In her pamphlet lauding *Borderline*, H.D. states that "film is the art of dream portrayal" (232). Helen in the Egyptian tomb muses, "*I move as one in a dream*" (*Helen* 43).

Memories sought and found in *Helen in Egypt* are treated as reworkable objects: "things remembered, forgotten, // remembered again, assembled / and re-assembled in different order" (289). The process parallels that of a filmmaker who cuts and reassembles camera shots as visual objectifications of time. Other cinematic parallels include visual close-up detail, "montage" successions of images, and superimposition by H.D.'s signature language practice of "word-dissolve"—as in "War, Ares, Achilles, Amor," whereby war is transposed into love (179; see Mandel, "Redirected Image").

H.D. uses herself as a visionary psychic lens. The transformative dynamics of her language work to dissolve boundaries of time and to interweave or revise mythological narratives. The final sequence of *Helen in Egypt* evokes

> *. . . the sea,*
> *its beat and long reverberation,*
> *its booming and delicate echo,*
>
> *its ripple that spells a charm*
> *on the sand, the rock-lichen,*
> *the sea-moss, the sand.* (304)

These auditory and visual images return to the earliest imagist poems in *Sea Garden*. H.D., from her first awareness of the possibilities of the moving picture, embraced cinema's artistic kinship with her transformative visions. Her art sought to read images in nature as hieroglyphic script of hidden meaning; she sought to see past our visible sun into the blindingly bright stars beyond. In 1927, her poem "Projector II," published in *Close Up*, composes a psalm to a god of light:

> This is his gift;
> light,
> light
> a wave
> that sweeps
> us
> from old fears
> and powers
> and disenchantments;
> . . . .
> old forms dispersed
> take fresh
> shapes
> out of nothingness;
> light
> renders us spell-bound,
> enchants us
> and astounds.
> (*Collected Poems* 354–55)

Such effects resonate with today's ubiquitous shifts of visual imagery.

Hilda Digital: Teaching H.D. in Cyberspace

Helen Sword

> All the light within light fascinates me, "satisfies" me, I feel like a cat playing with webs and webs of silver.
>
> —H.D., "Confessions-Questionnaire"

We tend to think of H.D., and to teach H.D., as a poet of the past. Wearing her Greek mask even when writing about contemporary issues, she obsessed about both her personal history and her textual history as a writer. Sigmund Freud encouraged this retrospective cast by urging H.D. to plumb her unconscious mind for images drawn from childhood. So did Norman Holmes Pearson, the solicitous Yale professor and close friend whose many queries about her literary friendships, travels, and source materials set H.D., especially from the 1940s onward, to writing endless notes and memoirs about the provenance of her earlier works. "It is obviously Penelope's web that I am weaving," H.D. wrote in "Advent," her 1933 record of her psychoanalytic sessions with Freud (*Tribute* 173). To read H.D.'s poetry and prose memoirs is to experience a writer who continually weaves and unweaves her texts, unmaking and remaking herself through literary language composed of so many sticky interwoven threads that even the most alert and dedicated reader might be forgiven for feeling occasional bouts of claustrophobia—not to say arachnophobia.

Webs figure in H.D.'s work as images of textual power but also as agents of imprisonment. In the same 1929 interview in which H.D. described herself as "a cat playing with webs and webs of silver" (in reference to her newfound fascination with cinema projection), she also noted:

> I fear the being caught in any one set formula or set of circumstances, I fear poverty in that it might catch me up in some ugly web of the wrong sort of things and the wrong sort of attitudes. I fear people from the future who may "trap" me. ("Confessions-Questionnaire" 366)

H.D. could not have anticipated the advent of that other web—the World Wide Web—that has come to rule our academic and personal lives. But I like to think that, rather than feeling trapped by the Internet's sticky strands, she would have welcomed, perhaps even reveled in, the world of hypermedia in all its endless, still unfolding potential: digital poetics, textual kinetics, cultural mnemonics, global networking.

In any event, we—the "people from the future" whom H.D. feared—ignore at our own peril that our students, the people of our future, are already citizens of cyberspace whose sophistication in the once arcane art of crafting hypertextual artifacts increases exponentially every year. As teachers, we can continue to introduce H.D.'s work as we have always done: through books and paper, perhaps with an occasional nod to orality and performance. Or we can use our knowledge of the past—twentieth-century history, modernist poetics—to help prepare our students for the intellectual challenges that lie ahead in a world entangled in and ensnared by communication technologies whose sociological impact we, like H.D. nearly a century ago, can only begin to fathom or predict.

Looking to the future as well as to the past, I want to suggest here some of the ways in which H.D., poet of webs and weaving, might be conceptualized and taught as a poet of the Web, that vast network of ethereal sites and hypertextual links in which our students today increasingly live, work, study, and (virtually) breathe. H.D. was one of the first modernist poets to establish a presence in cyberspace; in the mid-1990s, at a time when most English professors were still struggling to master their e-mail, Heather Hernandez—self-described "Technical Services Librarian at the San Francisco Maritime Library by day and H.D. fan by night"—set up the H.D. (*Hilda Doolittle*) *Home Page* (www.imagists.org/hd/), which quickly became a valuable resource site for H.D. scholars and remains the first hit from a *Google* search of "H.D. Hilda Doolittle." Unfortunately, the H.D. home page is not rich in teaching resources. The site contains links to books, archives, articles, and a scholarly newsletter but only to a few Web pages with H.D.'s poetry or prose, because most of her work remains under copyright. One of the great ironies of the digital age is that we can find stunning archival Web sites dedicated to the works of long-dead authors such as William Shakespeare, William Blake, and Dante Gabriel Rossetti but nothing comparable—neither edited texts nor manuscript facsimiles—on T. S. Eliot, James Joyce, H.D., or most other major twentieth-century authors, with the exception of living poets who, recognizing the value and excitement of having their poetry instantly available to a global audience, have built their own Web sites or given permission for their work to be reproduced online. Charles Bernstein's manifesto for the *PennSound* archive of recorded poetry begins with the words, "It must be free and downloadable." H.D.'s work, by and large, is neither.

All the same, half a cyberloaf is better than none. Most of H.D.'s poems are available electronically on *Literature Online*, a full-text digital database to which most major research libraries subscribe. The Beinecke Rare Book and Manuscript Library site, likewise, contains an ever-growing number of scanned manuscript facsimiles and images from its H.D. archive. Other types of multimedia resources, such as a recording of H.D. reading excerpts from *Helen in Egypt*, can be found on the Web as well. The suggestions that follow could be fruitfully applied to the teaching of any modernist author—or, indeed, to just about any other subject matter, literary or otherwise. But H.D.'s poetry lends itself particularly well to assignments that capitalize on new technologies. Her dense allusiveness, highly visual aesthetics, and palimpsestic overlay of past and present invite hypermedia responses that illuminate, complicate, and play on these crucial aspects of her work.

Digital Transformations

Picture this familiar scenario: having spent several class sessions listening with delight to their lively, insightful discussions of H.D.'s work, you have asked your students to produce interpretive essays on a single short H.D. poem, such as one of the early lyrics from *Sea Garden*. But when the completed assignments arrive on your desk, your heart sinks. Packaged as academic prose, your students' close readings have congealed into turgid sludge. Rather than bringing the poem to life, many of them have effectively killed it.

Digital transformation offers, for many students, a far more compelling means of climbing inside a poem than a standard academic essay and encourages them to produce more astute and energetic writing. The assignment might look something like this:

> Create a multimedia version of any poem in *Sea Garden*, taking advantage of technologies not available in H.D.'s day. What happens when the richly visual and aural qualities of her poetry are transported into a digital environment where text, image, and sound can be combined, transformed, and manipulated at will? Think of your assignment not merely as an impressionistic response to a complex and multidimensional poem but as a digital translation or interpretation of the original printed text. On a separate, linked page, provide a detailed (about 1,000-word) exegesis; that is, an explanation of what you've done with the poem and why.

Here, poetic interpretation becomes an act of personal engagement, not merely an exercise in academic gloss. (For a discussion of a similar assignment in a paper-based course, see Sword, "Teaching in Color.") The "digital transformation" portion of the assignment encourages explicitly creative, even playful responses: students can add graphic images and interactive elements, overlay voice or music or other sound effects, manipulate the font, use hyperlinks to direct or subvert the reader's progress, animate the imagery and typography—the possibilities are endless. (Such assignments work best when students are explicitly discouraged from producing predictable Hallmark-style Web pages that merely illustrate rather than interpret the text—for example, "Oread" superimposed in pretty italic font onto a photograph of some pine trees, with the sound of crashing waves in the background.) The analytical element—the exegesis—requires students to produce, in effect, a conventional academic essay, but one that chronicles their interpretive process rather than limning the text in a detached, impersonal mode. "The best way to understand how a text works . . . is to change it," advises Rob Pope in his book *Textual Intervention: Critical and Creative Strategies for Literary Studies* (1). If you really want to understand an H.D. poem in all its visual and verbal complexity, transform and adapt it for the Web.

Archival Assignments and Collective Resources

The hyperarchivist and digital pioneer Jerome McGann has noted the paradox that, in our brave new world of digital archiving, the arcane art of textual editing has become more crucially important than ever before ("Culture"). Yet very few of us explicitly teach such skills to our students, and the literary-critical elite still accord a far more exalted status to literary theory than to textual praxis. Digital archiving projects such as McGann's *The Complete Writings and Pictures of Dante Gabriel Rossetti: A Hypermedia Archive* or the *Modernist Journals Project* simply could not have been undertaken without the input of scholars who possess meticulous manuscript editing skills as well as sophisticated technological savvy. But such academic paragons remain in short supply. If we are to safeguard our literary heritage, argues McGann, we need to train a new generation of literature graduates capable of designing and executing the kinds of sophisticated digital resources on which our literary scholarship increasingly depends. At both the undergraduate and the graduate levels, students begin to acquire such skills when they design archival sites of their own, such as Web resources that explicitly take into account issues of audience, preservation, and access.

As of this writing, one of the most successful and fastest-growing sites on the World Wide Web is *Wikipedia*, a collaborative online encyclopedia that contains millions of entries in English alone, all contributed by volunteer "experts." In an ideal academic universe—one in which H.D.'s work were free of copyright protection—scholars could establish an H.D. wiki where both students and seasoned academics could post commentaries, resources, biographical materials, and links to other relevant sites. The value of such a site would be threefold. First, it would provide a one-stop shop for readers seeking information on H.D. Second, it would serve as a virtual meeting place for H.D. scholars—part salon, part café, part community hall—where conversations and collaborations could arise. Third (and most important for the purposes of this essay), it would allow teachers to develop assignments focused not just on the consumption of knowledge but on its production. Far from merely visiting the site to locate information, students could become contributors—experts in their own right—and their highest quality research projects would be accorded a public, permanent home. Instead of writing for a single, private reader (i.e., the teacher), they would be crafting essays and entries designed to reach a potentially global audience, and they would learn that such work must conform to the highest standards of content, style, and execution.

On a smaller scale, teachers can use wikis, blogs, *Facebook*, and other social software applications to create lively research communities in their classrooms. Imagine an annotated wiki version of *Trilogy*, with glosses on H.D.'s many references and allusions. Beginning undergraduates could be given the challenge of researching particular figures or tropes in the poem and producing brief scholarly commentaries. Advanced undergraduates and graduate students could be assigned more ambitious projects, as part of their training as the digital archivists of the future. For example, they could explore a particular poem's publication history and then produce a Web exhibit that might include a detailed bibliography; scanned facsimiles of manuscript drafts, magazine pages, and book pages; and a short interpretive essay exploring how one's reading of the poem changes as its publication history unfolds. In the coming years, as hypertext technologies grow more advanced and accessible and as rare-book libraries digitize more of their manuscript holdings, the potential for such projects will continue to expand—limited, once again, only by the constraints of the human imagination and the contingencies of copyright law.

The educationalists Betty Collis and Jef Moonen have demonstrated that such collaborative research sites can function as powerful teaching tools, providing not only a valuable learning experience for the students who create them but also an ever-expanding resource for future students. Why, Collis and Moonen ask, should teachers spend vast amounts of time assembling such resources themselves? When students, rather than teachers, produce and publish Web-based teaching resources, they engage in applied learning of the most active and intense kind and provide the students who come after them with the scaffolding for a growing body of increasingly detailed and complex assignments.

The collaborative ethos of an H.D. wiki would sit well both within the history of H.D. scholarship, which since at least the early 1980s has been characterized by cooperative, noncompetitive interchange among scholars, and within the production history of H.D.'s work, nurtured as it was by a network of close friends and sympathetic colleagues. Bonnie Kime Scott's classic anthology *The Gender of Modernism* contains a spiderweb-like diagram illustrating the many professional and personal interconnections among the modernist authors featured in her book. The World Wide Web takes such scholarly, artistic, and personal networks into a new dimension, enabling complex global interchanges at the push of a button.

A truly comprehensive H.D. wiki must remain, at least for the time being, an academic fantasy. A public Web site created around H.D.'s poetry and prose, without including H.D.'s actual words, would seem a shabby stepchild by comparison. Such a site might be worth establishing nonetheless, in the hope that eventually permission will be granted for posting at least a few poems, a few more manuscript materials to be set free into cyberspace. Only as scholars continue to lobby H.D.'s copyright holders (New Directions) and archivists (such as the Beinecke Library) to release more of H.D.'s work into the public domain can such a shift in publication culture take place.

The Web of the Future

I am aware that what I have written here may end up sounding naive, misguided, overoptimistic, or (I hope) blatantly obvious in five or ten years' time. Such is the breakneck speed of technological change, and such is the fragility of Web pages and hypertexts, which can establish themselves as invaluable teaching tools one day and then vanish without a trace the next. Indeed, I have deliberately cited in this essay only well-known, well-established institutional Web sites—those that seem most likely to maintain a presence in cyberspace beyond the publication of this book. As for the many wonderful Web-based teaching sites and student projects from which I have drawn inspiration in recent years but which I have reluctantly avoided mentioning in this essay, their most crucial work has already been accomplished, whether or not their content proves ephemeral. The creation, not the consumption, of such resources is the site where real learning takes place.

In a 13 December 1937 letter to Pearson, H.D. summed up her complex poetics of memory and desire in terms that anticipate the "radiant textuality" (to borrow McGann's evocative phrase) of hypermedia:

> Actual memory, repressed memory, desire to escape, desire to create (music), intellectual curiosity, a wish to make real to myself what is most real, the fragrant pages of the early Greek poets, to tear, if it be even the barest fragment of vibrant electric parchment from hands not always worthy to touch, fingers whose sterile "intellectuality" is so often an inverted curse of Midas—these are some of the ingredients of my poetry.
>
> (qtd. in Brown, Finch, and Kumin 72)

Recast and reimagined in digital form, H.D.'s poems can become, indeed, "vibrant electric parchment[s]"—animated by student hands untainted by "sterile 'intellectuality'"—that will glow in the weave and weft of the Web.

NOTES ON CONTRIBUTORS

Jane Augustine is a poet and independent scholar who has written four books of poetry and numerous essays on women in modernism. She is the editor of The Gift *by H.D.: The Complete Text* and H.D.'s *The Mystery* and has held the H.D. Fellowship in American Literature at Beinecke Library, Yale University. She is at work on a biography of H.D. and Lord Dowding during World War II.

Raffaella Baccolini is professor of English literature and gender studies at the University of Bologna, Forlì. She is the author of *Tradition, Identity, Desire: Revisionist Strategies in H.D.'s Late Poetry* and coeditor of the collections *Dark Horizons: Science Fiction and the Dystopian Imagination* and *Utopia Method Vision: The Use Value of Social Dreaming*. She is currently working on the representation of trauma in women's contemporary fiction and film.

Marsha Bryant is associate professor of English at the University of Florida, where she has received five teaching awards. She is the author of *Auden and Documentary in the 1930s* and the forthcoming *Women's Poetry and Popular Culture*. She is also editor of *Photo-Textualities: Reading Photographs and Literature*. Her essays have appeared in *Modernism/Modernity*, *American Literature*, *Mosaic*, *College Literature*, *Pedagogy*, and *The Unraveling Archive: Essays on Sylvia Plath*.

Rachel Connor is an independent researcher and writer in the United Kingdom. She is the author of *H.D. and the Image* and of chapters in *Literature and Visual Technologies: Writing after Cinema* and *A Companion to Twentieth-Century United States Fiction*. Her research interests are in modernist literature and film, contemporary writing, and creative writing. Her novel *Sisterwives* is forthcoming.

Annette Debo is associate professor of English at Western Carolina University and cochair of the H.D. International Society. Her monograph *The American H.D.: Nation and Modernist Identity* is forthcoming, and her essays have appeared in *African American Review*, *Callaloo*, *Paideuma*, *South Atlantic Review*, *Quarterly Review of Film and Video*, *CLA Journal*, and *College Literature*. She is at work on a study of women's poetry, violence, and the civil rights era.

Mary K. DeShazer is professor of English and women's and gender studies at Wake Forest University. She is the author of *Fractured Borders: Reading Women's Cancer Literature*; *A Poetics of Resistance: Women Writing from El Salvador, South Africa, and the United States*; and *Inspiring Women: Re-imagining the Muse*. She edited *The Longman Anthology of Women's Literature* and is completing a book entitled "Mammographies: The Cultural Discourses of Breast Cancer Narratives."

Madelyn Detloff is associate professor of English and women's, gender, and sexuality studies at Miami University, Oxford, OH. She is the author of *The Persistence of Modernism: Loss and Mourning in the Twentieth Century*. Her essays have appeared in the books *Approaches to Teaching Woolf's* Mrs. Dalloway; *Modernism and Mourning*; and *Incest and the Literary Imagination* and in the journals *ELN*, *Journal of Lesbian Studies*, *Women's Studies*, and *Hypatia*.

Mary Ann Eaverly is associate professor of classics at the University of Florida, where she has received two teaching awards. Her published work includes *Archaic Greek Equestrian Sculpture* and essays in archaeological journals. She has excavated in Greece, Israel, Italy, Cyprus, and Spain. She is interested in the connections between classical traditions and modern women writers, and her current book project is entitled "Brown Men, White Women: Color and Gender in Ancient Painting."

Susan Stanford Friedman is the Virginia Woolf Professor of English and Women's Studies at the University of Wisconsin, Madison. She is the author of *Psyche Reborn: The Emergence of H.D.*; *Penelope's Web: Gender, Modernity, H.D.'s Fiction*; and *Mappings: Feminism and the Cultural Geographies of Encounter* and the editor of *Analyzing Freud: Letters of H.D., Bryher, and Their Circle* and *Signets: Reading H.D.* She is working on books entitled "Planetary Modernism" and "Sisters of Scheherazade: Muslim Cultures and Women's Diasporic Writing."

Elizabeth Hirsh is associate professor at the University of South Florida. She is the author of *Women Writing Culture* and has published articles and book chapters on H.D., Luce Irigaray, Virginia Woolf, Adrienne Rich, Djuna Barnes, and Radclyffe Hall. She is completing a study of Virginia Woolf as historian.

Donna Krolik Hollenberg is professor of English at the University of Connecticut, Storrs. She is the author of *H.D.: The Poetics of Childbirth and Creativity*, and she has edited *Between History and Poetry: The Letters of H.D. and Norman Holmes Pearson* and the collection *H.D. and Poets After*. She has published essays about many other twentieth-century writers, and her biography, *A Poet's Revolution: The Life of Denise Levertov*, is forthcoming.

Bret L. Keeling is lecturer of English at Northeastern University. His essays have appeared in *Paideuma*, *Mosaic*, and *Twentieth Century Literature*, as well as the collection *Illuminations: New Readings of Virginia* Woolf. His interests are in modernism and postmodernism, gender studies and queer theory, feminism, minority literatures and postcolonialism, and pedagogies of literature and writing.

Charlotte Mandel is a poet and independent scholar. She has published seven books of poetry, including *Rock Vein Sky*, *The Life of Mary*, and *The Marriages of Jacob*. She edited the Eileen W. Barnes Award anthology *Saturday's Women*. Her essays on H.D. have appeared in *Women's Studies*, *Literature/Film Quarterly*, and *H.D.: Woman and Poet*. Her research on the role of cinema in the life and work of H.D. was supported by an alumni grant from Montclair State University.

James Maynard is assistant curator of the Poetry Collection at the University at Buffalo, State University of New York. His interests are in twentieth-century American poetry, pragmatism, and process philosophy. He coedited Robert Duncan's *Ground Work: Before the War / In the Dark* and has published essays and reviews in the *Journal of Modern Literature*, *Jacket*, *Mimeo Mimeo*, and *Process Studies*. He is the editor of the forthcoming collection *(Re:)Working the Ground: Essays on the Late Writings of Robert Duncan* and is editing a volume of Duncan's essays and other prose.

Susan McCabe is professor of English at the University of Southern California. She is the author of *Cinematic Modernism: Modern Poetry and Film* and *Elizabeth Bishop: Her Poetics of Loss*, as well as *Descartes' Nightmare*, winner of the Agha Shahid Ali Prize, and

Swirl. She wrote the introduction for *Visa for Avalon*, by Bryher, and is writing a critical biography of Bryher.

Adalaide Morris is John C. Gerber Professor of English at the University of Iowa. She is the author of *How to Live / What to Do: H.D.'s Cultural Poetics*; coeditor of *New Media Poetics: Contexts, Technotexts, and Theories*; and editor of *Sound States: Innovative Poetics and Acoustical Technologies*. She has published essays on H.D., contemporary innovative poetry, feminist fiction, and the academy. She is working on a manuscript entitled "What Else Can Poetry Do?"

Cyrena N. Pondrom is English Board of Visitors Professor of English at the University of Wisconsin, Madison. Her essays have appeared in *Modernism/Modernity*, *Agenda*, *American Literature*, *Contemporary Literature*, *Sagetrieb*, and *Journal of Modern Literature*, as well as the volumes *Signets: Reading H.D.*, *Marianne Moore: Woman and Poet*, the Blackwell *Companion to T. S. Eliot*, *Text and Meaning: Literary Discourse and Beyond*, and the forthcoming *Cambridge Companion to H.D.* She is working on a book manuscript, "T. S. Eliot and the Performativity of Gender."

Lisa Rado is instructor of English at Harvard-Westlake Upper School in Los Angeles. She is the author of *The Modern Androgyne Imagination: A Failed Sublime* and the editor of *Modernism, Gender, and Culture* and *Rereading Modernism: New Directions in Feminist Criticism*. Her essays have appeared in *Women's Studies*, *Twentieth Century Literature*, *Faulkner Journal*, and *Conradiana*.

Mara Scanlon is associate professor of English at the University of Mary Washington. Her essays have appeared in the *Writer's Chronicle*; *College Literature*; *LIT: Literature, Interpretation, Theory*; *Bucknell Review*; and *World Literature Today*. She is working on the digital humanities project "Looking for Whitman: The Poetry of Place in the Life and Work of Walt Whitman" and coediting a volume of essays on dialogism and poetry.

Helen Sword is head of the Academic Practice Group in the Centre for Academic Development at the University of Auckland, where she was corecipient of the 2007 Teaching Excellence Award for innovation in teaching. She has published essays on modernist poetry, digital poetics, higher education pedagogy, and scholarly writing. Her books include *Engendering Inspiration: Visionary Poetics in Rilke, Lawrence, and H.D.*; *Ghostwriting Modernism*; *The Writer's Diet*; *Pacific Rim Modernisms* (coeditor); and *Stylish Academic Writing*.

Heather H. Thomas is professor of English at Kutztown University of Pennsylvania. Her poetry books include *Blue Ruby*, *Resurrection Papers*, and *Practicing Amnesia*. Her publications include an article on H.D. and Wallace Stevens in the *Forum on Public Policy: A Journal of the Oxford Round Table* and essays in *We Who "Love to Be Astonished": Experimental Feminist Poetics and Performance Art*, the *Writer's Chronicle*, the *Emily Dickinson Journal*, and *Women's Studies*.

Lara Vetter is assistant professor of English at the University of North Carolina at Charlotte and cochair of the H.D. International Society. She is the author of *Modernist Writings and Religio-scientific Discourse: H.D., Loy, and Toomer*, and she has published articles in *Genre* and the *Journal of Modern Literature*. She is coeditor of *Emily Dickinson's Correspondences: A Born-Digital, Textual Inquiry*. She is at work on a book on H.D. and late modernism.

Rebecca Walsh is assistant professor of English at North Carolina State University. Her publications include essays in the collections *A Concise Companion to America Studies* and *Exclusions in Feminist Thought* and a coauthored essay in *PMLA*. She has guest-edited a special issue of *Interventions* on the topic of global diasporas. Her book project in progress is entitled "Modernism's Geopoetics: The Cultural Politics of the Near and Far."

Lesley Wheeler is professor of English and department chair at Washington and Lee University. She is the author of *Voicing American Poetry: Sound and Performance from the 1920s to the Present*; *The Poetics of Enclosure: American Women Poets from Dickinson to Dove*; and the books of poetry *Heathen* and *Heterotopia*. She is the coeditor of *Letters to the World: Poems from the Wom-Po Listserv* and is researching poetry and community in the twenty-first century.

SURVEY RESPONDENTS

The editors would like to thank the following teachers and scholars for responding so generously and thoroughly to a lengthy questionnaire on teaching H.D.'s texts. Several sections in "Materials" are based in part on the answers provided by them, and their contributions to this volume and to the future of teaching H.D. have been invaluable.

Barry Ahearn, *Tulane University*
Alma Rose Alvarez, *Southern Oregon University*
Katherine Arens, *University of Texas at Austin*
Jane Augustine, *independent scholar*
Raffaella Baccolini, *Università di Bologna, Forlì*
Christa Baiada, *Borough of Manhattan Community College, City University of New York*
Joyce Lorraine Beck, *Texas Christian University*
C. D. Blanton, *University of California, Berkeley*
Marsha Bryant, *University of Florida*
Catherine Carter, *Western Carolina University*
Kimberly Engdahl Coates, *Bowling Green State University*
Christine E. Coffman, *University of Alaska, Fairbanks*
Sasha Colby, *Simon Fraser University*
Alex Davis, *University College at Cork*
Mary K. DeShazer, *Wake Forest University*
Madelyn Detloff, *Miami University, Oxford, OH*
Maggie Dunn, *Rollins College*
Martha Greene Eads, *Eastern Mennonite University*
Mary Ann Eaverly, *University of Florida*
Delia Fisher, *Westfield State College*
Maria Stadter Fox, *Eckerd College*
Susan Stanford Friedman, *University of Wisconsin—Madison*
Julie Elaine Goodspeed-Chadwick, *Ball State University*
Elizabeth Greene, *Queen's University*
Dorys C. Grover, *Texas A&M University—Commerce*
Michael Hardin, *Susquehanna University*
Brenda Helt, *University of Minnesota*
Miranda B. Hickman, *McGill University*
Elizabeth Hirsh, *University of South Florida*
Donna Krolik Hollenberg, *University of Connecticut, Storrs*
Bret L. Keeling, *Northeastern University*
Georgia Kreiger, *Allegany College of Maryland*
Celena E. Kusch, *University of South Carolina Upstate*
Helane Levine-Keating, *Pace University, New York*
Charlotte Mandel, *Barnard College Center for Research on Women*
Kerry Manders, *York University*
Thomas Henry Martin, *Texas A&M University—Commerce*

James Maynard, *University at Buffalo, State University of New York*
Susan McCabe, *University of Southern California*
Adalaide Morris, *University of Iowa*
Betsy Nies, *University of North Florida*
Maureen Niwa-Heinen, *Camosun College*
Cyrena N. Pondrom, *University of Wisconsin—Madison*
Carrie Preston, *Boston University*
Lisa Rado, *Harvard-Westlake Upper School*
Deirdre Ray, *Cheyney University of Pennsylvania*
Martha Reid, *Moravian College*
Esther Sánchez-Pardo, *Universidad Complutense*
Mara Scanlon, *University of Mary Washington*
Ernest Smith, *University of Central Florida*
Helen Sword, *University of Auckland*
Heather H. Thomas, *Kutztown University of Pennsylvania*
Julie Vandivere, *Bloomsburg University*
Linda Wagner-Martin, *University of North Carolina at Chapel Hill*
Rebecca Walsh, *North Carolina State University*
Lisa Weihman, *West Virginia University, Morgantown*
Lesley Wheeler, *Washington and Lee University*

WORKS CITED

Academy of American Poets. *Poets.org*. Acad. of Amer. Poets, 2008. Web. 1 May 2008.

Aldington, Richard. *An Autobiography in Letters*. Ed. Norman T. Gates. University Park: Pennsylvania State UP, 1992. Print.

———. "The Case of Lieutenant Hall." Tate 77–91.

Ambelain, Robert. *La Kabbale pratique*. Paris: Bussière, 1990. Print.

Anderson, Margaret, ed. Little Review *Anthology*. New York: Hermitage, 1953. Print.

Anderson, Monica. *Women and the Politics of Travel, 1870–1914*. Madison: Fairleigh Dickinson UP, 2006. Print.

Atwood, Margaret. *Bluebeard's Egg*. Toronto: McClelland, 1983. Print.

———. *You Are Happy*. Toronto: Oxford UP, 1974. Print.

Augustine, Jane. "Sex, H.D. and Robert Kelly." Hollenberg, *H.D. and Poets* 45–52.

Baccolini, Raffaella. "'There Was a Helen before There Was a War': Memory and Desire in H.D.'s *Winter Love* and Pound's *Pisan Cantos*." *Sagetrieb* 15.1-2 (1996): 299–45. Print.

Barnes, Djuna. *Nightwood*. 1937. New York: New Directions, 2006. Print.

Barnstone, Aliki. Introduction. H.D., *Trilogy* vii–xviii.

Barthes, Roland. "The Death of the Author." *Image, Music, Text*. Trans. Stephen Heath. New York: Hill, 1977. 142–48. Print.

BBC. "World War II in Coventry." *Coventry and Warwickshire*. BBC, Dec. 2008. Web. 20 Dec. 2009.

Benstock, Shari. *Women of the Left Bank: Paris, 1900–1940*. Austin: U of Texas P, 1986. Print.

Bergonzi, Bernard. *Heroes' Twilight: A Study of the Literature of the Great War*. New York: Coward, 1966. Print.

Bernal, Martin. *The Black Athena: The Afroasiatic Roots of Classical Civilization*. New Brunswick: Rutgers UP, 1987. Print.

Bernstein, Charles. "PennSound Manifesto." *PennSound*. U of Pennsylvania, 2003. Web. 22 Feb. 2008.

Bertholf, Robert J., ed. *A Great Admiration: H.D. / Robert Duncan Correspondence, 1950–1961*. Venice: Lapis, 1992. Print.

The Bible. *Electronic Text Center*. U of Virginia Lib., n.d. Web. 1 May 2008. King James vers.

Birth of a Nation. Dir. D. W. Griffith. Perf. Lillian Gish. David W. Griffith Corp., 1915. Film.

Bishop, Elizabeth. *Questions of Travel*. New York: Farrar, 1965. Print.

"The Blitz." *The Times*. Times Newspapers, n.d. Web. 20 Dec. 2009.

Bloom, Harold, ed. *H.D.* New York: Chelsea House, 1989. Print. Modern Critical Views.

Bonheur, Rosa. *The Horse Fair*. 1855. Metropolitan Museum of Art, New York. *Metropolitan Museum of Art*. Web. 2 Dec. 2010.

Borderline. Dir. Kenneth Macpherson. Perf. Paul Robeson, H.D., Eslanda Robeson, Bryher. POOL Films, 1930. *Paul Robeson: Portraits of the Artist*. Criterion Collection, 2007. DVD.

Bornstein, George. "Pound and the Making of Modernism." *The Cambridge Companion to Ezra Pound*. Ed. Ira B. Nadel. Cambridge: Cambridge UP, 1999. 24–42. Print.

Boughn, Michael. *H.D.: A Bibliography, 1905–1990*. Charlottesville: UP of Virginia, 1993. Print.

Boughn, Michael, and Victor Coleman. Introduction. Duncan, *H.D. Book* 1–30.

Breasted, James Henry. *A History of Egypt: From the Earliest Times to the Persian Conquest*. 2nd ed. New York: Scribner's, 1912. Print.

Brontë, Charlotte. *Poems of Charlotte Brontë*. Ed. Tom Winnifirth. New York: Blackwell, 1984. Print.

Brooks, Gwendolyn. *A Street in Bronzeville*. New York: Harper, 1945. Print.

Brown, Bill, ed. *Things*. Chicago: U of Chicago P, 2004. Print.

———. "Thing Theory." B. Brown, *Things* 1–21.

Brown, Deborah, Annie Finch, and Maxine Kumin, eds. *Lofty Dogmas: Poets on Poetics.* Little Rock: U of Arkansas P, 2005. Print.

Brown, Judith. "*Borderline*, Sensation, and the Machinery of Expression." *Modernism/Modernity* 14.4 (2007): 687–705. Print.

Browning, Elizabeth Barrett. *The Complete Poetical Works of Elizabeth Barrett Browning*. 1900. Whitefish: Kessinger, 2005. Print.

Bryant, Marsha, and Mary Ann Eaverly. "Egypto-Modernism: James Henry Breasted, H.D., and the New Past." *Modernism/Modernity* 14.3 (2007): 435–53. Print.

Bryer, Jackson. "H.D.: A Note on Her Critical Reputation." *Contemporary Literature* 10.4 (1969): 627–31. Print.

Bryher. *The Days of Mars: A Memoir, 1940–1946*. New York: Harcourt, 1972. Print.

———. *The Heart to Artemis: A Writer's Memoirs*. New York: Harcourt, 1962. Print.

Buck, Claire. *H.D. and Freud: Bisexuality and a Feminine Discourse*. New York: St. Martin's, 1991. Print.

Budge, E. A. Wallis. *The Egyptian Book of the Dead*. New York: Dover, 1967. Print.

Bulfinch, Thomas. *Bulfinch's Mythology*. New York: Mod. Lib., 1998. Print.

Burnett, Gary. *H.D. between Image and Epic: The Mysteries of Her Poetics*. Ann Arbor: UMI, 1989. Print.

Butler, Judith. *The Psychic Life of Power: Theories in Subjection*. Stanford: Stanford UP, 1997. Print.

Butler, Octavia. *"Bloodchild" and Other Stories*. New York: Four Walls Eight Windows, 1995. Print.

Camboni, Marina, ed. *H.D.'s Poetry: "The Meanings That Words Hide."* New York: AMS, 2003. Print.

Carby, Hazel V. "'On the Threshold of Woman's Era': Lynching, Empire, and Sexuality in Black Feminist Theory." *Critical Inquiry* 12.1 (1985): 262–77. Print.

———. *Race Men*. Cambridge: Harvard UP, 1998. Print.

Carter, Angela. *The Bloody Chamber*. New York: Penguin, 1990. Print.

Caruth, Cathy. *Unclaimed Experience: Trauma, Narrative, and History*. Baltimore: Johns Hopkins UP, 1996. Print.

Castle, Terry. *The Apparitional Lesbian: Female Homosexuality and Modern Culture*. New York: Columbia UP, 1993. Print.

Chisholm, Dianne. *H.D.'s Freudian Poetics: Psychoanalysis in Translation*. Ithaca: Cornell UP, 1992. Print.

Chisolm, Lawrence W. *Fenollosa: The Far East and American Culture*. New Haven: Yale UP, 1963. Print.

Christian, Barbara. *Black Woman Novelists: The Development of a Tradition, 1892–1976*. Westport: Greenwood, 1980. Print.

Cixous, Hélène. "The Laugh of the Medusa." Trans. Keith Cohen and Paula Cohen. *Signs* 1.4 (1976): 875–93. Print.

Cobley, Evelyn. "History and Ideology in Autobiographical Literature of the First World War." *Mosaic* 23.3 (1990): 37–54. Print.

Collecott, Diana, ed. *H.D.* Spec. issue of *Agenda* 25.3-4 (1987–88): 1–201. Print.

———. *H.D. and Sapphic Modernism, 1910–1950*. Cambridge: Cambridge UP, 1999. Print.

Collis, Betty, and Jef Moonen. "The Contributing Student: Philosophy, Technology, and Strategy." *Finding Your Online Voice: Stories Told by Experienced Online Educators*. Ed. J. Michael Spector. Mahwah: Erlbaum, 2007. 36–59. Print.

Condell, Diana, and Jean Liddiard. *Working for Victory? Images of Women in the First World War, 1914–18*. London: Routledge–Kegan Paul, 1987. Print.

Connor, Rachel. *H.D. and the Image*. Manchester: Manchester UP, 2005. Print.

Cook, Elizabeth. *Achilles: A Novel*. New York: Picador, 2003. Print.

Cooper, Helen M., Adrienne Auslander Munich, and Susan Merrill Squier, eds. *Arms and the Woman: War, Gender, and Literary Representation*. Chapel Hill: U of North Carolina P, 1989. Print.

Curry, Renée R. "H.D., Dove, Glück, and Levin: The Poetry of Afroasiatic and White Greece." *Sagetrieb* 19.3 (2006): 173–200. Print.

Danielpour, Richard. *An American Requiem*. Assoc. Music, 2001. CD.

Debo, Annette. "Interracial Modernism in Avant-Garde Film: Paul Robeson and H.D. in the 1930 *Borderline*." *Quarterly Review of Film and Video* 18.4 (2001): 371–83. Print.

———. "Whiteness and the Black/White Border in H.D." *Paideuma* 33.2-3 (2004): 155–75. Print.

Dembo, L. S., ed. *H.D.: A Reconsideration*. Spec. issue of *Contemporary Literature* 10.4 (1969): 433–685. Print.

DeShazer, Mary K. *Inspiring Women: Reimagining the Muse*. New York: Pergamon, 1986. Print.

Dickinson, Emily. *The Poems of Emily Dickinson*. Ed. R. W. Franklin. Cambridge: Belknap–Harvard UP, 1999. Print.

"Digital Images Online." *Beinecke Rare Book and Manuscript Library*. Yale U, 15 Nov. 2005. Web. 30 Apr. 2008.

Doan, Laura. *Fashioning Sapphism: The Origins of a Modern English Lesbian Culture*. New York: Columbia UP, 2001. Print.

Dobson, Silvia. "Cloud of Memories: Books H.D. Shared with Me, 1934–1960." *H.D. Newsletter* 1.2 (1987): 26–41. Print.

———. "Remembering H.D." *Agenda* 25.3-4 (1987–88): 126–44. Print.

———. "'Shock Knit within Terror': Living through World War II." *Iowa Review* 16.3 (1986): 232–45. Print.

———. "Woof and Heave and Surge and Wave and Flow." King 37–48.

Donald, James, Anne Friedberg, and Laura Marcus, eds. Close Up, *1927–1933: Cinema and Modernism*. Princeton: Princeton UP, 1998. Print.

Doré, Gustave. *The Finding of Moses*. 1866. *The Doré Bible Illustrations*. New York: Dover, 1974. Print.

Dove, Rita. *Mother Love*. New York: Norton, 1995. Print.

duCille, Ann. *The Coupling Convention: Sex, Text, and Tradition in Black Women's Fiction*. New York: Oxford UP, 1993. Print.

Duffy, Carol Ann. *The World's Wife*. New York: Picador, 2000. Print.

Duncan, Robert. *The H.D. Book*. Ed. Michael Boughn and Victor Coleman. Berkeley: U of California P, 2011. Print.

———. "The H.D. Book: Outline and Chronology." *Ironwood* 22 (1983): 65. Print.

———. "In the Sight of a Lyre, a Little Spear, a Chair." *Poetry* 91.4 (1958): 256–60. Print.

DuPlessis, Rachel Blau, ed. *H.D.* Spec. issue of *Sagetrieb* 6.2 (1987): 1–199. Print.

———. *H.D.: The Career of That Struggle*. Bloomington: Indiana UP, 1986. Print.

———. *The Pink Guitar: Writing as Feminist Practice*. New York: Routledge, 1990. Print.

———. *Writing Beyond the Ending: Narrative Strategies of Twentieth-Century Women Writers*. Bloomington: Indiana UP, 1985. Print.

Edmunds, Susan. *Out of Line: History, Psychoanalysis, and Montage in H.D.'s Long Poems.* Stanford: Stanford UP, 1994. Print.

Edwards, Amelia. *A Thousand Miles up the Nile*. 2nd ed. London: Routledge, 1891. *Celebration of Women Writer's Project*. Ed. Mary Mark Ockerbloom. Web. 2 Sept. 2007.

"Eidolon." *Oxford English Dictionary*. 2nd ed. 1989. Print.

Eisenstein, Sergei. *Film Form: Essays in Film Theory*. Trans. and ed. Jay Leyda. New York: Harcourt, 1969. Print.

Eliade, Mircea. *The Sacred and the Profane: The Nature of Religion*. Trans. Willard R. Trask. New York: Harcourt, 1959. Print.

Eliot, T. S. *Collected Poems, 1909–1962*. New York: Harcourt, 1963. Print.

———. *The Sacred Wood: Essays on Poetry and Criticism*. London: Methuen, 1920. Print.

Fauset, Jessie Redmon. *Plum Bun: A Novel without a Moral*. Boston: Beacon, 1999. Print.

Felski, Rita. "Modernist Studies and Cultural Studies: Reflections on Method." *Modernism/Modernity* 10.3 (2003): 501–17. Print.

Fenollosa, Ernest. *The Chinese Written Character as a Medium for Poetry*. Ed. Ezra Pound. San Francisco: City Lights, 1968. Print.

Fitzgerald, F. Scott. *Tender Is the Night*. 1934. New York: Scribner's, 1995. Print.

Foothills. Dir. Kenneth Macpherson. 1929. Film fragment. Museum of Mod. Art, New York.

Forbes, Jill, and Sarah Street. "Ideology, Aesthetics and Power." *European Cinema: An Introduction*. Ed. Forbes and Street. New York: Palgrave, 2000. 26–47. Print.

Forster, E. M. "Anonymity: An Inquiry." 1925. *Two Cheers for Democracy*. London: Arnold, 1951. 77–88. Print.

———. *Maurice*. New York: Norton, 1971. Print.

Fraistat, Neil. "The Place of the Book and the Book as Place." *Poems in Their Place: The Intertextuality and Order of Poetic Collections*. Ed. Fraistat. Chapel Hill: U of North Carolina P, 1986. 3–17. Print.

Frazer, James George. *The Golden Bough: A Study in Magic and Religion*. New York: Macmillan, 1894. Print.

Freud, Sigmund. *The Interpretation of Dreams*. Trans. A. A. Brill. New York: Macmillan, 1913. Print.

———. *The Standard Edition of the Complete Psychological Works of Sigmund Freud*. 24 vols. London: Hogarth, 1900–53. Print.

Friedberg, Anne. "Approaching *Borderline*." King 369–90.

Friedman, Susan Stanford, ed. *Analyzing Freud: Letters of H.D., Bryher, and Their Circle*. New York: New Directions, 2002. Print.

———. "Hilda Doolittle (H.D.)." *Dictionary of Literary Biography* 45 (1986): 115–49. Print.

———. *Mappings: Feminism and the Cultural Geographies of Encounter*. Princeton: Princeton UP, 1998. Print.

———. "Modernism of the 'Scattered Remnant': Race and Politics in the Development of H.D.'s Modernist Vision." King 91–116.

———. *Penelope's Web: Gender, Modernity, H.D.'s Fiction*. Cambridge: Cambridge UP, 1990. Print.

———. "Periodizing Modernism: Postcolonial Modernities and the Space/Time Borders of Modernist Studies." Gikandi, *Modernism and Transnationalisms* 425–44.

———. *Psyche Reborn: The Emergence of H.D.* Bloomington: Indiana UP, 1981. Print.

———. "Who Buried H.D.? A Poet, Her Critics, and Her Place in 'the Literary Tradition.'" Bloom 45–61.

Friedman, Susan Stanford, and Rachel Blau DuPlessis, eds. *H.D. Centennial Issue*. Spec. issue of *Contemporary Literature* 27.4 (1986): 433–595. Print.

———. "'I Had Two Loves Separate': The Sexualities of H.D.'s *HER*." Friedman and DuPlessis, *Signets* 205–32.

———, eds. *Signets: Reading H.D.* Madison: U of Wisconsin P, 1990. Print.

Fritz, Angela DiPace. *Thought and Vision: A Critical Reading of H.D.'s Poetry*. Washington: Catholic U of America P, 1988. Print.

Frost, Robert. *North of Boston: Poems*. 1914. Ed. Edward Connery Lathem. New York: Dodd, 1983. Print.

Frow, John. "A Pebble, a Camera, a Man Who Turns into a Telegraph Pole." B. Brown, *Things* 346–61.

Fussell, Paul. *The Great War and Modern Memory*. London: Oxford UP, 1975. Print.

Geertz, Clifford. "Thick Description: Toward an Interpretive Theory of Culture." *The Interpretation of Cultures: Selected Essays*. By Geertz. New York: Basic, 1973. 3–30. Print.

Gelpi, Albert. *A Coherent Splendor: The American Renaissance, 1910–1950*. Cambridge: Cambridge UP, 1987. Print.

———. "Re-membering the Mother: A Reading of H.D.'s *Trilogy*." Friedman and DuPlessis, *Signets* 318–35.

Gikandi, Simon, ed. *Modernism and Transnationalisms*. Spec. issue of *Modernism/Modernity* 13.3 (2006): 419–606. Print.

———. "Preface: Modernism in the World." Gikandi, *Modernism and Transnationalisms* 419–24.

Gilbert, Sandra M., and Susan Gubar. *The Madwoman in the Attic: The Woman Writer and the Nineteenth-Century Literary Imagination*. New Haven: Yale UP, 1979. Print.

———. *No Man's Land: The Place of the Woman Writer in the Twentieth Century*. 3 vols. New Haven: Yale UP, 1988–94. Print.

Gould, Jean. *American Women Poets: Pioneers of Modern Poetry*. New York: Dodd, 1980. Print.

Graham, Jorie. *The End of Beauty*. Hopewell: Ecco, 1987. Print.

Gray, Janet. *She Wields a Pen: American Women Poets of the Nineteenth Century*. Iowa City: U of Iowa P, 1997. Print.

Greger, Debora. *Desert Fathers, Uranium Daughters*. New York: Penguin, 1996. Print.

———. *God*. New York: Penguin, 2001. Print.

Gregg, Frances. *The Mystic Leeway*. Ed. Ben Jones. Toronto: Carleton UP, 1995. Print.

Gregory, Eileen. *H.D. and Hellenism: Classic Lines*. New York: Cambridge UP, 1997. Print.

———. Preface. *H.D. Newsletter* 2.1 (1988): 5. Print.

———. "Rose Cut in Rock: Sappho and H.D.'s *Sea Garden*." Friedman and DuPlessis, *Signets* 129–54.

Gregory, Horace. "Speaking of Books." *New York Times Book Review* 22 Oct. 1961: 2. Print.

Grimm, Jacob, and Wilhelm Grimm. "Fichter's Bird." Trans. D. L. Ashliman. *University of Pittsburgh*. U of Pittsburgh, 2002. Web. 29 Apr. 2008.

Gubar, Susan. "The Echoing Spell of H.D.'s *Trilogy*." Friedman and DuPlessis, *Signets* 297–317.

Guest, Barbara. *Herself Defined: The Poet H.D. and Her World*. New York: Doubleday, 1984. Print.

Gunning, Tom. "Never Seen This Picture Before: Muybridge in Multiplicity." Prodger 222–72.

Hall, Radclyffe. *The Unlit Lamp*. New York: Cape, 1924. Print.

———. *The Well of Loneliness*. London: Jonathan Cape, 1928. Print.

Hamilton, Edith. *Mythology: Timeless Tales of Gods and Heroes*. New York: Warner, 1999. Print.

Hanley, Lynne. *Writing War: Fiction, Gender, and Memory*. Amherst: U of Massachusetts P, 1991. Print.

Hanscombe, Gillian, and Virginia L. Smyers. *Writing for Their Lives: The Modernist Women, 1910–1940*. Boston: Northeastern UP, 1989. Print.

Harad, Alyssa. "Resisting Crisis: Trauma, Pedagogy and Survival." *S&F Online* 2.1 (2003): 26 pars. Web. 21 Feb. 2008.

Harrison, Victoria. "When a Gift Is Poison: H.D., the Moravian, the Jew, and World War II." *Sagetrieb* 15.1-2 (1996): 69–93. Print.

Hatlen, Burton, ed. *H.D.* Spec. issue of *Sagetrieb* 15.1-2 (1996): 1–280. Print.

———. "The Imagist Poetics of H.D.'s *Sea Garden*." *Paideuma* 24.2-3 (1995): 107–30. Print.

———, ed. *Marianne Moore and H.D.* Spec. issue of *Paideuma* 33.2-3 (2004): 1–290. Print.

H.D. *Asphodel*. Ed. Robert Spoo. Durham: Duke UP, 1992. Print.

———. "Autobiographical Notes." H.D. Papers. Beinecke Rare Book and Manuscript Lib., Yale U, New Haven.

———. *Bid Me to Live (A Madrigal)*. New York: Dial, 1960. Print.

———. *Bid Me to Live: A Madrigal*. Redding Ridge: Black Swan, 1983. Print.

———. "The *Borderline* Pamphlet" ["*Borderline*: A POOL Film with Paul Robeson"]. Donald, Friedberg, and Marcus 221–36.

———. *By Avon River*. New York: Macmillan, 1949. Print.

———. "The Cinema and the Classics: Beauty, Restraint, the Mask and the Movietone." Donald, Friedberg, and Marcus 105–20.

———. *Collected Poems, 1912–1944*. Ed. Louis L. Martz. New York: New Directions, 1983. Print.

———. "Confessions-Questionnaire." *Little Review* 12.2 (1929). Rpt. in Margaret Anderson 364–66.

———. "Conrad Veidt: *The Student of Prague*." Donald, Friedberg, and Marcus 120–24.

———. *End to Torment*. New York: New Directions, 1979. Print.

———. "*Expiation*." Donald, Friedberg, and Marcus 125–30.

———. *The Gift*. Abr. Griselda Ohannessian. Introd. Perdita Schaffner. New York: New Directions, 1982. Print.

———. The Gift *by H.D.: The Complete Text*. Ed. Jane Augustine. Gainesville: UP of Florida, 1998. Print.

———. "H.D. by Delia Alton." *Iowa Review* 16.3 (1986): 174–221. Print.

———. H.D. Scrapbook. H.D. Papers. Beinecke Rare Book and Manuscript Lib., Yale U, New Haven.

———. *The Hedgehog*. New York: New Directions, 1988. Print.

———. *Hedylus*. 1928. Redding Ridge: Black Swan, 1980. Print.

———. *Helen in Egypt*. New York: New Directions, 1961. Print.

———. *Helen in Egypt*. *PennSound*. U of Pennsylvania, 2008. Web. 4 Oct. 2010.

———. *Hermetic Definition*. New York: New Directions, 1972. Print.

———. *HERmione* [*HER*]. New York: New Directions, 1981. Print.

———. *Hippolytus Temporizes [and] Ion*. 1927. New York: New Directions, 2003. Print.

———. "*Joan of Arc*." Donald, Friedberg, and Marcus 130–33.

———. "*The King of Kings* Again." *Close Up* 2.2 (1928): 21–32. Print.

———. *Kora and Ka*. 1934. New York: New Directions, 1996. Print.

———. "A Letter from England." *Bryn Mawr Alumnae Bulletin* 21.7 (1941): 22–23. Print.

———. *Majic Ring*. Ed. Demetres P. Tryphonopoulos. Gainesville: UP of Florida, 2009. Print.

———. *The Mystery*. Ed. Jane Augustine. Gainesville: UP of Florida, 2009. Print.

———. "Narthex." *The Second American Caravan*. Ed. Alfred Kreymborg, Lewis Mumford, and Paul Rosenfeld. New York: Macaulay, 1928. 225–84. Print.

——— [as John Helforth]. *Nights*. 1935. New York: New Directions, 1986. Print.

———. *Notes on Thought and Vision*. San Francisco: City Lights, 1982. Print.

———. *Paint It Today* [*Paint It To-day*]. Ed. Cassandra Laity. New York: New York UP, 1992. Print.

———. *Palimpsest*. 1926. Carbondale: Southern Illinois UP, 1968. Print.

———. *Pilate's Wife*. Ed. Joan A. Burke. New York: New Directions, 2000. Print.

———. "Russian Films." Donald, Friedberg, and Marcus 134–39.

———. "Sagesse." *Evergreen Review* 2.5 (1958): 57–117. Print.

———. *Selected Poems*. Ed. Louis L. Martz. New York: New Directions, 1988. Print.

———. *The Sword Went Out to Sea: (Synthesis of a Dream), by Delia Alton*. Ed. Cynthia Hogue and Julie Vandivere. Gainesville: UP of Florida, 2007. Print.

———. *Tribute to Freud*. 1945. New York: New Directions, 1984. Print.

———. *Trilogy*. 1944–46. Ed. Aliki Barnstone. New York: New Directions, 1998. Print.

———. "*Turksib*." *Close Up* 5.6 (1929): 488–92. Print.

———. "Two Americans." *New Directions in Prose and Poetry* 37 (1987): 58–68. Print.

———. *The Usual Star*. Dijon: Darantière, 1934. Print.

———. *Vale Ave*. Redding Ridge: Black Swan, 1992. Print.

———. *What Do I Love?* London: Brendin, 1950. Print.

———. *White Rose and the Red*. Ed Alison Halsall. Gainesville: UP of Florida, 2009. Print.

———. *Within the Walls*. Iowa City: Windhover, 1993. Print.

H.D. (Hilda Doolittle) Home Page. Ed. Heather Hernandez. Imagists.org, 2 Mar. 2008. Web. 30 Apr. 2008.

Hemingway, Ernest. *A Farewell to Arms*. 1929. New York: Scribner's, 1995. Print.

———. *The Garden of Eden*. 1986. New York: Scribner's, 1995. Print.

———. *In Our Time*. 1930. New York: Scribner's, 1996. Print.

———. *The Sun Also Rises*. 1926. New York: Scribner's, 2006. Print.

Henke, Suzette A. *Shattered Subjects: Trauma and Testimony in Women's Life-Writing*. London: Macmillan, 2000. Print.

Herman, Judith Lewis. *Trauma and Recovery: From Domestic Abuse to Political Terror*. New York: Basic, 1997. Print.

Higonnet, Margaret Randolph, et al., eds. *Behind the Lines: Gender and the Two World Wars*. New Haven: Yale UP, 1987. Print.

Hogue, Cynthia. *The Incognito Body*. Los Angeles: Red Hen, 2006. Print.

Hollenberg, Donna Krolik, ed. "Art and Ardor in World War One: Selected Letters from H.D. to John Cournos." *Iowa Review* 16.3 (1986): 126–55. Print.

———, ed. *Between History and Poetry: The Letters of H.D. and Norman Holmes Pearson*. Iowa City: U of Iowa P, 1997. Print.

———, ed. *H.D. and Poets After*. Iowa City: U of Iowa P, 2000. Print.

———. *H.D.: The Poetics of Childbirth and Creativity*. Boston: Northeastern UP, 1991. Print.

———. Introduction. Hollenberg, *H.D. and Poets* xi–xxii.

———. "'Obscure Directions': Interpreting Denise Levertov's Ambivalence about Ezra Pound." *Biography* 27.4 (2004): 737–50. Print.

———. "'Within the World of Your Perceptions': The Letters of H.D. and Denise Levertov." *Paideuma* 33.2-3 (2004): 247–74. Print.

Hollenberg, Donna Krolik, and Eileen Gregory, eds. *H.D.* Spec. issue of *Sagetrieb* 14.1-2 (1995): 1–278. Print.

Holy Bible. Grand Rapids: Zondervan, 1996. Print. New intl. vers.

Howe, Susan. *My Emily Dickinson*. Berkeley: North Atlantic, 1985. Print.

Hughes, Glenn. *Imagism and the Imagists: A Study in Modern Poetry*. Stanford: Stanford UP, 1931. Print.

Hughes, Langston. *Collected Poems of Langston Hughes*. Ed. Arnold Rampersad and David Roessel. New York: Vintage, 1994. Print.

———. "The Negro Artist and the Racial Mountain." *Nation* 23 June 1926: n. pag. Print.

———. *Selected Poems of Langston Hughes*. New York: Vintage, 1990. Print.

Hull, Gloria T. *Color, Sex, and Poetry: Three Women Writers of the Harlem Renaissance*. Bloomington: Indiana UP, 1987. Print.

Hulme, T. E. *Speculations: Essays on Humanism and the Philosophy of Art*. Ed. Herbert Read. New York: Harcourt, 1924. Print.

Huntington, Samuel P. *The Clash of Civilizations and the Remaking of World Order*. New York: Simon, 1998. Print.

Irigaray, Luce. "The Power of Discourse and the Subordination of the Feminine." *This Sex Which Is Not One*. 1977. Trans. Catherine Porter with Carolyn Burke. Ithaca: Cornell UP, 1985. 68–85. Print.

Jackson, Thomas H., ed. *A Celebration of H.D. and Marianne Moore*. Spec. issue of *Poesis: A Journal of Criticism*. 6.3-4 (1985): 1–137. Print.

Joyce, James. *Portrait of the Artist as a Young Man*. New York: Viking, 1964. Print.

The Joyless Street. Dir. G. W. Pabst. Perf. Werner Krauss, Valeska Gert, Asta Nielsen, and Greta Garbo. Sofar-Film, 1925. Film.

Kaplan, Caren. "The Politics of Location as Transnational Feminist Critical Practice." *Scattered Hegemonies: Postmodernity and Transnational Feminist Practices*. Ed. Inderpal Grewal and Kaplan. Minneapolis: U of Minnesota P, 1994. 137–52. Print.

———. *Questions of Travel: Postmodern Discourses of Displacement*. Durham: Duke UP, 1996. Print.

Kelly, Robert. "H.D.: A Joining." Hollenberg, *H.D. and Poets* 32–44.

Kenner, Hugh. *The Pound Era*. Berkeley: U of California P, 1971. Print.

King, Michael, ed. *H.D.: Woman and Poet*. Orono: Natl. Poetry Foundation, 1986. Print.

Kingston, Maxine Hong. *The Woman Warrior: Memoirs of a Girlhood among Ghosts*. New York: Knopf, 1976. Print.

Kircher, Athanasius. *Oedipus Aegyptiacus*. 3 vols. Rome: Ex Typographia Vitalis Mascardi, 1652–54. Print.

Kirkpatrick, Sidney D. *The Revenge of Thomas Eakins*. New Haven: Yale UP, 2006. Print.

Kloepfer, Deborah Kelly. *The Unspeakable Mother: Forbidden Discourse in Jean Rhys and H.D.* Ithaca: Cornell UP, 1989. Print.

Korg, Jacob. *Winter Love: Ezra Pound and H.D.* Madison: U of Wisconsin P, 2003. Print.

Kossman, Nina. *Gods and Mortals: Modern Poems on Classical Myths*. New York: Oxford UP, 2000. Print.

Lacan, Jacques. *Écrits: The First Complete Edition in English*. Trans. Bruce Fink. New York: Norton, 2006. Print.

LaCapra, Dominick. *History and Memory after Auschwitz*. Ithaca: Cornell UP, 1998. Print.

———. *Writing History, Writing Trauma*. Baltimore: Johns Hopkins UP, 2001. Print.

Laity, Cassandra. *H.D. and the Victorian Fin de Siècle: Gender, Modernism, Decadence*. New York: Cambridge UP, 1996. Print.

Landseer, Edwin Henry. *Stag at Bay*. 1846. Watercolor. Courtauld Inst. of Art, London.

Last Year in Marienbad. By Alain Robbe-Grillet. Dir. Alain Resnais. Perf. Giorgio Albertazzi, Delphine Seyrig, and Sacha Pitoeff. Argos Films, 1961. Film.

Lawrence, D. H. *The Man Who Died*. 1929. New York: Harper, 1995. Print.

———. *The Rainbow*. Ed. James Wood, Mark Kinkead-Weekes, and Anne Fernihough. New York: Penguin, 2007. Print.

———. *Sons and Lovers*. Ed. Geoff Dyer. New York: Mod. Lib., 1999. Print.

Lemke, Sieglinde. *Primitivist Modernism: Black Culture and the Origins of Transatlantic Modernism*. New York: Oxford UP, 1998. Print.

Lendinara, Patrizia. "Binding Words and Feelings: Nominal Compounds in the *Trilogy*." Camboni 115–41.

Levertov, Denise. *Breathing the Water*. New York: New Directions, 1987. Print.

———. *The Jacob's Ladder*. New York: New Directions, 1961. Print.

———. *Life in the Forest*. New York: New Directions, 1978. Print.

———. *Light Up the Cave*. New York: New Directions, 1981. Print.

———. *Poems, 1960–1967*. New York: New Directions, 1967. Print.

———. *Poems, 1968–1972*. New York: New Directions, 1987. Print.

———. *The Poet in the World*. New York: New Directions, 1973. Print.

———. *Relearning the Alphabet*. New York: New Directions, 1970. Print.

———. *Sands of the Well*. New York: New Directions, 1996. Print.

———. "Scenes from the Life of the Peppertrees." *Evergreen Review* 2.5 (1958): 86–87. Print.

———. *The Stream and the Sapphire*. New York: New Directions, 1997. Print.

———. *To Stay Alive*. New York: New Directions, 1971. Print.

Longenbach, James. "Modern Poetry." *The Cambridge Companion to Modernism*. Ed. Michael Levenson. Cambridge: Cambridge UP, 1999. 100–29. Print.

Lorde, Audre. *The Black Unicorn*. New York: Norton, 1995. Print.

Lowe, Lisa. *Critical Terrains: French and British Orientalisms*. Ithaca: Cornell UP, 1991. Print.

Lowell, Amy. *Selected Poems of Amy Lowell*. Ed. Melissa Bradshaw and Adrienne Munich. New Brunswick: Rutgers UP, 2002. Print.

Malek, Jaromir. *Egypt: 4,000 Years of Art*. New York: Phaidon, 2003. Print.

Mandel, Charlotte. "Garbo/Helen: The Self-Projection of H.D." *Women's Studies* 7.1-2 (1980): 127–35. Print.

———. "Letters across the Atlantic: H.D., Bryher, May Sarton, during World War II." *A Celebration for May Sarton: Essays from the National Conference "May Sarton at 80: A Celebration of Her Life and Work."* Ed. Constance Hunting and Mary Anne Wallace. Orono: Puckerbrush, 1994. 89–104. Print.

———. "Magical Lenses: Poet's Vision beyond the Naked Eye." King 301–18.

———. "The Redirected Image: Cinematic Dynamics in the Style of H.D." *Literature/Film Quarterly* 11.1 (1983): 36–45. Print.

———. Rev. of *The Gift*, by H.D. *English Literature in Transition, 1880–1920* 42.3 (1999): 344–48. Print.

Mansfield, Katherine. "The Fly." Tate 68–72.

Mathis, Mary S., and Michael King. "An Annotated Bibliography of Works about H.D.: 1969–1985." King 393–511.

McCabe, Susan. "Borderline Modernism: Paul Robeson and the Femme Fatale." *Callaloo* 25.2 (2002): 639–53. Print.

———. *Cinematic Modernism: Modernist Poetry and Film*. New York: Cambridge UP, 2005. Print.

McGann, Jerome J. "Culture and Technology: The Way We Live Now, What Is to Be Done?" *Interdisciplinary Science Reviews* 30.2 (2005): 179–89. Print.

———. *Radiant Textuality: Literature since the World Wide Web*. New York: Palgrave, 2001. Print.

McIntosh, Peggy. "White Privilege and Male Privilege: A Personal Account of Coming to See Correspondences through Work in Women's Studies." *Race, Class, and Gender: An Anthology*. Ed. Margaret L. Anderson and Patricia Hill Collins. Belmont: Wadsworth, 1988. 94–105. Print.

Millay, Edna St. Vincent. *The Selected Poetry of Edna St. Vincent Millay*. Ed. Nancy Milford. New York: Mod. Lib., 2001. Print.

Miller, Meredith. "Enslaved to Both These Others: Gender and Inheritance in H.D.'s 'Secret Name: Excavator's Egypt.'" *Tulsa Studies in Women's Literature* 16.1 (1997): 77–105. Print.

Monkey's Moon. Dir. Kenneth Macpherson. POOL, 1929. *Beinecke Rare Book and Manuscript Library*. Web. 24 Nov. 2010.

Moore, Marianne. *Complete Poems*. New York: Macmillian, 1981. Print.

———. *The Selected Letters of Marianne Moore*. Ed. Bonnie Costello, Celeste Goodridge, and Cristanne Miller. New York: Knopf, 1997. Print.

Moravian Church in North America. Moravian Church in North Amer., 2008. Web. 1 May 2008.

Morris, Adalaide. "The Concept of Projection: H.D.'s Visionary Powers." *Contemporary Literature* 25.4 (1984): 411–36. Print.

———, ed. *H.D. Centennial Issue*. Spec. issue of *Iowa Review* 16.3 (1986): 1–303. Print.

———. *How to Live / What to Do: H.D.'s Cultural Poetics*. Urbana: U of Illinois P, 2003. Print.

———. "Signaling: Feminism, Politics, and Mysticism in H.D.'s War Trilogy." *Sagetrieb* 9.3 (1990): 121–33. Print.

Murray, Margaret A. *Ancient Egyptian Legends*. London: Murray, 1920. Print.

Murry, John Middleton, ed. *Katherine Mansfield's Letters to John Middleton Murry: 1913–1922*. London: Constable, 1951. Print.

Muybridge, Eadweard. *Muybridge's Complete Human and Animal Locomotion: All 781 Plates from the 1887 Animal Locomotion*. 1887. 2 vols. New York: Dover, 1979. Print.

Nelson, Cary, ed. *Modern American Poetry*. U of Illinois, Urbana, 2002. Web. 1 May 2008.

Ngũgĩ wa Thiong'o. "For Peace, Justice, and Culture: The Intellectual in the Twenty-First Century." *Profession* (2006): 33–39. Print.

Nielsen, Aldon Lynn. *Reading Race: White American Poets and the Racial Discourse in the Twentieth Century*. Athens: U of Georgia P, 1988. Print.

Nims, John Frederick. "Off the Main Road: Some Maverick Meters." *An Exaltation of Forms: Contemporary Poets Celebrate the Diversity of Their Art.* Ed. Annie Finch and Kathrine Varnes. Ann Arbor: U of Michigan P, 2002. 95–104. Print.

October: Ten Days That Shook the World. Dir. Sergei Eisenstein. Sovkino, 1928. Film.

Olson, Charles. *Call Me Ishmael.* San Francisco: City Lights, 1947. Print.

Orange, Tom. "William Carlos Williams between Image and Object." *William Carlos Williams and the Language of Poetry.* Ed. Burton Hatlen and Demetres Tryphonopoulos. Orono: Natl. Poetry Foundation, 2002. 127–56. Print.

Ostriker, Alicia Suskin. *Feminist Revision and the Bible.* Cambridge: Blackwell, 1992. Print.

———. "No Rule of Procedure: The Open Poetics of H.D." Friedman and DuPlessis, *Signets* 336–51.

———. *Stealing the Language: The Emergence of Women's Poetry in America.* Boston: Beacon, 1986. Print.

———. "What Do Women Poets Want? H.D. and Marianne Moore as Poetic Ancestresses." *Contemporary Literature* 27.4 (1986): 475–92. Print.

———. *Writing Like a Woman.* Ann Arbor: U of Michigan P, 1983. Print.

Owen, Wilfred. *The Collected Poems of Wilfred Owen.* Ed. C. Day Lewis. New York: New Directions, 1963. Print.

Pandora's Box. Dir. G. W. Pabst. Süd-Film, 1929. Film.

Parada, Carlos. *Greek Mythology Link.* Parada and Maicar Förlag, 1997. Web. 4 Oct. 2010.

The Passion of Joan of Arc. Dir. Carl Dreyer. Perf. Maria Falconetti and Eugene Silvain. Société Générale des Films, 1928. Film.

Pearson, Norman Holmes. Foreword. *Trilogy.* By H.D. New York: New Directions, 1973. v–xii. Print.

Pearson, Norman Holmes, and L. S. Dembo. "Norman Holmes Pearson on H.D.: An Interview." *Contemporary Literature* 10.4 (1969): 435–46. Print.

Phelan, Peggy. "Weapons and Scalpels: The Early Poetry and H.D. and Marianne Moore." Willis 403–18.

Poe, Edgar Allan. *Edgar Allan Poe: Poetry and Tales.* Ed. Patrick F. Quinn. New York: Lib. of Amer., 1984. Print.

Pondrom, Cyrena N. "H.D. and the Origins of Imagism." Friedman and DuPlessis, *Signets* 85–109.

———. "Marianne Moore and H.D.: Female Community and Poetic Achievement." Willis 371–402.

———. "Selected Letters from H.D. to F. S. Flint: A Commentary on the Imagist Period." *Contemporary Literature* 10.4 (1969): 557–86. Print.

Pope, Rob. *Textual Intervention: Critical and Creative Strategies for Literary Studies.* London: Routledge, 1995. Print.

Pound, Ezra. *ABC of Reading.* New York: New Directions, 1960. Print.

———. *The Cantos of Ezra Pound.* New York: New Directions, 1970. Print.

———, ed. *Des Imagistes: An Anthology.* London: Poetry Bookshop, 1914. Print.

———. "A Few Don'ts by an Imagiste." *Poetry* 1 (1913): 200–06. Print.

———. *The Letters of Ezra Pound, 1907–1941*. Ed. D. D. Paige. New York: Harcourt, 1950. Print.

———. *Literary Essays of Ezra Pound.* Ed. T. S. Eliot. Boston: Faber, 1985. Print.

———. *Selected Poems of Ezra Pound*. New York: New Directions, 1957. Print.

———. "Vorticism." *Fortnightly Review* 96 (1914): 461–71. Print.

Powell, Barry B. *Classical Myth.* Upper Saddle River: Prentice, 2006. Print.

Preminger, Alex, Terry V. F. Brogan, and Frank J. Warnke, eds. *New Princeton Encyclopedia of Poetry and Poetics*. Princeton: Princeton UP, 1993. Print.

Prodger, Phillip. *Time Stands Still: Muybridge and the Instantaneous Photography Movement*. New York: Oxford UP, 2003. Print.

Quinn, Vincent. *Hilda Doolittle (H.D.).* New York: Twayne, 1967. Print.

Ramazani, Jahan. "Modernist Bricolage, Postcolonial Hybridity." Gikandi, *Modernism and Transnationalisms* 445–64.

Rembrandt van Rijn. *The Anatomy Lesson of Dr. Nicolaes Tulp.* 1632. Oil on canvas. Mauritshuis, The Hague.

Rich, Adrienne. *Diving into the Wreck: Poems, 1971–1972*. New York: Norton, 1973. Print.

Richards, James. "The Blitz: Sorting the Myth from the Reality." *British History In-Depth*. BBC, 2010. Web. 15 Nov. 2010.

Rilke, Rainer Maria. *Sonnets to Orpheus*. Trans. M. D. Herter Norton. New York: Norton, 2006. Print.

Rinn, Fauneil J., ed. *Emily Dickinson–H.D. Dual Centennial*. Spec. issue of *San José Studies* 13.3 (1987): 1–144. Print.

Robins, Gay. *The Art of Ancient Egypt*. Cambridge: Harvard UP, 1997. Print.

Robinson, Janice S. *H.D.: The Life and Work of an American Poet*. Boston: Houghton, 1982. Print.

Roediger, David R. *The Wages of Whiteness: Race and the Making of the American Working Class*. London: Verso, 2007. Print.

Said, Edward W. *Orientalism*. New York: Vintage, 1978. Print.

Saussure, Ferdinand de. *Course in General Linguistics.* Trans. Wade Baskin. Ed. Charles Bally and Albert Sechehaye. New York: Philosophical Lib., 1959. Print.

Sbisa, Marina. "Subject and Gender in H.D.'s *Trilogy*." Camboni 91–113.

Scarry, Elaine. *The Body in Pain: The Making and Unmaking of the World*. New York: Oxford UP, 1985. Print.

Schaffner, Perdita. Introduction. H.D., *Hedgehog* vii–xiii.

———. Introduction. H.D., *Nights* ix–xvi.

———. "Keeper of the Flame." King 27–33.

———. "Merano, 1962." *Paideuma* 4 (1975): 513–18. Print.

———. "Pandora's Box." H.D., *HERmione* vii–xi.

———. "A Profound Animal." H.D., *Bid* [1983] 185–94.

———. "Running." *Iowa Review* 16.3 (1986): 7–13. Print.

———. "A Sketch of H.D.: The Egyptian Cat." Friedman and DuPlessis, *Signets* 3–6.

———. "They Lived to Write." *New Directions for Women* 18 (1989): 18–19. Print.

———. "Unless a Bomb Falls . . ." H.D., *Gift* ix–xv.

Schussele, Christian. *The Power of the Gospel*. 1862. Moravian Archives, Bethlehem. *Moravian Archives*. Web. 2 Dec. 2010.

Schweik, Susan. *A Gulf So Deeply Cut: American Women Poets and the Second World War*. Madison: U of Wisconsin P, 1991. Print.

Scott, Bonnie Kime, ed. *The Gender of Modernism: A Critical Anthology*. Bloomington: Indiana UP, 1990. Print.

Sexton, Anne. *Transformations*. Boston: Houghton, 1971. Print.

Shakespeare, William. *As You Like It*. Ed. Agnes Latham. London: Oxford UP, 1975. Print.

———. *The Merchant of Venice*. Ed. John Russell Brown. London: Oxford UP, 1959. Print.

Shelley, Percy Bysshe. *"A Defence of Poetry" and a Letter to Lord Ellenborough*. Folcroft: Folcroft Lib., 1973. Print.

Shohat, Ella. *Taboo Memories, Diasporic Voices*. Durham: Duke UP, 2006. Print.

Sidney, Philip. *A Defence of Poetry*. 1579–80. Ed. J. A. van Dorsten. New York: Oxford UP, 1971. Print.

Silko, Leslie Marmon. *Storyteller*. New York: Seaver, 1981. Print.

Silverstein, Louis. "H.D. Chronology." *H.D. (Hilda Doolittle)*. Imagists.org, 10 Dec. 2006. Web. 18 Sept. 2007.

Smith, William. *Smaller Classical Dictionary*. New York: Dutton, 1958. Print.

Smyers, Virginia. "H.D.'s Books in the Bryher Library." *H.D. Newsletter* 1.2 (1987): 15–25. Print.

Some Imagist Poets: An Anthology. 3 vols. Boston: Houghton, 1915, 1916, 1917. Print.

Spiro, Joanna. "Weighed in the Balance: H.D.'s Resistance to Freud in 'Writing on the Wall.'" *American Imago* 58.2 (2001): 597–621. Print.

Spoo, Robert. Introduction. H.D., *Kora* v–xv.

Stanton, Domna C. Introduction. *Profession* (2006): 7–12. Print.

Stein, Gertrude. *The Autobiography of Alice B. Toklas*. 1933. New York: Vintage, 1990. Print.

———. *Everybody's Autobiography*. 1937. New York: Exact Change, 2004. Print.

———. *Gertrude Stein: Writings, 1903–1932*. Ed. Catharine R. Stimpson and Harriet Chessman. New York: Lib. of Amer., 1998. Print.

———. *The Making of Americans*. New York: Boni, 1926. Print.

———. *Selected Writings of Gertrude Stein*. Ed. Carl Van Vechten. 1946. New York: Vintage, 1990. Print.

Stewart, Susan. *Poetry and the Fate of the Senses*. Chicago: U of Chicago P, 2002. Print.

Stoler, Ann Laura. "Tense and Tender Ties: The Politics of Comparison in North American History and (Post) Colonial Studies." *Haunted by Empire: Geogra-*

phies of Intimacy in North American History. Ed. Stoler. Durham: Duke UP, 2006. 23–70. Print.

Strachey, James. "Preliminary Notes upon the Problem of Akhenaten." *International Journal of Psycho-analysis* 20 (1939): 33–42. Print.

The Student of Prague. Dir. Henrik Galeen. Perf. Conrad Veidt. Sokal-Film, 1926. Film.

Surette, Leon. *The Birth of Modernism: Ezra Pound, T. S. Eliot, W. B. Yeats, and the Occult*. Buffalo: McGill–Queen's UP, 1993. Print.

Swann, Thomas Burnett. *The Classical World of H.D.* Lincoln: U of Nebraska P, 1962. Print.

Swinburne, A. C. *Poems and Ballads*. London: Chatto, 1914. Print.

Sword, Helen. *Engendering Inspiration: Visionary Strategies in Rilke, Lawrence, and H.D.* Ann Arbor: U of Michigan P, 1995. Print.

———. "Teaching in Color: Multiple Intelligences in the Literature Classroom." *Pedagogy* 7.2 (2007): 223–50. Print.

Tate, Trudi, ed. *Women, Men and the Great War*. Manchester: Manchester UP, 1995. Print.

Taylor, Georgina. *H.D. and the Public Sphere of Modernist Women Writers, 1913–1946: Talking Women*. Oxford: Clarendon, 2001. Print.

Tinker, Carol, ed. "H.D.: A Friendship Traced: Letters to Silvia Dobson and a Poem." *Conjunctions* 2 (1982): 115–57. Print.

Tobin, Vincent Arieh. "Amun and Amun-Re." *Oxford Encyclopedia of Ancient Egypt*. Vol. 1. Ed. Donald B. Redford. Oxford: Oxford UP, 2001. 82–84. Print.

Torgovnik, Marianna. *Gone Primitive: Savage Intellects, Modern Lives*. Chicago: U of Chicago P, 1990. Print.

The Torrent. Dir. Monta Bell. MGM, 1926. Film.

Truettner, William H. "The Art of History: American Exploration and Discovery Scenes, 1840–1860." *American Art Journal* 14.1 (1982): 4–31. Print.

Twitchell-Waas, Jeffrey. "Seaward: H.D.'s *Helen in Egypt* as a Response to Pound's *Cantos*." *Twentieth Century Literature* 44.4 (1998): 464–83. Print.

Van Zanten, David. "Second Empire Architecture in Philadelphia." *Philadelphia Museum of Art Bulletin* 74.322 (1978): 9–24. Print.

Vendler, Helen. "Marianne Moore." *Marianne Moore.* Ed. Harold Bloom. New York: Chelsea House, 1987. 73–88. Print. Modern Critical Views.

Walton, Jean. "'Nightmare of the Uncoordinated White-Folk': Race, Psychoanalysis, and *Borderline*." *Discourse* 19.2 (1997): 88–109. Print.

———. "White Neurotics, Black Primitives, and the Queer Matrix of *Borderline*." *Out Takes: Essays on Queer Theory and Film*. Ed. Ellis Hanson. Durham: Duke UP, 1999. 243–70. Print.

Warner, Sylvia Townsend. *Mr. Fortune's Maggot*. 1927. New York: New York Review Classics, 2001. Print.

West, Rebecca. *The Return of the Soldier*. 1918. New York: Penguin, 1998. Print.

Wheeler, Lesley. "Both Flower and Flower Gatherer: Medbh McGuckian's *The Flower Master* and H.D.'s *Sea Garden*." *Twentieth Century Literature* 49.4 (2003): 494–519. Print.

Whitman, Walt. "Exposition Building—New City Hall—River Trip." *Complete Prose Works*. Full Books, n.d. Web. 24 June 2008.

———. *Leaves of Grass*. 2nd ed. New York: Norton, 2002. Print.

Wilde, Oscar. "The Decay of Lying." *The Best-Known Works of Oscar Wilde*. New York: Blue Ribbon, 1927. 597–620. Print.

———. *The Picture of Dorian Gray*. Ed. Joseph Bristow. New York: Oxford UP, 2006. Print.

Wilkinson, Richard H. *Symbol and Magic in Egyptian Art*. London: Thames, 1994. Print.

Williams, William Carlos. *Collected Poems: 1909–1939*. New York: New Directions, 1986. Print.

———. *In the American Grain*. Norfolk: New Directions, 1925. Print.

———. *Paterson*. New York: New Directions, 1948. Print.

———. *Selected Poems*. Ed. Charles Tomlinson. New York: New Directions, 1985. Print.

———. "A Sort of a Song." *The William Carlos Williams Reader*. Ed. M. L. Rosenthal. New York: New Directions, 1965. 46–47. Print.

Willis, Patricia C., ed. *Marianne Moore: Woman and Poet*. Orono: Natl. Poetry Foundation, 1990. Print.

Wing Beat. Dir. Kenneth Macpherson. 1927. Film fragment. Museum of Mod. Art, New York.

Woolf, Virginia. *Mrs. Dalloway*. New York: Harcourt, 1925. Print.

———. *Orlando*. New York: Harcourt, 1928. Print.

———. *A Room of One's Own*. New York: Harcourt, 1929. Print.

———. *Three Guineas*. New York: Harcourt, 1966. Print.

———. *To the Lighthouse*. New York: Harcourt, 1927. Print.

World War II Poster Collection. Northwestern U Lib., 1997. Web. 6 Feb. 2008.

Yeats, William Butler. *Collected Poems of William Butler Yeats*. Ed. Richard J. Finneran. New York: Scribner's, 1996. Print.

Young, James E. *At Memory's Edge: After-images of the Holocaust in Contemporary Art and Architecture*. New Haven: Yale UP, 2000. Print.

Zilboorg, Caroline. "Letters across the Abyss: The H.D.–Adrienne Monnier Correspondence." *Sagetrieb* 8.3 (1989): 115–34. Print.

———, ed. *Richard Aldington and H.D.: The Early Years in Letters*. Bloomington: Indiana UP, 1992. Print.

———, ed. *Richard Aldington and H.D.: Their Lives in Letters, 1918–61*. Manchester: Manchester UP, 2003. Print.

———, ed. *Richard Aldington and H.D.: The Later Years in Letters*. Manchester: Manchester UP, 1995. Print.

Zukofsky, Louis. *Bottom: On Shakespeare*. Austin: Ark, 1963. Print.

INDEX

Akhenaten, 78, 81–82
Aldington, Richard, 1, 9, 10, 15, 18, 26, 27, 29, 30, 34, 40, 41, 44, 94, 120, 122
Ambelain, Robert, 69
Amenophis II, 111
Anderson, Monica, 112
Atwood, Margaret, 19, 20
Auden, W. H., 19
Augustine, Jane, 11, 62n1, 69n1, 144, 159n1

Baccolini, Raffaella, 34
Balzac, Honoré de, 26
Barnes, Djuna, 19, 20, 93
Barnstone, Aliki, 9, 16, 102, 135
Barthes, Roland, 71, 73, 74
Beach, Sylvia, 28, 129
Beaton, Cecil, 82, 131
Beauvoir, Simone de, 71
Benstock, Shari, 13, 31
Bentley, Barbara, 20
Bergonzi, Bernard, 121
Bernal, Martin, 141
Bernstein, Charles, 17, 173
Bertholf, Robert J., 15, 150, 152n1
Bishop, Elizabeth, 47
Blake, William, 173
Blaser, Robin, 143
Bloom, Harold, 1, 13
Bonaparte, Marie, 72, 73
Bonheur, Rosa, 60–61
Bornstein, George, 34
Boughn, Michael, 1, 13, 15, 42, 151
Bowering, George, 143
Bowles, Jane, 19
Breasted, James Henry, 77, 111, 112
Brogan, Terry V. F., 84
Brontë, Charlotte, 20
Brooke, Rupert, 114
Brooks, Gwendolyn, 47
Brown, Bill, 57, 58, 59–60
Brown, Deborah, 177
Brown, Judith, 165n1
Brown, Robert McAfee, 146
Browning, Elizabeth Barrett, 20
Browning, Robert, 20
Bryant, Marsha, 17, 20, 21, 22, 82, 111, 112
Bryer, Jackson, 14
Bryher, 9, 10, 11, 12, 14, 15, 17, 27, 28, 29, 30, 31, 50, 65, 68, 70, 72, 77, 79, 81, 93, 94–95, 97, 101, 108–09, 111, 122, 150, 160, 161–62, 164, 168–69, 170
Buck, Claire, 15
Budge, E. A. Wallis, 16
Bulfinch, Thomas, 16
Burnett, Gary, 12, 13
Butler, Judith, 91, 133
Butler, Octavia, 19
Butts, Mary, 28

Caesar, Gaius Julius, 72, 76
Campbell, David A., 93
Carby, Hazel V., 109, 165n1
Carruth, Hayden, 143
Carter, Angela, 19
Caruth, Cathy, 134n1
Castle, Terry, 95
Chadwick, Mary, 28, 73
Champollion, Jean-François, 77
Charcot, Jean-Martin, 72
Chekhov, Anton, 145
Chisholm, Dianne, 77
Chisolm, Lawrence W., 60
Christian, Barbara, 109, 110
Cicero, 135
Cixous, Hélène, 71, 73, 74
Clifton, Lucille, 20
Coates, Kimberly Engdahl, 20, 21
Cobley, Evelyn, 121
Coffman, Christine E., 20, 21
Coleman, Emily Holmes, 19
Coleman, Victor, 151
Collecott, Diana, 15, 16, 48n2, 93
Collis, Betty, 176
Condell, Diana, 121
Connor, Rachel, 160, 162, 165n1
Conrad, Joseph, 114
Cook, Elizabeth, 19
Cooper, Helen M., 121
Cooper, Jane, 143
Cournos, John, 15, 26
Creeley, Robert, 143, 145
Cunard, Nancy, 28, 107
Curry, Renée R., 143

Dahlen, Beverly, 143
Danielpour, Richard, 18
Darantière, Maurice, 11
Da Vinci, Leonardo, 65
Debo, Annette, 107, 108, 109, 162, 165n1, 170
Dembo, L. S., 12, 14, 16
DeShazer, Mary K., 13
Dickens, Charles, 135
Dickinson, Emily, 16, 19, 43, 148
di Prima, Diane, 143

Doan, Laura, 99
Dobson, Silvia, 14, 15
Donald, James, 12, 165n1, 166, 169
Doolittle, Charles, 25, 27, 56, 57, 62, 63, 72, 73, 166
Doolittle, Gilbert, 27, 72
Doolittle, Helen Wolle, 25, 29, 63, 68–69, 72, 73, 76, 86, 98
Doré, Gustave, 64, 66, 72, 73, 76
Dorn, Edward, 145
Dove, Rita, 19, 143
Dowding, Hugh Caswall Tremenheere, 68, 86, 144
Dreyer, Carl, 18, 170
duCille, Ann, 110
Duffy, Carol Ann, 19
Duncan, Robert, 1, 15, 18, 114–15, 118, 143, 148–52, 152n1
DuPlessis, Rachel Blau, 13, 14, 15, 16, 19, 31, 100, 148, 153, 159
Durand, Lionel, 144

Eakins, Thomas, 57, 60, 61, 62
Eaverly, Mary Ann, 82, 111, 112
Edmunds, Susan, 15, 16, 77, 81, 86
Edwards, Amelia, 112
Eisenstein, Sergei, 28, 98, 161, 167–68
Eliade, Mircea, 147
Eliot, T. S., 18, 20, 25, 26, 32, 34, 35, 37, 38, 42, 96, 114, 136, 138, 140, 150, 173
Ellerman, John, 27, 29
Ellerman, Winifred. *See* Bryher
Ellis, Havelock, 27, 94
Emerson, Claudia, 18
Engel, Bernard F., 12
Euripides, 9, 27, 85, 86, 92

Fauset, Jessie Redmon, 110
Felski, Rita, 127
Fenollosa, Ernest, 18, 60, 62
Finch, Annie, 177
Fish, Stanley, 71
Fitts, Dudley, 150
Fitzgerald, F. Scott, 18, 20
Fletcher, John Gould, 26
Flint, F. S., 15, 26, 34, 40
Forbes, Jill, 163
Ford, Ford Madox, 19, 26
Forster, E. M., 19, 117, 118
Foucault, Michel, 71
Fraistat, Neil, 40
Franklin, Benjamin, 61
Frazer, James George, 64
Freud, Sigmund, 1, 5, 7, 8, 11, 15, 25, 28, 29, 54–55, 66, 70–76, 86, 90, 91, 93, 95–96, 98, 150, 172
Friedberg, Anne, 12, 108, 109, 165n1, 166, 169
Friedman, Susan Stanford, 1, 11, 13, 14, 15, 16, 25, 31, 41, 42, 47, 48n2, 70, 77, 86, 92, 95, 100, 101, 103, 107, 128, 148, 150, 153, 165n1
Fritz, Angela DiPace, 13
Frost, Robert, 32, 42, 47
Frow, John, 57
Fussell, Paul, 114, 121

Garbo, Greta, 98, 162–63
Geertz, Clifford, 57
Gelpi, Albert, 9, 13, 16
Gikandi, Simon, 100, 105
Gilbert, Sandra M., 13, 71, 73, 121, 143
Gilman, Charlotte Perkins, 19
Ginsberg, Allen, 21
Glück, Louise, 143
Gould, Jean, 13
Graham, Jorie, 20
Grahn, Judy, 143
Graves, Robert, 20
Gray, Cecil, 9, 10, 27, 94
Gray, Janet, 43
Greger, Debora, 19
Gregg, Frances, 9, 26, 27, 56, 60, 62, 64, 72, 93, 94, 95, 129
Gregory, Eileen, 15, 16, 47, 148
Gregory, Horace, 9, 12
Griffith, D. W., 109
Grimm, Jacob, 64
Grimm, Wilhelm, 64
Gubar, Susan, 13, 15, 16, 71, 73, 80, 100, 121
Guest, Barbara, 13, 15, 31, 63, 94, 143
Gunn, Thom, 143
Gunning, Tom, 61

Hall, Donald, 143
Hall, Radclyffe, 19, 25, 99
Hamilton, Edith, 16, 86
Hanley, Lynne, 121
Hannibal, 72, 75
Hanscombe, Gillian, 31
Harad, Alyssa, 125
Harper, Frances Ellen Watkins, 43
Harrison, Victoria, 132
Hatlen, Burton, 16, 41
Hatshepsut, 77, 79, 81, 82, 125
Hemingway, Ernest, 18, 19, 20, 28, 120, 122, 123
Henke, Suzette A., 128
Herman, Judith Lewis, 134n1
Hernandez, Heather, 129, 173
Herring, Robert, 107
Heydt, Erich, 28, 86
Hickman, Miranda B., 20, 21
Higonnet, Margaret Randolph, 121
Hitler, Adolf, 28
Hogue, Cynthia, 19

Holland, Norman N., 12
Hollenberg, Donna Krolik, 15, 16, 42, 44, 142, 143, 144, 149, 152n1
Homer, 19–20, 85, 92
Hough, Lindy, 143
Howe, Susan, 143, 148
Hughes, Glenn, 166
Hughes, Langston, 18, 32, 38–39, 49, 112
Hull, Gloria T., 110
Hulme, T. E., 40, 93
Hunt, Violet, 26
Huntington, Samuel P., 120

Irigaray, Luce, 90–91

Jackson, Helen Hunt, 43
Jackson, Thomas H., 16
Jarrell, Randall, 150
Johnson, Emily Pauline, 43
Joyce, James, 19, 28, 49, 114, 138, 145, 150, 173

Kaplan, Caren, 100, 104, 105
Keeling, Bret L., 20, 21
Kelly, Robert, 143, 148
Kenner, Hugh, 96
King, Michael, 11, 13, 14, 15, 148
Kingston, Maxine Hong, 19
Kircher, Athanasius, 69
Kirkpatrick, Sidney D., 61
Kloepfer, Deborah Kelly, 13, 44
Koch, Kenneth, 145
Korg, Jacob, 34
Kossman, Nina, 20
Kristeva, Julia, 91
Kumin, Maxine, 177
Kushner, Dale, 143

Lacan, Jacques, 71, 73, 74, 75
LaCapra, Dominick, 134n1
Laity, Cassandra, 9–10, 15, 96
Landseer, Edwin Henry, 72, 73
Lang, Fritz, 160
Lawrence, D. H., 9, 10, 17, 19, 20, 26–27, 54, 55, 55n2, 150
Lawrence, Frieda, 10
Leeuw, Gerardus van der, 73, 74
Lemke, Sieglinde, 108
Lendinara, Patrizia, 103
Levertov, Denise, 15, 19, 120, 124, 125, 142–47, 148
Levin, Phillis, 143
Lewis, Wyndham, 26
Liddiard, Jean, 121
Livesay, Dorothy, 143
Lo Fu, 51
Longenbach, James, 157
Lorde, Audre, 19
Lowe, Lisa, 112
Lowell, Amy, 17, 18, 19, 26, 40, 41, 42
Lucas, A., 77

Macpherson, Kenneth, 10–11, 12, 28, 94–95, 97, 107, 108–09, 160, 161, 162, 168–70
Malek, Jaromir, 82n1
Mandel, Charlotte, 11, 15, 61, 98, 143, 160, 167, 168, 171
Mansfield, Katherine, 120, 122, 124, 145
Marcus, Laura, 12, 165n1, 166, 169
Martz, Louis L., 8, 29
Mathis, Mary S., 148
McAlmon, Robert, 28
McCabe, Susan, 109, 163, 165n1
McCullers, Carson, 145
McGann, Jerome J., 175, 177
McIntosh, Peggy, 108
Millay, Edna St. Vincent, 19, 42, 43
Miller, Meredith, 112
Monnier, Adrienne, 15, 28
Monroe, Harriet, 26, 41
Moonen, Jef, 176
Moore, Marianne, 16, 18, 19, 26, 27, 28, 32, 34, 35–36, 42–43, 56, 60, 62, 140
Morley, Hilda, 143
Morris, Adalaide, 15, 16, 47, 61, 79, 127, 165n1
Mueller, Sarah, 48n1
Munich, Adrienne Auslander, 121
Murnau, F. W., 160
Murray, Margaret, 77, 111
Murry, John Middleton, 124
Muybridge, Eadweard, 57, 61–62

Nelson, Cary, 17
Ngũgĩ wa Thiong'o, 120, 126
Nielsen, Aldon Lynn, 107, 170
Nims, John Frederick, 41

O'Brien, Tim, 120
O'Connor, Flannery, 20
O'Keeffe, Georgia, 97
Olson, Charles, 148
Orange, Tom, 34
Ostriker, Alicia Suskin, 13, 16, 19, 27, 34
Ovid, 19, 20, 92
Owen, Wilfred, 32–33, 35, 36–37, 114

Pabst, G. W., 18, 28, 98, 160, 162, 164, 170
Parada, Carlos, 17
Pearson, Norman Holmes, 1, 9, 10, 11, 12, 14, 15, 17, 29–30, 68, 104, 144, 149, 152n1, 172, 177
Peck, John, 143
Penn, William, 59
Phelan, Peggy, 34

Pinsky, Robert, 143
Plath, Sylvia, 19
Plato, 71
Poe, Edgar Allan, 20, 49, 98
Pondrom, Cyrena N., 15, 34
Pope, Rob, 175
Pound, Ezra, 1, 8, 9, 10, 11, 14, 18, 20, 25, 26, 27, 30, 32, 33, 34–35, 40, 41, 56, 60, 61, 62, 72, 85, 91n1, 93, 94, 96, 97, 114, 120, 122, 136, 138, 143–44, 150, 156, 157, 158, 166
Powell, Barry B., 16
Preminger, Alex, 84
Prodger, Phillip, 61, 62

Quinn, Vincent, 1, 12

Rachewiltz, Mary de, 14
Ramazani, Jahan, 101, 104, 105
Ray, Man, 28
Reese, Lizette Woodworth, 43
Reid, Ian, 145
Rembrandt, 72, 73
Rennard, Michael, 48n1
Rettallack, Joan, 143
Rich, Adrienne, 19, 104, 143
Richards, James, 128
Richardson, Dorothy, 19, 28, 93, 145
Riddel, Joseph N., 12
Rilke, Rainer Maria, 20
Rinn, Fauneil J., 16
Robbe-Grillet, Alain, 170
Robeson, Eslanda, 11, 97, 109, 169, 170
Robeson, Paul, 11, 28, 97, 109, 161, 166, 169, 170
Robins, Gay, 82n1
Robinson, Janice S., 13, 15, 31
Roediger, David R., 108
Rosenberg, Isaac, 114
Rossetti, Christina, 20, 43
Rossetti, Dante Gabriel, 29, 68, 173
Rukeyser, Muriel, 19

Sachs, Hanns, 28, 72
Said, Edward W., 111, 112, 126
Sandburg, Carl, 32
Sappho, 20, 27, 41, 92, 93
Sarton, May, 15
Sassoon, Siegfried, 114
Saussure, Ferdinand de, 71, 73, 74
Sbisa, Marina, 103
Scarry, Elaine, 130
Schaffner, Perdita, 9, 10, 11, 14, 27, 50, 65, 94, 129
Schmideberg, Walter, 72
Schussele, Christian, 60–61
Schweik, Susan, 81, 105–06
Scott, Bonnie Kime, 13, 176
Sexton, Anne, 19
Shakespeare, William, 27, 72, 75, 76, 95, 173
Shange, Ntozake, 18
Shelley, Percy Bysshe, 71, 136
Shohat, Ella, 111
Siddall, Elizabeth, 29, 68
Sidney, Philip, 71, 136
Silko, Leslie Marmon, 19
Silverstein, Louis, 17, 28, 31, 77, 129
Sinclair, May, 26
Sitwell, Edith, 19
Smith, William, 16
Smyers, Virginia, 15, 31, 77
Spiro, Joanna, 76
Spoo, Robert, 10, 115, 116, 117
Squier, Susan Merrill, 121
Stanton, Domna C., 126
Stein, Gertrude, 6, 18, 19, 20, 25, 28, 32, 33, 37–38, 57, 62
Stein, Leo, 58
Stesichorus, 85, 86, 92, 99
Stevens, Wallace, 33, 34
Stewart, Susan, 155
Stoler, Ann Laura, 107
Stowe, Harriet Beecher, 154
Strachey, James, 81
Street, Sarah, 163
Surette, Leon, 25
Swann, Thomas Burnett, 12
Swenson, May, 143
Swinburne, A. C., 26, 64, 93
Sword, Helen, 22, 82, 174
Symonds, J. A., 93

Taylor, Georgina, 100–01, 104
Thutmose III, 79
Tinker, Carol, 15
Tobin, Vincent Arieh, 77
Toklas, Alice B., 28
Torgovnik, Marianna, 107–08
Tostevin, Lola Lemire, 143
Truettner, William H., 61
Tutankhamun, 77, 82, 112
Twitchell-Waas, Jeffrey, 34

Uccello, Paolo, 61

Van Duyn, Helen, 20
Van Vechten, Carl, 107
Van Zanten, David, 59
Veidt, Conrad, 164, 170
Vendler, Helen, 35

Wagner, Linda W., 12
Wagoner, Michael, 48n1
Walcott, Derek, 18
Walden, Edith, 143
Waldman, Anne, 143
Walsh, John, 10
Walton, Jean, 109, 165n1
Warner, Marina, 120, 125

Warner, Sylvia Townsend, 19
Warnke, Frank J., 84
Weatherhead, A. Kingsley, 12
Weigall, E. P., 77
Weigl, Bruce, 120
Weinberg, Herman G., 12
Welty, Eudora, 145
West, Rebecca, 114, 115–17
Wheeler, Lesley, 48n2
Whitman, Walt, 18, 32, 59
Wiene, Robert, 160
Wilde, Oscar, 19, 49, 93, 99
Wilkinson, Richard H., 82n1
Williams, William Carlos, 17, 18, 20, 26, 32, 33, 34, 35, 42, 56, 60, 62, 143–44, 148, 150
Winterson, Jeanette, 19
Wolle, Francis, 61, 166
Wolle, Hartley, 63
Woolf, Virginia, 19, 49, 71, 73, 93, 96, 101, 114, 115–17, 130–31, 138

Yeats, William Butler, 19, 20, 26, 33, 42, 114, 115
Yorke, Dorothy "Arabella," 10, 27, 94
Young, James E., 131–32

Zeisberger, David, 60
Zilboorg, Caroline, 15, 41
Zinzendorf, Nicholas von, 64, 66–67, 68–69
Zukofsky, Louis, 32, 148